PEARLS
Their Origin, Treatment and Identification

PEARLS
Their Origin, Treatment and Identification

Jean Taburiaux

Translated by David Ceriog-Hughes

Illustrations by Jean-Paul Ehrmann

Chilton Book Company,
Radnor, PA.

First Published (in English) 1985
Reprinted 1986

Translated from the French edition, 'La Perle - et ses secrets'

Copyright © English-language edition: N.A.G. Press and
Jean Taburiaux, 1985

This edition published in the U.S.A in 1985 by Chilton Book Company,
Chilton Way, Radnor, PA 19089

PUBLISHER'S NOTE

The following illustrations were based on drawings
published by Kunihiko Miwa of the Mitsuwa Co
Ltd, Tokyo, Japan, who originated those methods
of presentation of the knowledge he had researched.
Page 110. Three-dimensional view of the structure
of an oyster shell.
Page 113. Lustre and orient as a surface effect.

ACKNOWLEDGEMENTS
In addition to the colour photographs supplied by
the author, the Publishers are grateful to Mikimoto
Pearls Ltd, E. Allen Jobbins, *Gems and Gemology* and
The Goldsmith for permission to reproduce other
colour photographs in this edition.

British Library Cataloguing in Publication Data
Taburiaux, Jean
    Pearls : their origin, treatment and identification.
    1. Pearls
    I. Title
    639' .412   SH375

ISBN 0-8019-7713-4

Printed in Great Britain by Anchor Brendon Ltd, Tiptree, Colchester,
Essex, and bound in the U.S.A.

Contents

PART TWO: PEARL SHELLFISH AND THE FORMATION OF PEARLS

PART THREE: CULTURED PEARLS

PART FOUR: PEARL WORKING AND SELLING

Preface

Here at last is a well-documented book about the pearl. For more than twenty years many of us have been searching for such a work. The pearl still poses questions even after years of study. But this book is not merely a series of scientific answers; it is a compilation including actual experiences as well. Neither is it a dictionary; so do not hesitate in travelling around the world with the author to visit each important area of production. Let yourself be carried along with the flow of the account, and in the analysis of the biological processes which gave birth to the pearl, where science is anything but forbidding. Jean Taburiaux speaks of what he knows and loves. He fosters a special relationship with the pearl. One day, perhaps, he will tell us how to 'work' in pearl. There are not twenty people on this earth who have kept that tradition. He is the sort of man 'whose eye listens and whose hand understands'.

Daniel Piat
Founder, National Institute of Gemmology, France

Introduction

Of all the jewels which we admire, perhaps pearls are the least appreciated in depth. Yet when closely observed, they show some qualities that are incomparable though humble and discreet, because they can enhance latent beauty in other things. Set in a necklace on a silken thread, they light up the face of the woman who wears them; they inspire admiration in many, even envy in others.

Throughout history, emperors, kings and queens have sought to possess them. Priceless collections of pearls exhibited in museums today exhibit only a fraction of those ancient possessions. Indeed the admiration for, and even the worship of pearls - symbols of beauty, purity and wealth - seems to have spread through every culture, in every age, over the expanse of the world since civilisation began.

Frequently worn in the past by men as often as by women, pearls nevertheless seem to have been pre-destined for a woman and to be the tribute which every man dreams of paying his mate. Just as Aphrodite emerged from the foam of the ocean waves, the pearl has its birthplace in the oceans. Delicate and discreet, it does not sparkle; it glows.

For millenia, in every latitude bathed by the warm seas so favourable to the proliferation of oyster-beds, in all communities, pearls have been obtained by collecting shells from the depths of the sea. Indigenous methods were used on a small scale, employed for the most part intermittently by families of fishermen for whom the pearls represented a seasonal occupation and constituted an additional means of supporting or enriching themselves beyond their normal way of life.

The man would dive and hurriedly gather as many loose oysters as he could. These were left on the shore in piles to be opened and searched for pearls. The discovery of a fine pearl was a special occasion which assured a small fortune for the fisherman and his family. Nevertheless, the pearl fishermen's life was one of the harshest in the world - continually working to the limits of his strength and thus curtailing the length of his life. In addition he had to run the risk of squalls and tempests, as well as encounters with the poisonous fish and sharks which haunted the marine depths.

From the 15th century onwards, Europeans who subjugated native populations in pearling areas saw a fast way of becoming rich by the intensive development of fishing-grounds. Many natives were unscrupulously exploited by adventurers hungry for treasure, and were sometimes reduced to slavery and forced to dive hopelessly and unceasingly until they died. This chapter of pearl history is one of the strangest, in which adventure, cruelty, beauty, suffering and death are closely linked. In the 19th century, with the increasing demand for pearls on the world market, large sailing ships were introduced; then steam ships allowed the undertaking of large projects of intensive fishing. The introduction of the diving suit at the start of the 20th century enabled divers to collect enormous numbers of oysters. It threatened devastation of the oyster-beds and was on the verge of endangering the survival of entire species of these molluscs. But a crisis in 1929 caused the destruction of large numbers of pearl fisheries and put an end to this danger. Since then, the beds have not really been exploited and there is every reason to suppose that vast fortunes now lie on the ocean bed.

The cultured pearl was first developed in Japan at the turn of the century, before spreading throughout the Pacific. With pearl culture, it is not fisheries using divers which provide the bases necessary for pearl production, but specialised farms using a qualified workforce for the complex and delicate work involved.

At first the cultured pearl was totally disregarded by traditional dealers for whom it was no more than an 'ersatz' natural pearl. In a few decades, the cultured pearl compelled recognition by the increasing demand of the public and has acquired its letters of patent of nobility from the greatest jewellers in the world; the proof being that today it constitutes the major part of the market supply.

This book takes the reader from the historic and romantic beginnings of pearling, through its exploitation, to the modern sophisticated industry that still depends on knowledge of the oyster's habits and on the romanticism of the buyer of pearls.

PART ONE
NATURAL
PEARLS

The Pearl

Pearl is a word of magical import for many people, being a symbol of beauty and purity. It gave rise to legends of mystical birth from the seas. It is impossible to say with any certainty when the first pearl was brought from under the sea, but ever since man gathered his first shellfish to feed himself and to make small tools, the discovery of pearls was obviously soon to follow. Thereafter, one can easily imagine one of our ancestors giving a pearl to his beloved. So the symbol of purity and wealth became also a symbol of love, as testified by the following anecdote in the history of the Roman Empire.

Cleopatra possessed two magnificent pear-shaped pearls. One day, when she was with Mark Antony, he proclaimed that he was unsure of her love for him. In answer, Cleopatra dissolved one of her most precious possessions, one of her pearl ear-rings, in a goblet of wine and toasted him by swallowing the wine.

Throughout history, the Arabs and Hindus have been the greatest admirers of pearls. To the Hindus they were dewdrops fallen at night into the sea and collected on the body of the oyster. If this phenomenon occurred during a full moon, the pearl would be of real beauty, but if the sky were overcast, the pearl would be dull and of poor quality.

The Hindus also attributed to the pearl the power of bringing good luck. It is said that Lord Krishna discovered the first pearl at the greatest depth of the sea and offered it to his daughter, Pandaia, on the day of her marriage. Nowadays, the Indians still respect this legend and no marriage takes place without pearls being given for luck to the bride.

To protect themselves, the Mogul Emperors of India and then the Rajahs wore pearls in different ways: on rings and collars, but also threaded on gold and silver wires for attachment to their clothes. Their head-dresses and the harnesses of their horses and elephants were richly embroidered with them.

The Greeks believed that pearls came from lightning when it struck the sea. Women wore pearls mainly on ear-rings; men only on their right ears. This custom, as with many others, was probably originated by the Persians, because-ancient coins have been found bearing the effigies of queens of Persia wearing hanging pearls.

The Arabs wore pearls set in gold with other sumptuous jewels embroidered on their head-dresses and clothing. They even collected them for the pleasure of looking at them, enclosing their treasures in simple jars filled with water - unique pearls, lovingly collected one by one over the years, each with its own history, either because of the particularly dangerous conditions in which it was discovered or the particular qualities of the pearl itself. Jars containing such pearls were placed in chests of precious wood, inlaid with mother-of-pearl in shimmering colours of troca, abalone and Pintadine shells - chests with locks and hinges of copper and steel, shaped by man and fire, and engraved by unknown artists.

A sheik would take each jar and place it on a rich carpet covered by a white cloth so that nothing could change the colour of the pearls. The first few jars would contain pearls of rare quality but of small diameter. As more jars were taken from the chest, the diameter of the pearls increased. In a short while the guest, sitting cross-legged before about ten pearl jars, some more beautiful than others, would probably be seized by a strange emotion before the fairyland of gems.

Now for the greatest attraction: the sheik draws forth the final jar, containing a single pearl. What a joy! Alone, it is worth more than all the others. Watch the face of the sheik. He has let nothing show, but his eyes betray him; it is his pearl and he loves it more than anything in the world. But, as the visitor leaves the palace he will be given, as a sign of friendship, a pearl which will remind him of an unforgettable spectacle.

In Europe it is well known that pearls have been coveted by emperors, kings and queens since time immemorial. Given as presents and proof of friendship, they have played their small roles in the context of history: consider the number of historical portraits in museums showing ancient monarchs clothed in sumptuous pearl ornaments. The prestige with which pearls have always been held is not testified by history alone. It is equally expressed in numerous legends.

According to one, this is the origin of pearls. A raindrop fell from the clouds. Upon seeing the vast sea, it became confused. 'What am I?' it asked, 'beside the ocean? I am truly lost and have vanished in its vastness'. As a reward for such a modest avowal, it was gathered in the mother-of-pearl of a shell and, through the care of Providence, it became the expensive pearl which adorned the diadems of monarchs.

Another legend, entitled 'Offerings to the Gods', tells this tale: The air offered him the rainbow, fire, meteor, earth, ruby, sea, and pearl. The rainbow formed the god's halo, the meteor his lamp, the ruby adorned his forehead, and he carried the pearl on his heart. Of all the presents, the pearl was incontestably the one dearest to him.

The value attached to pearls by Semitic peoples is reflected in the Old

Testament's frequent references to them, especially in the Book of Job and the Proverbs of Solomon. In the Epistle according to St. Matthew, Christ said, in the Sermon on the Mount: 'The Kingdom of Heaven is like a merchant searching for beautiful pearls, who, finding one at great cost, sells all his possessions to buy it.' For St. Matthew, the pearl was the symbol of wisdom which led the believer through trials and tribulations to renounce all his belongings in this world in preference for the Kingdom of God.

CHAPTER 1
Fisheries Throughout the World

Pearls are gathered throughout the world by people very different in colour, religion and custom. The climate, the nature of the sea, the proximity or distance of the coast, the fertility or sterility of the maritime soil, all these factors have resulted in fishing techniques and the sale of the produce being very different from one country to another.

Pearl fisheries used to be situated almost entirely in warm waters. The most important were undoubtedly those in the Persian Gulf which borders Iran, Kuwait, Saudi Arabia and Quatar. The most productive gulf regions were situated some 240 to 320 km (150 to 200 miles) from the Arabian coast.

When the harvest was over, the fishermen transacted their pearl business on the island of Bahrein. From there, some were sold and sent to India (let us not forget the virtues which the Hindus believed the pearls to possess); others were sold to river-side sheiks.

The Red Sea has surrendered some magnificent pearls. The town of Massaona was a well-known centre. From Port Sudan to Aden and Djibouti, the sea is strewn with groups of islands whose edges are rich in oyster-beds. The heat, sea turbulence, and piracy made pearl fishing particularly dangerous in these areas.

Australia too offers pearl-fishing sites, chiefly on the west coast between Kimberley and Port Medland. A main town, Broome, backs on to the coast and its inhabitants have no exit other than the sea to avoid meeting the perils entailed by a long desert crossing. Thursday Island too, on the tip of Cape York right in the middle of the Torres Straits on the great Coral Reef, is renowned for its pearl oyster-beds.

Further to the north is a whole region encompassing New Guinea, Indonesia, Malaysia and the Philippines where pearls are found. Then let us go to the East, the Solomon Islands, New Caledonia, Fiji, Samoa, Tuamotu and finally the Marquises Islands.

Let us dream for a moment of a voyage which, putting ourselves at the mercy of the wind and tide, would lead us to Queen Pomare, who, according to the legend, possessed such large pearls that only she could pick them up to play with.

Other places are equally well known. Ceylon (Sri Lanka) provided bright pearls of good colour, but of small diameter. Venezuela provided an abundance of brilliantly white small pearls which were collected by dragging the depths from a boat, instead of having recourse to diving. Panama possessed pearls of a large diameter but dull and brown in colour.

Finally, the freshwater or river pearls of Europe and America were plentiful and pretty, but not as beautiful as pearls from the sea. Although generally milky in appearance, with traces of bluish pink and less well appreciated than seawater pearls, they sometimes equalled them in price.

Persian Gulf

The fisheries of the Persian Gulf have been known for more than 2,000 years. Through the centuries, they have been regular suppliers of pearls of great beauty. Both Greeks and Romans knew of their existence. Tylos was the Roman name given to the isle of Bahrein.

Pliny, the great Latin naturalist, related in his 'Historia Naturalis (Book IX)', that pearls of the Persian Gulf were the most beautiful, and mentioned the town of El Katiff (on the Arabian coast, opposite Bahrein) as a great pearl centre.

In the 16th century all the gulf ports were controlled by the Portuguese. They charged pearl fishers 75 abassis (about £1) per boat plus a certain percentage of the oyster catch. In the 17th century, the Persians replaced them and reduced the taxes considerably.

In the years 1925-1930, the various rights of licences granted to fishing boats maintained the Bahrein treasury and those of the Arabian coastal sheiks in those days the entire Gulf economy was based on pearls. The wealthy, the poor and the slaves all relied on the fishing industry. Boat builders, sail merchants, rope, cable, rice, tobacco and date merchants all saw their accounts rise and fall in conjunction with the pearl harvests. In 1930 it was reckoned that 3,000 boats were dragging the Gulfs and 7,000 men formed their crews.

The Persian Gulf, about 965 km (600 miles) in length by 160 km (100 miles) in width, becomes narrow at the Straits of Hormuz, to burst into the Gulf of Oman, which is open to the Arabian sea. Over all its area, its depth rarely exceeds 55 metres (180 ft). The oyster-beds are widely distributed throughout the Gulf. However, the largest concentration is found near Bahrein. The oyster found in the greatest number is the *Pinctada radiata* or *vulgaris*. It attaches itself to rock and coral beds, but can also be found on the sand itself.

Let us imagine we are in the Gulf when pearl fishing was the main activity there. Fishing is carried on throughout the year by the tribesmen of Hasa, Oman and the pirate coast, to name only the most famous. According to the season, and thus the water temperature, fishing takes place at several places. In the winter-time, the cold north-westerly winds blow violently, and the gales are a grave danger to any vessel which sails far from the coast. The fishermen then explore the beds and passages which are less deep. In April and May they go further afield, and it is only from June to September that they explore the far depths.

The boats vary in size, and are perfectly adapted to the sort of fishing which they undertake. The smallest take on three or five men and only work the coastal areas. The largest, whose crew can number 80 men, drag the Gulf in all directions and leave for three to four weeks at a time.

The boat's owner is usually an Arab whose only wealth lies in his vessel. Before setting out on a fishing trip, he must buy all the material and provisions (rice, coffee, spices, sugar and so on) his men will need. It is a large expenditure because the average crew numbers 25 to 30 or more. In order to cover his

Sea-going gaff-rigged pearling schooner, one of the larger boats that fished in the Persian Gulf for three or four weeks at a time and had a crew of as many as 80.

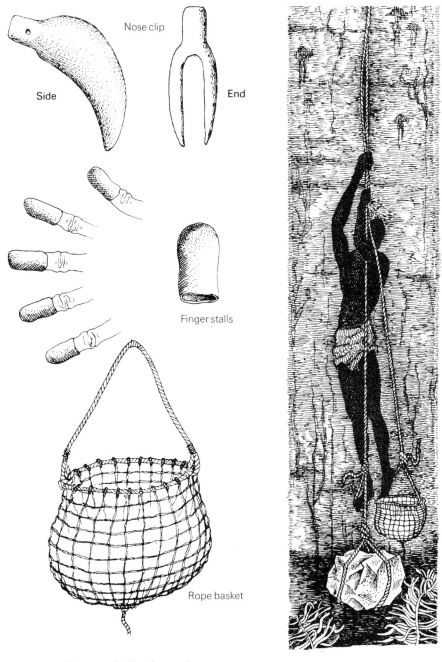

Nose clip

Side

End

Finger stalls

Rope basket

The pearl diver's equipment

expenses, he enters into an agreement with a financier who makes him a loan at exorbitant interest rates. In addition, the first 'sight' of the pearls is reserved by the financier, an infallible way of assuring himself of a steady supply of cheap pearls. In fact, at the time of the sale, the feeble offers for what are left hardly cover the rising cost of the loan, interest included. When there is a poor catch, the boat owner is literally subjugated by his financier to undertake several more trips until the debt is paid.

The fishermen's life is extremely rough on board ship. He and his crew dive in loin cloths and are tied to the boat by a rope. The only pieces of equipment they possess are large stones to serve as ballast, rope baskets to hold the catch, and bones to pinch their nostrils so that their ears can be decompressed in the dives. They generally work at depths of from about 10 to 20 metres (say 30 to 60 ft).

Fishing methods have not changed for centuries. At the beginning of this century, the Iranians tried to introduce diving- suits, but these were rejected by all the divers and totally banned by the coastal sheiks. People in many countries that are not industrialised soon realise that modern methods applied to their ancient activities of fishing and mining will quickly destroy their livlihoods. The Arabs knew this with pearling, just as the governments of Sri Lanka and Thailand do today by protecting family gem mining. Modern methods would exhaust in a few weeks a small gem mine that will keep a family alive for a generation or more.

Fishing takes place in the following way: When the Nakhuda (owner-captain) judges the oyster-bed to be favourable, he drops anchor. Then oars are fixed on to the boat in horizontal fashion and three ropes are attached to them. One, ending in a loop, allows the diver to rest on the surface between dives; the second, the ballast line, weighed down by a large stone, pulls him swiftly to the bottom; the final rope raises him to the surface with his precious load of oysters.

Divers work to the limits of their strength, and without the help of the third rope pulled by the rope-man, they would be unable to rise up by their own means.

This is how it happens: the diver in the water, clinging to the safety line, seizes the ballast line on which a loop has been previously knotted. He passes one foot through this loop and places the other on the basket, which allows him to take it down without any hindrance. He takes three or four deep breaths, pinches his nose with the bone-pinch which always hangs tied around his neck, and disappears under the surface, under the influence of the ballast. When the

Left: A Persian Gulf diver descends with his stone weight for ballast and his basket for the oysters he collects. He keeps one foot in a loop in the rope and the other on the basket, to stop it floating up when it is empty. On the left from the top are his nose clip, seen from the front and from the side, finger stalls of rubber or leather for protection, and a cord basket.

ballast line slackens, he has arrived. The rope-man pulls the ballast line back and fixes it on to the oar. He watches the other rope very closely, because the life of his companion rests on the speed with which he pulls it up.

Once at the bottom, collecting oysters, the diver slowly lets out the air which he has trapped in his lungs, and it is only when he is out of breath and strength that he gives a strong tug on the line, meaning that he must be brought to the surface immediately. The rope-man then pulls this line up as fast as he can. Near the surface the diver lets go and, with his arms along his body, emerges from the sea like a dolphin. At the surface, the rope-man takes the oyster basket and discards all but the empty shells and pebbles which the diver has gathered in his haste, while tipping the oysters on to the deck.

Each diver works hourly shifts, six times a day, and stays about one to one-and-a-half minutes underwater during each dive. With rest time, that makes about one dive every five minutes.

A diver's team is often a strange mixture of normal men, cripples (divers injured by shark bites or ray-fish stings) and even blind men. When the boat is anchored on a fairly rich bed, blind divers do their work just as well as the others. More than one fisherman who had lost a leg as well as his sight has declared that he was more at home underwater than on dry land.

The oysters are opened every morning before sunrise and before the diving begins. The man who opens the shells is completely naked so that he is not

The camp of a small group of independent pearl fishers on the west coast of the Persian Gulf. The squatting men are opening shells.

tempted to hide one or two pearls for himself. He works under the surveillance of the Nakhuda and the other members of the crew, because the profit from the catch is split among them. The largest part of the haul is composed of small pearls. It is believed that 10 per cent of oysters contain pearls, but only 3 per cent a pearl of value.

Opening oysters is routine. A sharp movement of a knife placed against the hinge and the oyster opens easily. The flesh is examined with the point of the knife, then carefully removed from the shell and gently prodded by the finger. When, from the folds of a bruised piece of flesh, a large and beautiful pearl suddenly appears, the whole boat rejoices. Hearing the conversation as time presses on into the night, one would think that the pearl is even more exceptional. Its beauty, shape, orient, the purity of its skin all make it priceless in the eyes of the fishermen. Only a queen will be fit to wear it, and the men on board will all be rich!

More than one rival boat fishes in the same area. The discovery of such a pearl cannot go unnoticed, such is the joy on board the ship. From boat to boat, the news is passed on and arrives at the bank where, yet again, the incomparable beauty of the pearl arouses people's imagination.

On the return to port, the harvest is first presented to the financier who guards against sharing the enthusiasm of the fishermen. His first offer is moderate. Bids and counterbids follow it. The boat owner is hampered by the increase in his debt, the accumulating interest, and his divers, who are in a hurry to return home. With a heavy heart he is often obliged to accept the price which is forced on him. But occasionally the presence of a foreign buyer enables him to hold his own against his financier and to do business for a larger sum of money. Proud and happy on his return to his boat, he can free himself from his debt and share with his men a fair price for their hard work.

The sale of the pearls often takes place on board ship with merchants who arrive at the fishing-grounds in motor boats.

It is not easy to approach the Nakhuda; this is often done by the intermediary of an agent who is usually of the same tribe or family. The small lots are often exchanged for fresh provisions, dates or tobacco, but the important lots are the subject of long and difficult transactions that can last for several days.

The Nakhudas do not really know the price of their merchandise, so they often ask from ten to 100 times its value in order to obtain, by successively lowering the price, an idea of a fair one, and to make the best possible deal.

The intermediary agent is indispensable, because he knows about both pearls and men. He judges, appreciates, advises, even becomes angry and talks with both parties. When he senses a possible agreement, everyone sits down, their hands hidden by a cloth. The agent tells them each bid and counterbid by successive pressing of such and such a finger or knuckle. Not a single word is spoken. The agent's role is to ensure that the two adversaries come to an agreement and shake hands on it. Then he announces the price at which the deal closed. There are kisses and congratulations. But the matter is not finished: there has to be agreement about the present and the tips which the purchaser must give to the family of the vendor and his servants. When that is done, there are renewed congratulations and wishes of good fortune.

All transactions in the earlier days were paid in roupees or Austrian silver talers.

Continuing our journey in the past, at the end of the season, the main dealers, who have performed ten or a hundred deals, go to Bombay to sell their pearls. Here the pearls will be polished, dried and pierced by Hindu experts.

Sharing the sale money is done in the form of loans which the Nakhuda makes to his crew. The Koran forbids all money-loans, so the credit which the businessman gives the Nakhuda and he in turn gives to his men is therefore in the form of sacks of rice, sugar, tobacco and so on, counted at 20 per cent above the market price in the low season and 80 to 100 per cent above in the high season.

The divers are always in debt, and the better they are at their job, the more important their debts. Indeed, the Nakhuda who wishes to have a good diver stay in his service lends him more than he needs. The official loans are put down in a book which can be consulted by the authorities at any time. But the Nakhuda agrees an official loan and then makes the diver sign a receipt which is

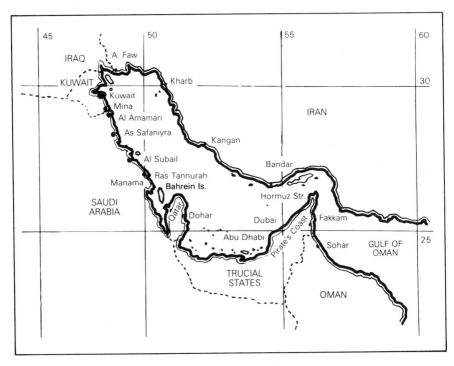

The Persian Gulf

not in the book. In this way, the diver thinks that he is obliged to work for the leader, but in reality he is not.

The Nakhuda who claimed that he was obliging his diver to work for him because of his debt would see his claim rejected by the court. But the divers do not know this. Most of them are totally illiterate and after a year do not know how much they owe the Nakhuda, who does not keep regular accounts of his debts or credits. It is in this way that, when a diver dies, his sons are often forced to dive to wipe out their father's debts and those which they begin to build up themselves with the Nakhuda.

The divers are supposed to share in the profit from the sale, after deduction of the fishing licence fee and the advance payment made to them and to their families by the Nakhuda or by the rich financier on dry land.

The Nakhuda gets 20 per cent of the catch and profit, the remainder is divided into nine equal parts, three for the divers, two for the rope-men, one for the apprentices and three for the second in command.

Ceylon/Sri Lanka

The fisheries of Ceylon, just as famous as those of the Persian Gulf and known for just as long, have seen intense activity in earlier years. The oyster-beds are found in abundance in the strait which separates India from Ceylon. This strait is divided into two parts; the first formed by the Gulf of Manaar, the second by the Palk Strait.

One of the first precise descriptions that we possess of these fisheries is due to Marco Polo visiting the area in about 1294. He reported that a large number of boats stopped each year from April to mid-May at a place called Battelar, and soon afterwards they penetrated 99 km (60 miles) into the Gulf. Once there, the men embarked on the smallest vessels to go fishing. Dealers who wished to obtain pearls had to take on, there and then, a certain number of divers and servants for this short period. Moreover, they had to undertake to hand over 10 per cent of their haul to the King and 12 per cent to the 'charmer of the great fish', who protected the divers from dangers with his prayers!

In 1350 the missionary Friar Jordanus reported the presence of more than 8,000 vessels sometimes working from three months at a stretch under the authority of the King of Kandy.

The region fell under the control of the Portuguese in 1510. They allowed the fishermen to continue their activities on the condition that the catch was divided into four. One part was for the religious leaders, one for the King, one for the soldiers, and the last one to reward the pearlers' own efforts.

In 1658, this area was passed into the control of the Dutch, who changed none of their predecessors' rules. Then it came under British occupation. From 1796, under their guidance, fishing developed considerably until suddenly in 1887 a layer of sand and mud engulfed a large part of the beds.

Since then, extensive research has been done on oysters, and fishing was as severely restricted. It was realised that the pearls from oysters less than four years old were almost worthless. At the age of six the value increased twofold, at seven it quadrupled. Eight was about the average age for an oyster from Ceylon. If one waited any longer, a great number died naturally and many others cast off the pearls which had become embedded in their flesh.

This is how a visitor would have described the fisheries before 1947-48 when Ceylon gained its independence, and was given an additional name, Sri Lanka.

The oyster-beds are regularly inspected and no-one has the right to begin before the fishing season is declared officially open. When this begins, the authorities act in the following way. Batches of 1,000 oysters are raised by diving and dragging the beds in three different places. The three batches are kept in sacks for about ten days. So that there is no risk of damaging the pearls with a knife edge, the oysters are allowed to open by themselves; then flies lay eggs on them, and the maggots burrow into them. They are handed to the washers, who empty sacks of oysters into large tubs full of running water. The washers stand in a line beside the tubs. They are naked and are not allowed to let their hands leave the water except to drop the empty shells at their feet. When the washing is over, there is nothing left at the bottom of the tubs but pearls and scraps of flesh which are carefully inspected by the washers, then by their wives and children who, thanks to the keenness of their sight and the delicacy of their touch, find a large number of small pearls in this rubbish.

The pearl batches obtained in this way are offered to dealers. Still imagining how a visitor in the past would have described the scene: As batches are sold, the outcome is relayed to the Colonial Secretary who, according to the price obtained, will accept or reject proposed fishing on such or such a bed. Fishing generally takes place towards the end of February/beginning of March. At this time, the sea is fairly calm, the currents not too strong and the chance of storms and gales very unlikely.

When permission to fish has been given, the news spreads like wildfire on every coast. Two weeks before the opening date the boats start to arrive at a temporary port, hurriedly built by the English authorities. From these boats come men, women, children and a whole host of building materials to construct huts, shops and all kinds of businesses. In fact, on a deserted stretch of sand situated between the sea and the jungle, a town of several thousand inhabitants is constructed for only a few weeks. The English authorities oversee the positioning of the huts, prison, police station, hospital, cemetery, reservoir, post office, bank and so forth.

The population unites divers, businessmen, dealers, servants, entertainers, dancers, doctors, mechanics and all the people one would encounter in a large town of three or four thousand. The ethnic races are equally diverse, the four main ones being Sinhalese, Hindu, Chinese and Arab.

The fishing technique is the same as that used by the Arabs in the Persian Gulf. Only the details are different. Just before midnight, the divers have a large meal, finish their prayers and set sail to be at the location by dawn. The boat's position has been determined before their departure and marked with buoys by the authorities. When they arrive, they must wait to start fishing for a signal, given by the guardboat, and may not stop until a new signal is given well before nightfall, so that there is time to return to port under observation. The reason is that the English keep about two-thirds of each boat's produce. But when returning to shore, the fishermen manage to take large pearls from the oysters, which start to open during the three or four hours which the journey takes. If the

Divers working over a bed of oysters in the Gulf of Manaar between India and Sri Lanka in the 19th century, when the British administration controlled fishing. The boats would leave at dawn for designated fishing areas. Divers work from both sides of the boat.

winds are against them, they will not reach land until after nightfall, which is a godsend to the pearlers as they can open up a number of oysters and surreptitiously throw the waste into the sea.

When they reach land, the fishermen must unload their pearls in special enclosures. There they are searched by the authorities to ensure that no pearls have been hidden. It appears that a great many pearls are recovered in this way. Then the batch is divided into three equal parts, and one part is given to the fishermen by the officer responsible. They take the pearls outside the enclosure where a crowd of dealers will be waiting to buy them in part or as a whole. Certain batches have been sold oyster by oyster, but the most usual transaction is for batches of eight to twelve shells.

The prices vary a great deal and depend on the number of pearls discovered in the first few sales. It is a lottery which few people can resist.

As for the government's pearls - they are put up for sale by auction each evening at 9 o'clock. Whoever pays the most can choose as many oysters as he wants for this price in multiples of a thousand. This goes on until the tubs are empty. Most of the buyers are Hindus who specialise in polishing and piercing pearls.

The pearls of Sri Lanka are generally of a very high quality in their colour and shape. But it is sadly very rare to find one which weighs more than 10 grains.

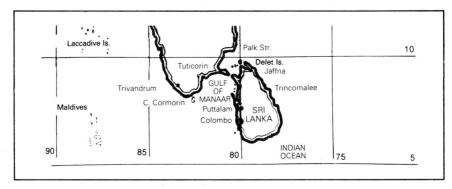

Sri Lanka (Ceylon)

Red Sea

The Red Sea fisheries were well known before the birth of Christ. The oysters *Margaritifera erythroeensis* are found there in abundance. Of a type close to those found in the Persian Gulf they are 10 to 12 cm (4 to 5 in) in diameter and can weigh 1 kilogramme (2.2 lb) or more. The shell is bordered by a fine band of dark mother-of-pearl. These oysters, called *sadof* by the Arabs, have a double value, of the mother-of- pearl shells and the pearls which they contain. They are found in the area from Jidda Suakin to the Gulf of Aden, at depths of 9 to 20 metres (30 to 65 ft).

A smaller type of oyster is also fished, called *Bul Bul* locally, which is of interest only for the pearls which it contains, although its shell is very fine. Of a hundred oysters only three or four will contain pearls.

Lou-Lou means pearl in Arabic, and it is associated with *Ya-mal*, meaning fortune. Yet the fishermen's life on the Red Sea is one of the hardest in the world and very few are left since oil was discovered in such quantities in the area. The poor divers receive only a pittance from the pearls they collect. But from this hard, dangerous life, which injures the body so severely that a man of thirty is old, they take a pride and gain a knowledge which, in the eyes of many, is the greatest fortune of all.

Diving is a hereditary profession, passing from father to son. The young man is not happy until his eardrums have burst. Then he descends even deeper. He will be deaf, but who cares? The *dol*, a sort of fish, brushes past him, releasing an electrical charge which marks him for life. The *loethi*, another fish, does not burn

A sambouk on the Red Sea, which has been fished for pearls since pre-Christian times and was one of the most dangerous areas, the divers working in pairs for this reason. The canoe being towed is used for spotting oysters, as shown in the next sketch.

him but cuts into his flesh like the marks of a whip. He is proud of all that, because at last he is like his father.

Fishing takes place from three kinds of boat: the *boom*, which is a large wide boat able to take 60 men, the *sambouk*, smaller one holding 15 or 25 crewmen and divers, and six or eight canoes, called *houri*.

The owner of the *boom* or the *sambouk* hardly ever sails. He puts his boat at the service of the divers, provides the necessary food and gives each member an advance payment to support their families during the voyage. He puts two of his men on board - the Nakhuda, who is responsible for the boat, and his agent who is his informer.

From the *boom*, the men fix four or five oars on each side of the boat. From these oars go two lines, one holding a weight of 4 or 5 kg (around 9 or 10 lb), the other to raise the diver and his precious load at the slightest signal.

The divers work in pairs, returning to the sea-bed in turns. Their only equipment is a loin-cloth, leather finger coverings to protect them from cuts and a *Pince-nez* made of bone or horn. At the end of the day the oyster opening begins. The whole crew is silently united; from the first blow of the knife, shouts of '*Ya Mal, Ya Mal*' ring out in unison.

On a *sambouk*, fishing is practised in a different way. Early in the morning, the divers on the *houri* leave the *sambouk* to go to the oyster-beds which are some way away, and do not return until evening. The divers in the same *houri* are closely linked and struggle together against the dangers which constantly face them.

Red Sea divers in their canoe. The man in the middle is using glass-bottomed box to see through the surface of the water to the bottom.

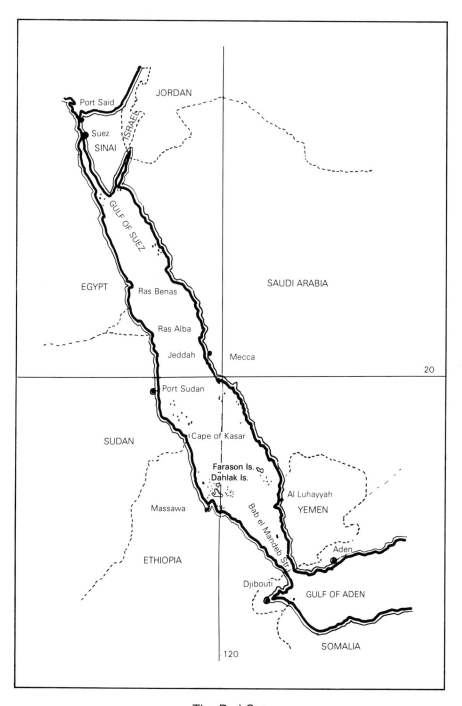

The Red Sea

While one man paddles at the back, another explores the depths at the front through a box with a glass bottom. When he sees an oyster, he dives. His companion then takes the glass and watches the movement of his friend. Armed with a long stick with a pick on the end, he is ready to strike and see off any enemy in sight such as a shark, or other predator. These areas are also full of clams, which represent constant danger. Because these men dive without goggles, their field of vision is very limited. If by mischance a hand or foot catches in a clam as the man tries to tear away an oyster, the clam closes with such force that it can break the bone. The diver's life then rests with the man on the surface, who will dive immediately to save his companion from such a cruel death.

The oysters are opened at night on the *sambouk* before the whole crew. When a pearl is found, everyone claims that it is his oyster and that he is the best diver. The quarrels and controversies which arise for the sake of prestige are all in fun; the proceeds of the trip are in any case put into a common kitty.

On their return to the shore after the voyage, the Nakhuda, the representative of the owner, and one of the divers, seek to sell their goods, which are kept in fine red fabric. For this they contact agents of the great sheiks and Hindus or buyers for foreign firms like Bienenfeld, Rosenthal and many others. These agents are easily distinguishable in the bustling crowd of the bazaar: they are the best dressed by far and stand talking in front of the shops in small groups.

Sometimes the Nakhuda has to travel to Massaouhn, Aden or Djibouti before finding a fair price for his pearls. After numerous transactions and insults, the deal is finally concluded. Then a new one begins.

The Nakhuda and the owner's agent make an agreement and bribe the diver's representative so that he will tell his men he received only about half the actual sum. Then the division of the funds take place - one-third to pay for the boat, one-third divided into three parts (two for the owner and one for his agent) and one-third (which has already been halved) for the crew.

With such an unfair division, and the additional embezzlement, it is easy to suppose that almost nothing is left for the divers, who must repay the advances made by the owner at the start, plus the money which their wives have had to borrow during the long voyage. So almost all the profit is taken up and they have no other course of action but to set out again and try and provide for their needs.

Madagascar

The pearl oysters of Madagascar are from the *pinctada* family. They split into three distinct categories - *margaritifera*, *irradians*, and *andocca*. The natives have never dived to fish for oysters. They were happy to collect them at low tide, the most adventurous diving up to 2 metres (6.5 ft). The oysters are attached to *cymodachies*, forming beds which can reach tens of metres (dozens of yards) in length.

At the start of the century, a census of the oyster-beds was taken and this revealed the presence of important pearl deposits on the north and south-west coasts of the country, particularly in the Tulear region, inside the zone between Moromba and Androka. These deposits, totally untouched, were full of potential. Located at depths of 10 to 15 metres (32 to 48 ft) the beds were easily exploited by men in diving suits. Unfortunately we have few details about the way in which fishing was carried out. But however this happened, the mother-of-pearl and pearls of Madagascar were mainly sent to France.

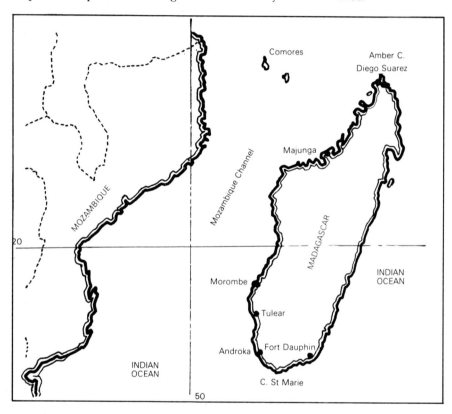

Madagascar

India

India has three regions, a long way from one another, where oyster-beds are found: the Madras coast, certain reefs on the Malabar coast and the area surrounding Bombay.

The Tuticorin fisheries in Madras province are closely linked with those in Ceylon because the channel of sea separating them is only a few miles wide. The oysters there are fished in the same way and by the same men.

According to Dr. Edgar Thurston of Madras Museum, in the estuary of the river Sonnapore close to Berhampore, and in Pulicat lake near Tuticorin, two types of shellfish are found: *Mytious smaragdinus* and *Placuna placenta*, which produce cheap pearls used for cheap jewellery. The fishermen, working from a barge, place a long cane into the water which does not exceed 10 to 12 metres (32 to 39 ft) in depth. At the bottom, the diver holds on to the bamboo with one hand, while he loosens the shells with the other. The bamboo is used to haul him to the surface with his cluster of oysters, which is often very heavy.

On the west coast near Bombay, more precisely in the southern part of the Gulf of Cutch, fishing is not done by divers. The oysters are gathered from rocks at low tide by women and children.

On the coast of Ratnagir, south of Bombay, and at Kananur in Malabar district, a variety of mollusc is found called *Placuna*, which has the popular name of 'window shell' because it was used by the Chinese in the past for windows. A modern use is in lampshades. This mollusc is plentiful from Karachi to the coast

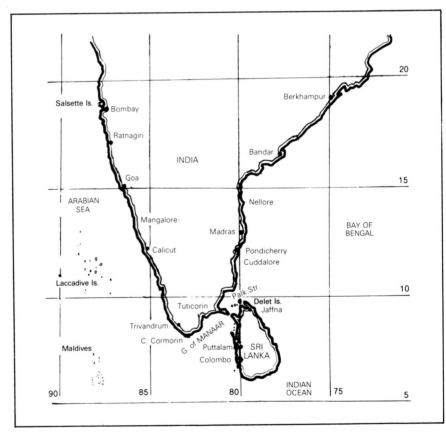

India and Sri Lanka (Ceylon)

by Kanara, but the pearls which it produces are often strange, small and dull. Most of them are sold to be ground to powder as a medicine which is mixed with betel nuts and is consumed by millions of Hindus.

Although India has never produced many pearls, the largest market is found at Bombay. The Hindus love pearls because of the Krishna legend and have always tried to collect the largest number possible. When the Arab dealers from the Indian Ocean coast have finished looking for rough pearls with the divers, fishermen and agents of the Red Sea or the Persian Gulf, they go to Bombay to sell them. The Hindus buy the crude pearls, sand them, polish them, pierce them, class them, pile them in small groups and divide them into categories to await buyers from all over the world.

Purchases are not made by the pearl jewellers direct, but through agents and dealers. Seated on a light cushion, the buyer studies each group of pearls shown to him. To do this, he separates them according to size with the help of a small sieve, then according to their quality and shape. The only aid which he has is his memory, since the light changes with every hour, with the weather, the reflected colour of the paint on the walls and so on.

To make a good purchase he has to assimilate all these factors, without forgetting the market for which the goods are destined. Indeed, for the same colour and quality the English, Scandinavians and Americans will pay different prices.

When the perusal is ended, the seller and buyer cover their hands with a white or red cloth. They stay seated opposite each other for many minutes, without a word being uttered. All the offers take place under the cloth. Pressure applied to such and such a knuckle signifies one price, gripping one or another finger means a different one. It is fascinating to watch the cloth move in total silence, watched by ten or so people. At this moment it seems that the world has stopped turning. No expression appears on their features. Buyer and seller measure each other up, weigh this up, and make a judgment. Finally the cloth is thrown off to signal a firm handshake in front of witnesses sealing a deal which is known only by the seller and buyer.

With the business over, the good news is spread at last that a deal has been struck. But at what price? It is another Arabian nights tale, with the price dropping as the night advances. These machinations form part of the charm and secrecy of the East. The dealings always end with a celebration, conforming with the secular rules of Eastern hospitality.

The Mergui Archipelago

Situated in the gulf of Bengal near the coast of Burma, the Mergui Archipelago is composed of a group of numerous small isles separated from each other by shallow channels which contain *Pinctada vulgaris* and *maxima* in great numbers.

This region, which for centuries was isolated from the outside world, was

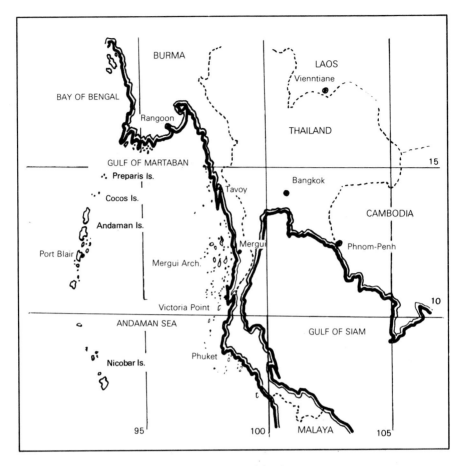

The Mergui Archipelago

inhabited by the Salang people. The Malayasians are thought to be their direct descendents.

The Salangs, a sort of marine nomadic people, live for almost the whole year on wide rustic boats which are well suited to their way of life. It is only during the monsoon period that they take cover on dry land, where they build very simple shelters with bamboo and palm trees. These people lived for the most part from fishing for mother-of-pearl and pearls, which they sold to Chinese dealers who visited them from time to time on their big junks.

In 1826, the British government tried to exploit the fishing grounds by bringing in teams of experienced divers from Southern India. These men hardly knew the area and the rewards in pearl and mother-of-pearl were so meagre that the attempt was abandoned.

The Salangs, excellent divers themselves, men and women, had an exact knowledge of the reefs. With the ever-increasing demand for mother-of-pearl and pearls on the market, they themselves were more and more in demand. It is said that at the end of the last century, knowing little about money, they were still prepared to exchange very beautiful pearls for a small amount of opium or tobacco. Such a windfall could not be hidden from the outside world for long.

In 1888, expeditions from the Red Sea met with great success, to such an extent that it was shortly impossible to find a single piece of mother-of-pearl in the shallow waters. So the method of exploitation of the archipelago was changed. Because they had access to particularly cheap work-forces who were brought from Malaysia, Singapore, Philippines and even Japan, rich Hindus and Chinese had boats which were equipped with all the material necessary for divers to carry out their fishing projects.

Faced with this exploitation of the reefs, the Burmese government had to take some action. They divided the archipelago into three zones, each measuring about 5,200 sq km (2,000 square miles). The exploitation rights were sold by auction. They also took a percentage of the retrieved mother-of-pearl, but none of the pearls.

The catches were sold on the spot to the Chinese and Hindus who had a business monopoly in the area. Pearls which left for Bombay came on to the world market soon afterwards.

Those which went to China were sold to rich mandarins who had, one may say, the annoying habit of piercing the pearls at the base and sewing them on to their cloths, which depreciated the pearl by about 60 per cent.

The natural pearls of the Mergui archipelago are very like cultured pearls from Burma, because they are produced in the same water by the same oysters.

China

The vastness of such a country with so many waterways, streams and rivers, the steepness and length of its coast, have made it a large producer of pearls.

In records of the ancient Chinese civilisations, the pearl is often mentioned as the indispensable present to the Emperor by every foreign visitor. The book of King Shu, 2350 BC, tells how Yu offered pearls from the river Hwai on behalf of King Kau as well as a string of pearls which were not perfectly round.Historians inform us that they were a welcomed way for the Heavenly Empire to receive taxes from wealthy mandarins.

In the ancient dictionary Nh'ya of 13 BC, the discovery of pearls in Sh'en-Sin province is mentioned.

According to different beliefs of the Chinese, the origin of the pearl can vary. Some believe them to have come from the brain of a magic dragon, others that they are plentiful and bring good luck during the reign of great Emperors. The luminosity of the pearl is often mentioned. At the start of Christianity in Kiang-Su province, the story is told of a pearl so brilliant that it could be seen at night three miles away. Other pearls were so bright that one could cook rice by the heat of their rays.

Che-Kiang province has had a long reputation for pearls. In 200 BC the story was told of a merchant in Shao-Hing, an ancient town in Hang-Chau bay, who sold to the Empress a pearl which was 60mm (2.3 in) in diameter, and shortly-afterwards one of 240 mm (9.4 in) diameter to a princess. The Emperor learnt of this discovery and sent his agent to find the largest pearl, which he would call 'the Moon pearl'. But the largest one brought back was no more than 20 mm. (0.78 in).

In the Chinese encyclopedia, Keh Chi Kiug Yuen, the presence of fisheries is shown in the south of Kwang-Yung province, in Lien-Chau department near Hohpu.

The fishing began in spring, but first a horse, a cow, a sheep, a pig and a bird had to be sacrificed to the Gods so that the season was good and the fishermen were protected from the dangers of the sea. In order to economise, animals were often replaced by cardboard models.

Fishing was carried out in a classical way. When he left the boat, the diver, ballasted by a stone to accelerate his descent, searched the sea-bed, filling a rope bag he had with him. As soon as he pulled on the line connected to the boat his companion pulled him up swiftly.

But this type of fishing entailed a certain number of dangers, chiefly due to sharks and other sorts of fish. The inventive Chinese progressed quickly to the technique of dragging a number of nets along the sea-bed, pulled by one or two junks.

A great number of pearls have been found in rivers and lakes. They came from the *Unio* varieties - which are larger than our European ones - *Unio mongolicus*, *Unio dahuricus* and *Unio dinsas plicatus*, types which are spread throughout eastern Asia from Siberia to the Indian Ocean and from the Himalayas to the Pacific.

These were important fisheries in Manchuria in the Amur, Gan and Sangarie rivers and in the Ming Chau Men lakes. Around Canton, *Unio dipses plicatus* has been used to produce a sort of cultured pearl.

Japan

Few documents survive about pearl finds in Japan. Before the arrival of the Chinese, it appears that the Japanese held pearls in little esteem, apart from their medicinal properties. One finds mention of these in two volumes, the Saiminki (1573) and the Yoyakusuwa (1726).

In 1760, the French jeweller and traveller, Jean-Baptiste Tavernier, described pearls from Japan which had been shown to him by a Dutch merchant.

Kaempfer, in 1727, wrote that oysters were very plentiful on the major coastal stretches and that it was possible to gather them at low tide or by diving to depths of 5 to 6 metres (16 to 20 ft). Everyone was allowed to take part in this activity and there was no contrary rule or regulation. For the most part the diving was undertaken by women, who were reputed to be more robust than the men and better able to stand the cold water.

It was the Chinese people who taught the Japanese to appreciate the pearls as well as the ways in which to wear them. Very quickly, pearls came into fashion among the upper middle-classes and acquired a monetary value. From then on, pearl fishing and business with China intensified considerably.

Kamepfer remarked on the presence of two types of pearl shell in the Arima gulf. One was a type of snail, the *Placuna*; the other came from the gastropod family, the *Haliotis*. Both these molluscs had never before been gathered for their pearls but as foods, which is why pearls had occasionally been found in the folds of their flesh when they were being eaten.

The pearl oyster of Japan is the *Pinctada martensi*, which is found in great quantities over much of the coastline. But nowadays most of the oyster-beds are occupied by cultured pearl farms.

The Philippines and Malaysia

The Sula archipelago is made up of a multitude of islands and inlets. Around them pearl and mother-of-pearl fishing is carried out, and was for a long time the region's only source of wealth. Because of the slave and piracy trades, and the attitude of the surrounding populations who violently rejected Western civilisation, very little information of the true life-style of the fishermen and their ancient fishing techniques has been disclosed.

In Malaysia and the Philippines, the pearl is called *mutya* or *mootars*. These two words are very similar to the Sanskrit *mukutaa* and the Sinhalese *mootoo*, which are also words used to describe pearls. This undoubtedly gives us some indication as to the origin and spread of pearl and mother-of-pearl fishing in the whole vast area.

In order to gather pearls at depths of 20 to 40 metres (65 to 130 ft), the people of Sula have long been using a sort of drag-line (*badja*) made in a very special way. This drag is balanced by two stones and has from five to ten long wooden teeth, which are slightly curved outwards and are capped by finer bamboo teeth, about 5 metres (16 ft) in total length. When pulled along behind a dug-out canoe, itself driven by the wind and currents, the drag is tied by two ropes: one being used to pull the drag and the other to hold the teeth in a horizontal position so that the drag slides along the sea-bed on the curve of its teeth.

As soon as the teeth enter the yawning shells of the oysters, the shells close with a great deal of force and can then be brought to the surface. This type of fishing can be used only in areas where the sea-bed is not littered with rocks or blocks of madrepore.

In rocky places, the Moros use another method which relies on the same principle. Working from a dug-out canoe, they peer closely into the water. When they see an oyster hidden between two rocks, they lower into the water a sort of trident tied to a rattan rope. As soon as the teeth enter the oyster it closes and, as in the previous case, becomes the victim of its own trap. Once the shell is shut, the oyster is brought to the surface. Obviously, a trident can be used only in clear and shallow water, and requires great skill on the part of the fishermen.

By far the greatest part of the fishing is done by divers, who were found in their hundreds at Maimbun, Tapul, Lagos and many other places. In their small boats, the fishermen visit the reefs with only a knife to detach the oysters and, on occasion, to defend themselves against sharks and other fish. They enter the water feet first and quickly turn around to dive down. The fishermen of Sulu

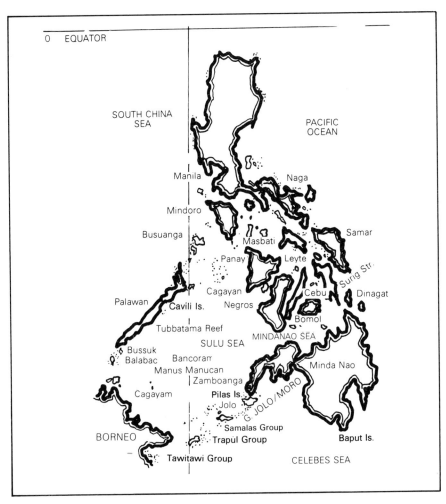

Philippines

and, more precisely, those of Parang, Patian and Sicubun, are among the most expert in the world. They can easily dive 30 to 40 metres (97 to 130 ft). However, they are not very industrious and rarely complete more than twelve to fifteen dives a day.

Several dives are needed to locate and take an oyster, but the sale of the shell is generally enough to satisfy the needs of the fisherman for several days. The discovery of a pearl is regarded as a valuable but unexpected bonus.

After a short day's work the fishermen return to dry land, open the oysters and examine the contents with great care in their search for pearls. The animals' flesh is dried in the sun for later consumption and the shells carefully cleaned and sheltered until they are bartered or sold.

In 1820, in a report about development in the Philippines, John Crawford revealed that 25,000 Spanish dollars-worth of pearls and 70,000 dollars-worth of mother-of-pearl were exported that year from Sulu to China.

For many years, successive Sultans of Sulu exerted total control over the fishermen who, in order to work, had to keep back a certain percentage of the sale of their catch for the Sultan. Moreover, every pearl exceeding six chuchuk was declared by law to be the property of the Sultan and thus could not be sold by the poor fisherman unless he took enormous risks to bypass the law.

The market for pearls and mother-of-pearl was on the island of Sulu, where the catches were brought from many other islands including Maimbun, Parang Tapul, Lagos and Laminusa.

Strong currents circulate between these islands, and the sea-beds of gravel and rock are very favourable for the development of large Pintadines. A smaller quantity of *Margaritifera* is also found.

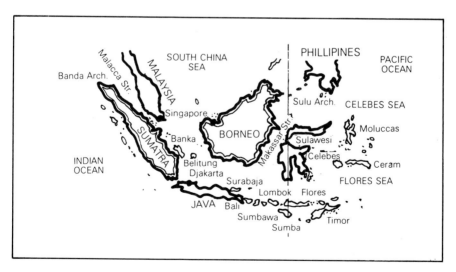

Malaysia

According to a report published by the Manilla trading office in 1906, there were ten boats registered to fish for pearl and mother-of-pearl. In total, the licence fees for a fiscal year were 3,375 pesos from these ten boats. The boats were mainly moros, a type of dug-out canoe with an out-rigger, able to tow two or three canoes, which were used to explore places inaccessible to the large moros.

On each moro, there were one or two divers, a cook, four crewmen and a skipper. The crewmen and cook received 15 pesos a month, the skipper and divers 40 pesos with a bonus for each oyster fished, plus their food.

Near Jolo, the boats worked almost all year round, but further north, because of monsoons, fishing was interrupted for the period from December to April. After a fishing trip, each skipper was obliged by law to declare the number of oysters fished and the total weight of the catch to the Customs officers at the ports of Jolo and Zamboanga.

Nowadays, fishing is still carried on in these regions, but the difference is that the oysters are carefully kept alive to be sold to the various cultured pearl farms dotted about the area.

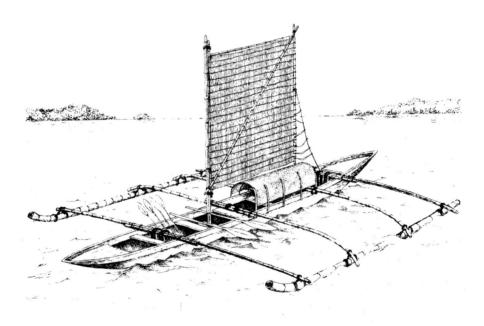

In the Philippines and off Malaysia, a large canoe, called a moro, with two outriggers and a rattan sail is favoured because it can reach otherwise inaccessible areas. It carries a skipper, one or two divers, a cook, and a crew of four. Today the fishermen seek live oysters for the cultured pearl industry instead of pearls.

New Guinea

New Guinea is one of the most primitive places in the world where, until a few years ago, mother-of-pearl was the coin of exchange for the coastal people.

Fishing takes place from dug-out canoes which carry two men who dive in turn, dressed only in loin-cloths. The fishing is never very plentiful, because it does not represent an essential way of life: indeed the forests are rich in wild game, berries and fruit, enough to supply the people with their everyday needs.

Fishing was introduced from overseas. The buyer would charter a boat which he filled with fabrics, kitchen articles and novelties. Going along the coasts and travelling up the rivers, he would hail villagers and natives on their own. Deals would be made on board ship because, even when armed, going on to dry land was running a risk. The buyers would exchange shirts, trousers, pots and pans for primitive statues, crocodile skins, rare birds and of course pearls and mother-of-pearl. Such adventurers were in constant contact with the great dealers of Sydney and Brisbane, with whom they would renegotiate their purchases. Almost by chance these men have been among the best purveyors of primitive objets d'art for museums.

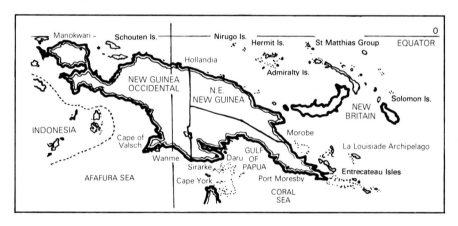

New Guinea

Australia

The most widespread beds of pearl-oysters are found in Australia. They are spread out irregularly over a distance of about 4,800 km (3,000 miles) from Freemantle in the south west to Cooktown in the north east.

In Queensland, the fisheries of the Torres Straits (the channel which separates them from New Guinea) have been very prolific. Fishing is also carried out all along the Great Barrier Reef in the east.

According to an official report in 1905, there were 348 boats and 2,850 men living from fishing for pearls and mother-of-pearl. They collected a catch that

45

year worth £135,000. In the west of Shark's Bay near Broome, at the same time, there were 365 boats, 3,000 men and £196,000-worth of pearl and mother-of-pearl. Further south, the figures were 60 boats, 375 men and £25,000- worth of pearls and shell.

Three sorts of pearl-oysters are found along these coasts. By far the most plentiful is the *Pinctada maxima*, known to give the most beautiful mother-of-pearl in the world. Its shell is totally white inside and is commonly called 'silver lip'. In certain channels between the islands on the rocky sea-bed, a variety of the same species is found whose colour is slightly different, as it has golden yellow tints. It is called 'gold lip' and is less well priced on the world market.

The oysters are found on the sea-bed, firmly attached by their byssus and normally concealed by algae in the water. The largest number of species are found in areas with a strong current; the stronger the current, the more oxygenated the water and the more plentiful the food supply.

The second species is the *Pinctada margaritifera*, smaller than the *maxima*. Its shell has a black border, and it is called 'black lip'. It is from the same family as found in Touamoutou and is reckoned to number 26 per cent of the total of silver and gold lips.

The third species is the *Pinctada carcharium*, which is found almost exclusively in Shark's Bay and the surrounding area. This oyster is the closest to those fished in the Persian Gulf. Its shell is too thin to be used in the button or fancy-goods industry, and it has no value other than the pearls which it contains. But pearls are found more often in *Pinctada carcharium* than in the species previously mentioned.

Fishing for large Pintadines in Australia dates back to 1861: their discovery is attributed to an American named Tays. This navigator, who was constantly searching for mother-of-pearl for the Singapore market, realised that it was possible to collect a great number of oysters at low tide on the north-west coast. With the help of the coastal inhabitants, a great clearing of the reefs began, which quickly exhausted them. Then Tays taught the locals how to dive and by about 1867 a large number of locals were fishing from two- to three-man canoes. At first they dived only to depths of 2 to 4 metres (6.5 to 13 ft), but with practice, they quickly became the equals of the fishermen of Barein and Ceylon. A new industry had been born.

This new activity attracted many adventurers to the semi-desert coasts. Fishing trips were carefully organised. Each boat was placed under the management of two or three Whites who had control of fifteen black divers. On board, the discipline was very strict. When working, the Blacks were not allowed to speak first and indeed could speak only when the Whites asked them questions. In the morning, three or four divers would go on to a barge with a white man. His main job was to calculate the drift of the barge in relation to the current, in order to retrieve the divers as soon as they re-appeared on the surface. Currents could reach speeds of 5 to 10 km (about 3 to 6 miles) per hour.

Fishing in such conditions was extremely hazardous and divers disappeared frequently.

Towards 1879, with the arrival of the first diving-suits, the living conditions of the divers improved considerably. They swiftly adapted to the new way of working, and it is thought that by 1910 no ship employed any naked divers.

The main source of the diver's revenue came from the sale of mother- of-pearl. The boat owner was normally Chinese with a crew made up of about fifteen men recruited from the island population, men of a black race resulting from marriages between Aborigines and the people of New Guinea. Their strength was outstanding. They worked under the control of a skipper who was normally the strongest and biggest man.

Fishing from boats equipped with diving-suits was very different from the old way. The boats were motor-sailers, which had the advantage that they could also work when the wind dropped. They operated for periods from eight to fifteen days, but never went far from the coast, so that they could shelter at night and find fresh water and necessary food.

Australia had very extensive pearl beds spread over 3,000 miles from Freemantle to Cooktown. Most revenue came from shells for mother-of-pearl, here seen being washed on a beach.

The divers, each weighted with lead and simply equipped with a diving helmet and two baskets, dived in groups of four, for a length of 15 minutes to a depth of 10 to 20 metres (32.5 to 65 ft). Linked to a boat by a rope, a diver gave the rope a tug as soon as his basket was full. The basket would be pulled up and the divers would have time to fill the second. Two pulls on the rope meant the diver was asking for more air to scare off a shark or an over-curious barracuda. Three tugs was the signal to be brought to the surface.

Opening of the oysters took place only in front of the men who had caught them. When a pearl was discovered, the men on the air pumps had to be closely watched so that in their excitement they would not change the rhythm of the air being pumped. Each shift took a turn of 15 minutes on the air pumps.

Apart from the pearls and shells, the adductor muscles of the oysters were also kept, being twisted around the guy-ropes to be dried by sun and wind. On the return to dry land, the dried muscles were added to rice or curry and eaten as a delicacy.

The fine pearls of Australia are generally coloured white, with a faint silvery tint. Among the gold lips pearls, named after the golden colour of the mother-of-pearl, are frequently found with a whitish pink shade and cream tint on a silvery background. Because of the size of the oysters, pearls often weigh 20 and sometimes as much as 80 to 100 grains. (A grain is 0.05 gramme.)

The divers were employed by the boat owner to whom, according to the contract, the total value of the catch should pass. But the truth is often very different. By common agreement between skipper and divers, only a small part of the catch was delivered to the owner; the remainder, usually containing the finest pearls, was sold by the skipper, who then divided the profit amongst the crew.

Every week, on Friday evening, the boats returned to port. It was easy to tell how successful the catch had been from the number of muscles drying on the guy ropes. On the quays, women and children bustled, dressed in stunning colours, and amid the shouting, singing and dancing, a celebration was begun which would not end until late at night.

The pearl buyer remained at the edge of the crowd, hoping to catch the skipper's eye. When he did so, the skipper winked to show that he had pearls to sell.

At nightfall a messenger fetched the buyer and both would set off through the narrow streets, in the dark, trying to avoid tripping over roots, with which the ground was covered. Finally they would see the faint light of the skipper's cottage, where a dozen people had gathered, as well as a gaggle of children.

The skipper and buyer retire to a small room lit only by an oil lamp. There, seated on a mat, the skipper tells of the adventures of the last voyage, and the hazards and dangers which he and his men had faced in order to snatch such marvellous pearls from the ocean.

At last, almost regretfully, he decides to open the small bag in his hand and place the contents on a piece of white linen. There they lie, freshly plucked from

Diving-suits were swiftly adopted by divers in Australia, working from motor sailers, and by 1910 there were probably no naked divers left. Divers worked in groups of four, each with two baskets.

the water. The light from the oil lamp prevents the true colour from being seen and all the pearls appear yellow and dull. So the buyer has to guess what the pearls would look like in the cold light of day. When the classifying of shapes and weights is over, the bids and counter-bids alternate. Contrary to Indian and Arab customs, the trading is concluded fairly swiftly, because everyone is waiting behind the door for the result of the sale so that more celebrations can begin.

On his return to his own home, the buyer had to wait impatiently for dawn so that he could appreciate the true value of the pearls he had bought.

The large mother-of-pearl trading centres, and the rendezvous for all the boats, were Broome, Port Darwin, Port Kennedy and Thursday Island.

Through the intensive development of fishing, the beds were swiftly exhausted, forcing the boats to go further afield into areas where it was impossible to shelter from the frequent storms and tempests of the region. The world economic crisis of 1930, as well as the development of plastics in the button industry, caused the collapse of the world mother-of-pearl market. It became pointless to maintain a fleet, and many boats disappeared during that period.

Fortunately for the small boats that had still remained active, the cultured pearl industry was to pick up again. Starting from about 1955, a demand was created for mother-of-pearl beads and once more the best fishing-grounds were sought after and guarded as valuable sources of revenue.

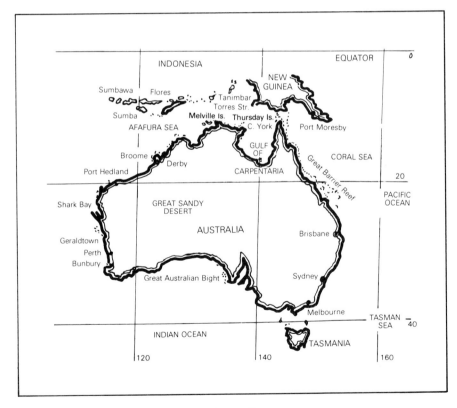

Australia

Tahiti

Before the arrival of the Europeans, the Tahitians did not value pearl or mother-of-pearl very highly, although they used it to decorate clothing, cutting tools and fishing lures. According to ancient legends, the wealth of the oyster-beds was inexhaustible, so that women and children could wade into the water to gather up to 100 kg (220 lb) of mother-of-pearl a day. After large sailing ships were introduced, the beds were quickly exhausted but the demand for mother-of-pearl continued to increase. The Tahitians traded their catches for all kinds of goods.

It was in 1827 that the first white man became interested in commercial exploitation of the mother-of-pearl beds of Touamotou. His name was Morenhout and in order to employ the native work-force he had to obtain permission from Queen Pomare. However, she asked him to bring her such a large amount of money that he decided to go elsewhere and deal directly with the people; but his attempt was a total failure, and he was forced to give up.

Nevertheless, news of the discovery of large oysters and pearls in the region spread quickly. In 1830 and the years that followed, expeditions sent from Valparaiso in Chile had considerable success. In 1846, under the guidance of a Mormon named Grouard, fishing took on a greater importance, and Grouard is supposed to have made a fortune.

The first accurate reports which are available about the production of mother-of-pearl date from 1880, when the French government of the time reckoned that about 15,000 tonnes of mother-of-pearl had been gathered during the year.

So intensive had fishing become that in 1883 the Ministry of the Sea and Colonies ordered a census of the beds. It was carried out by G. Bouchon Grandely in 1885. In his report, he advised strict restriction of the fishing season as well as formal prevention of fishing on some banks so that they could regenerate themselves.

The plan was adopted without opposition and each year the names of islands and islets where fishing was allowed were published in the official Colonial Journal.

In 1890, the diving-suits were tried, but they were never totally accepted by the natives. Luckily they were forbidden two years later in order to preserve the numerous fishermen's livelihoods, as well as the oyster-beds which would never have withstood this type of fishing. Later, the use of diving-suits was permitted, but they were never exploited in any extensive way. At the start of the century, a report from London showed that 450 tonnes of mother-of-pearl was fished each season and that 4,000 fishermen and others depended on this industry.

The two main species of pearl-oyster fished in Touamotou are *Pinctada maculata* and *Pinctada margaritifera*. The first type has almost no value, as its shell is too thin to be worth anything to the mother-of-pearl industry; moreover its pearls are very small, golden yellow, and unpopular on the world market, where they acquired the nickname 'pippi'. The second variety with its large, wide shell is, with copra, the greatest source of the archipelago's wealth. Its black, thick mother-of-pearl was in great demand for fancy-goods and button making, and the black or grey pearls which it forms were always much sought after by the jewel houses.

Fishing was done from dug-out canoes with out-riggers, which left early in the morning and were out all day long. On board each canoe, apart from two divers, food and water, there was also a large stone.

Once over the oyster-beds, the canoe was moored by a rope about 100 metres (325 ft) long; the large stone was tied to another rope and used as ballast. The diver passed a hand through a running knot in this rope and jumped into the water. He guided his descent with his free hand. As soon as he touched the bottom he collected as many oysters as possible in a basket and, when out of

Off Tahiti, divers worked in pairs or singly, like this one, from a canoe with an outrigger. Their methods were so ruthless that they entirely destroyed many beds.

breath, freed his hand and rose quickly to the surface. While he was resting, the rope man pulled up the oysters and ballast, winding up about 10 metres (32.5 ft) of rope. This operation was repeated throughout the day. A few divers were so strong, they rejected the substantial help of the weighty stones.

At night, the canoes returned to the village where the divers opened their catch, cleaned the shells and searched for pearls. The finds were sold to dealers (normally Chinese) who came to live in the village for the season.

Divers from the same canoe split the profit in half. As in Australia, the adducent muscle was saved; mixed with coconut, it made up the main part of the evening meal.

The natives believed that the largest pearls were found in oysters aged about ten years, which was why Tahitian divers went deeper than others. They collected every oyster they came across, young or old, down to 30 metres (nearly 100 ft), totally destroying some beds and leaving no possibility of repopulating them.

The ruthless methods of the Tahitians forced the authorities to close off certain lagoons for a number of years, rather than risk total extinction of the species.

New Caledonia

Pinctada margaritifera are fairly abundant along the coast of New Caledonia. They are found in shallow water between the land and the coral reef which borders the island, as well as around the isles of Lifou, Konienne and Wallis. The natives were brought up to fish for pearls and mother-of-pearl, which they traded with the crews of passing ships.

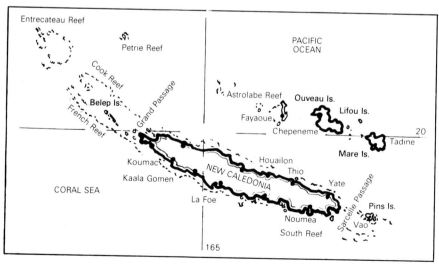

New Caledonia

At the start of this century, diving-suits were introduced, which caused rapid exhaustion of the beds. The greater part of the pearls and mother-of-pearl catch was sent to France. But the mother-of-pearl market collapsed just after pearling became uneconomic.

Today, fishing having been interrupted for many years by the market collapse, the beds have been repopulated. In recent times production of cultured pearls has met with success. Several farms have their products on the market. They produce pearls from light grey to dark black. It is impossible to differentiate between them and similar pearls from Tahiti, Gambiera, Fiji and other regions.

Mexico

With the discovery of Mexico by Hernando Cortes in 1522, the Old World saw the sea in the New World bursting with treasure, including pearls of many colours and shades - black, white, blue, brown and so on. These pearls are generally small in size, although several specimens of 100 to 300 grains have been recovered.

The fisheries are in the Gulf of California, more particularly between the Lucas Point and the Bay of Mulage and the beds are found at depths from 5 to 40 metres (16 to 130 ft). The oysters, *Margaritifera mazatlantica*, are normally found singly, firmly embedded on the coral sea-bed.

Relations between the Spanish and the coastal Indians were as master and slave. The invaders forced the natives to dive for them and, under such conditions, every expedition into the Gulf was dangerous.

With the arrival of the Jesuits in 1642, relations improved between both communities. The Spanish organised fishing trips, for which they used divers from the Yaqui and Mayo tribes and from which they took most of the profit. It is said that there not a sailor or soldier who was not involved in a pearl-fishing deal; so much so that many left their posts shortly after their arrival in the New World.

This state of affairs could not last. In 1740, Father Silvatierra, the official authority, prohibited all sailors and soldiers from pearl dealing; but he had to make certain concessions so that the natives were not suddenly deprived of their income.

In 1825, an English company tried to exploit the beds by using a diving bell. It was a catastrophe. Lieutenant Hardy, in charge of the expedition, gave the reasons in a report 'It is practically impossible to dive with the bell because the sea is often rough and even when it is calm, the jagged sea bottom and the strength of the currents makes the use of such equipment very hazardous.'

In traditional fishing, divers, normally from the Yaqui tribe, went to the oyster-beds on board a large ship. From this, dug-out canoes were sent out, each with three or four divers, who carried a net tied to their legs or their neck to hold the oysters they gathered. In one hand, a diver held a hefty stick with which to detach oysters stuck between rocks or coral and also to defend himself against possible enemies.

Fishing took place from May to September, when the water was not too cold in the morning. Indeed, every afternoon shortly after midday a strong breeze blew up, which could upset the frail boats and made any fishing impossible.

By the start of this century, diving techniques had progressed considerably. Then, expeditions went off for two to three months at a time. The main boat was really a small cargo ship, and the canoes were barges able to transport six men, an air pump and diving equipment. The well-ordered, intensive fishing resulted in rapid depletion of the oyster-beds.

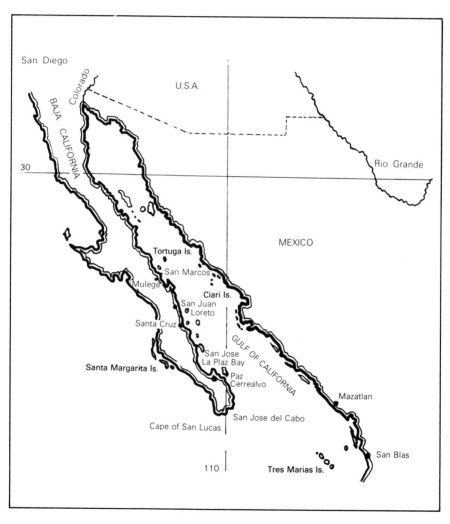

Gulf of California

Panama

The fisheries of Panama were discovered by the Spaniard Balboa, who in 1513 reached the Gulf of Saint Michael, known today as the Gulf of Panama. While scouting the land, he met the Indian Chief, Tomaco. As he seemed astonished at the amount of gold and pearls which were worn by the men and women of the tribe, the chief presented him with gold, 240 large pearls and a great number of smaller ones. Seeing the surprise and wonder of the Spaniards, Tomaco sent his men fishing and in a few days presented the foreigners with 2,000 grammes of pearls. The great chief told Balboa that these pearls were fairly modest in comparison with others which had been found off the Isle of Tararequi, where pearls as large as a human eye could be taken from oysters as wide as sombreros.

The Spaniards returned the following year. An interesting report on Balboa's 1514 expedition has been found, which contains the following words, 'The chief of Tararequi Island tried to repel the Spaniards three times but at the fourth attempt they succeeded in landing . When they had disembarked, the chief took them to his own home, gave them food and a basket of pearls weighing 110 marcs (27,280 grammes/about 60 lb). In return he was given spectacles, hammocks, bells, scissors, axes, and all sorts of trinkets which he valued more than the pearls'.

In the 16th century, Ouiedo concluded that the majority of the pearls set in the Spanish crown, as well as those found in Seville and Toledo cathedrals, came from the coasts of Panama.

The Spanish conquered the region and reduced certain natives to a state of slavery, forcing them to dive to great depths. They believed that the deeper the oysters were fished, the larger the pearl would be which lay inside. This was quite false and many divers died because of the bad treatment meted out to them by the conquistadors, so slaves were imported from Africa. According to the record of Admiral Antonio De Ulloa of 1735, the slaves had to give their masters all the pearls that had been gathered and in return they could keep the shells.

These were the ancestors of the black divers who still live on the islands of the Saint Miguel archipelago.

After Panama became independent in 1820, the black divers continued to fish for oysters and pearls, but for their own profit. They sailed in fours in dug-out canoes, and fished from June to December. On islands which were fairly near the coast, they erected huts in which they stayed for two to three weeks, only fishing during daytime and using low tides to reach the far depths.

Oyster and pearl fishing became very popular in 1855. In 1859 a report tells us that, in that one year, 957 tonnes of mother-of-pearl were exported to the English market, which was only one of many in the world. One can only wonder at the millions of pearls that were torn from the ocean bed.

In order to satisfy the growing demand for mother-of-pearl at this time, boats were sent with diving gear on board. But they did not always get the expected results. A story is told of a Scottish boat which arrived in Panama with a crew of thirty men equipped with air pumps and diving-suits. This experienced team expected to make a fortune in a few months. But they were struck by yellow fever and in six weeks two-thirds of them had succumbed. The rest of the crew swiftly raised anchor and left for more friendly climes. Luckily not every expedition met with the same bad fortune.

This was how a fishing trip was arranged. It was a feat of team-work which needed large resources and a small fleet which included a sailing ship of 80-100 tonnes, a schooner of 15-20 tonnes, a motor boat and five or six canoes propelled by oars and sails to carry the air pumps.

The large sailing ship carried the diving equipment, the galley, food supplies and spare parts. The schooner was used to transport the mother-of-pearl back to dry land each day. It was also used as a source of contact between the main ship and the outside world. The motor boat towed the canoes to the fishing area, helped out if needed, and returned them to the main ship at night.

Each canoe took about six men on board. As soon as it arrived at the fishing-ground it would drop anchor. Two men worked the air pump and the diver tested his equipment for the last time. When he reached the bottom, if he saw any oysters, he signalled for two baskets to be sent down, which he gradually filled. When one was full he sent it up to the surface and filled the second, and so

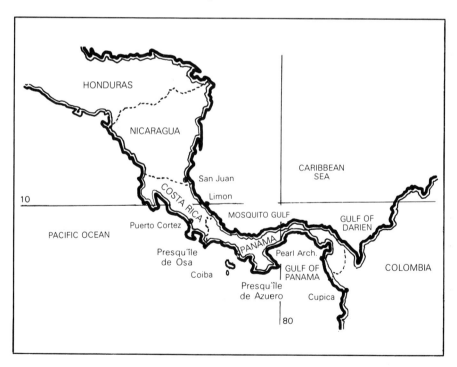

Panama

on. On the canoes, the oysters were put into bags bearing the number of the diver who had gathered them.

Each dive lasted two to three hours, depending on the tide and the depth at which the diver was working. Throughout this activity the rhythm of the air pump was carefully watched by a man in the canoe.

When the fishing was over, the motor boat took the canoe back to the main ship, where the oysters were finally opened.

The oyster-beds stretched from the Bay of Panama to the coasts of Costa Rica, but the divers were often Mexican refugees. The flotilla's owner would sign a contract with every diver and make him an advanced payment. Wine, women and betting on card games took up most of this money in a few days. At dawn on the departure date, the boss would have to round up his men from all the bars and brothels. It is easy to imagine the trouble he would have to make such an unruly gang obey his orders. Moreover, he had to ensure the safe conduct of the pearl buyer, who generally travelled on the ship and carried a great deal of gold on him.

The divers were paid according to the tonnage of the oysters caught. Deductions were made for expenses and advance payments, but the pearl dealings were counted as separate payments.

Venezuela

Before the arrival of Europeans or Americans, the natives of Venezuela did not attach any great value to gold or pearls because they were so plentiful. They wore them freely and used them to decorate their temples richly.

After his third voyage to America in 1498, Christopher Columbus recorded that as his boat entered the Gulf of Paria it was escorted by a large number of canoes, whose rowers wore chains and plates of gold against their chests as well as pearl bracelets. In a letter written to the Court in 1500, he explained his delay and begged the clemency of his sovereign for his stay to collect pearls and gold in the Gulf of Paria and the neighbouring coast.

Franciso Lopez of Gomara, in his 'Historia General De Las Indias' published in 1554, claimed the existence of more than 400 lagoons rich in pearls between Cape Vela and the Gulf of Paria. He also said that during the same voyage, Christopher Columbus discovered the island of Cubagua, which he named 'The Island of Pearls'. Having let a few of his men disembark on scouting trips, he was surprised when they hurried back laden with gold and pearls which they had exchanged for glassware.

The Venezuelan oyster-beds were still being fished very actively between the wars. Fishing was done in two ways, by a single diver in a small boat, or by dragging the sea-bed. Several attempts were made to use diving gear, but luckily they were rejected by the locals who were afraid that their oyster-beds would be rapidly exhausted, and they would lose their livelihoods.

The oyster found in Venezuela is the *Pinctada margaritifera radiata*, closely related to the type found in Ceylon. The shell has very little commercial value. The colour of the pearls is very varied, going from white to brown and even black. The pearls rarely weigh more than 20 grains.

Most of the Venezuelan goods are sold in Paris and more precisely by the Binenfeld firm, who have made them something of a speciality. Indeed this company owns its own fleet in the region, thus maintaining a virtual monopoly of this type of pearl in France.

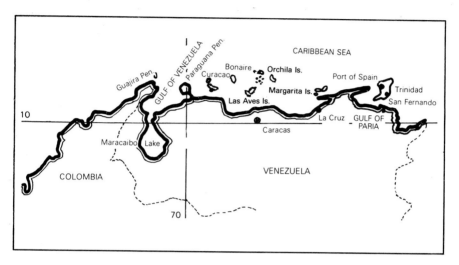

Venezuela

United States

It is said that the first pearl from the USA was discovered in 1857 by a cobbler named David Howell. Howell used to search the rivers for mulette, a kind of edible mussel, of which he was very fond. One day, on the banks of Notch Brook near Peterson in New Jersey, he collected a sufficient number of mulette, returned home and prepared them by frying them in oil. Then he sat down and tasted his favourite dish. Suddenly his teeth grated against something hard. He spat out a pearl weighing 400 grains. The next day he took it to a jeweller, who told him, 'If the pearl had not been damaged by the heat, oil and teethmarks, it would have been worth 25,000 dollars.'

The news spread quickly and a few days later, another pearl was discovered by a carpenter, Jacob Quackenbush. It weighed about 100 grains. In order to get the best price, he went to New York, where after much discussion, the jeweller Charles Tiffany bought it for 1,500 dollars.

After both finds, Notch Brook was over-run by amateur prospectors coming from far and wide, but no more large pearls were ever discovered. In the years that followed however, it is thought that between 120,000 and 150,000 dollar's-worth of pearls were taken from the river. The day soon arrived when not a single mollusc was left. Notch Brook was exhausted.

Notices in the press about the two large finds unleashed a huge rush for pearls. They were found in numerous lakes and rivers in Ohio, Texas, Colorado, Mississippi and Wisconsin. The names Sugar Apple, Rock Wisconsin and Mississippi River became famous for the pearls which had been found in their waters.

Depending on the river where the pearls had been found, they had different colours and values. Those from Wisconsin were reputed to be the finest, and the story of their discovery is well worth telling.

A salesman in Prairie Les-Chiens noticed some children playing marbles with coloured balls he had never seen before. He went up to them, had a look at the 'marbles' and asked where they had been found. They told him they had come from the grocer's.

The grocer's shop was a well-stocked emporium with almost everything that one could wish to buy. The salesman asked for marbles for his children and the grocer pointed to a corner of the shop where there were five or six barrels from which he bought a selection.

Back in New York, he showed the strange marbles to one of his friends who worked in a jeweller's business and immediately recognised them as freshwater pearls. He told his boss, who immediately sent him to Prairie-les-Chiens to buy all the marbles available. The news spread and soon millions of pearls were being found throughout the State.

In Arkansas it was said that every river contained pearls. Black River was by far the richest.

In 1898, Tennessee Valley had its moment of glory, as well as Mystic River in Connecticut, Pearl River in Rockland, Ocklackonee River in Florida and many others too numerous to mention.

A great number of rivers containing pearls were discovered by the children of farmers who chose land near water to build their farmstead. Most children could not resist water and when they went swimming, they discovered American mulettes and pearls.

When the true value of pearls became known, thanks to articles in the press, whole families joined in the search and exploited the rivers to supplement their incomes.

The intensive gathering of mulettes without regard for their age, as well as industrial development and pollution of entire rivers, caused the total extinction of the species in many waters. Most of the pearls were slightly irregular in shape, whereas the world market tended to prefer pearls which were totally round, pear-shaped or button-shaped. At the same time pearl discoveries which were becoming rarer did not offer such lucrative rewards.

Curiously enough, the successful development of the cultured pearl industry was based on mulettes (also called 'pig-toes'), and now all cultured pearl cores come from this shellfish.

Europe

Pearls found in Europe are mainly freshwater pearls and an important source of supply in the past. Nowadays, very few rivers or lakes are worth exploring to find them.

English and Scottish Pearls

English pearls were always much sought after as well as those from Scotland. In his work 'Ecclesiastical History of the English People', St. Bede, the English monk (673-735) gave a detailed description of the English method of pearl production at the time. He declared that there was a great variety of shellfish, producing pearls of every colour, red, purple, green, violet, but most frequently white.

In 1070, Marbodius, Bishop of Rennes, stated that English pearls were as beautiful as those from the Far East. But John II, King of France, did not share this point of view. In 1355, in a treaty confirming the privileges of goldsmiths and jewellers, one can read: 'Craftsmen cannot use gold with silver, or Scottish pearls with Eastern pearls in their work except in large precious ecclesiastical objets d'art'.

Throughout history there are eye-witness accounts of English pearls being given and received by sovereigns as presents. It is said that Queen Victoria owned the finest collection of pearls including one of 40 guineas (£42). The Duchess of Hamilton sold her necklaces for £350 in 1863. A report in 1864 estimated that the total value of pearls gathered in Scotland was £12,000.

Most of these fine pearls came from the shellfish *Unio margaritifera*, which has a shell 7.5 to 18 cm (3 to 7 in) long by 4 to 6.5 cm (1.5 to 2.5 in) in width. The outer shell is dark brown, the interior a milky white. It is found here and there on pebbly river-beds, and also in clusters in holes in the river-beds where the water is deep. Pearling rivers in Scotland included the Tay, Earn and Teith rivers in Perthshire; the Dee, Don and Ythan in Aberdeenshire; Spey and Findhorn in Invernesshire, and many others such as the Doon, Burns, Nith, Annan, Clyde and Tweed. Only one professional pearl fisherman, Bill Abernethy, is left in Scotland today.

Ireland

Pearls have been found in rivers in Ireland - Kerry, Donegal, Tyrone, Antrim and elsewhere. In 1892, the River Bann gave up one of the most beautiful pearls that Ireland had seen. A year later Lady Dudley, wife of the Viceroy of Ireland, presented Queen Alexandra with a brooch made up totally of pearls from the river Connemara.

Fishing for the *Unio* is only carried out when the water is low. The fisherman's equipment is very simple; apart from waders, he has a stick about two metres (6.5 ft) in length, pointed at one end, and a tube about 5 cm (2 in) across with a glass end which allows him to scrutinise the river-bed and direct the movement of his stick in order to catch the mulette. This sort of fishing is sometimes carried out from a barge. The stick is then longer, but the technique is identical.

Despite pollution, it is likely that individual prospectors still fish in the lakes and rivers because a Parisian dealer says that in 1980 he bought a small collection of pearls which, from the colour, had been fished only recently.

French Pearls

The Vologne, a river in Lorraine, and more precisely the stretch between Arche and Bruyeres, was well known for its pearls in the 16th century. In 1530, Volcy, a chronicler of the time, mentioned it in a small volume, as did Francis Reues in 1566. He explained that near the Vosges mountains was a river which contained white, dull pearls, and that when pigeons were made to swallow them, the pearls emerged pure and shining. At the same time, a legend claimed that the pearls were carried and placed in the mulettes by pigeons. Remembering the phenomenon observed by the Arabs in the Red Sea, (page 30), one can see a link.

The Dukes of Lorraine maintained a certain amount of control over the pearls, for fishing was authorised only during the summer months, which had the effect of preserving the species.

In 1779, in an essay on the Vologne fisheries, Durival noted that during the sixty previous years the pearl catches had been plentiful but they were now becoming scarcer.

The Empress Eugenie, on holiday at Plombière in 1862, expressed a desire to have several mulettes transported to her ponds at Malmaison, because the pearls were so famous. This was immediately carried out, but to my knowledge no pearl was ever discovered there.

In west France, many pearls were found, notably at the confluence of the Ille and the Vilaine, in the Steir and the Odet, near Quimper, and in the Menech near Lesneven, north of Brest. All of these were small, but reputed to have a good colour.

Further south a type of mulette is found which is slightly different from the previous one - the *Unio sinuatus pictorum*, which for a long time was exploited for its pearls and shell in the Gironde estuary, in the Garonne, Dordogne and its tributaries, and in the Seugne in Charentes.

German Pearls

Fisheries are known to have existed in Bavaria from the 16th century and to have produced a great number of pearls. The main fisheries were found in Upper Franconia (along the Main and the Lower Upper Rhine), Upper Palatinate (on the Czech border) and in the small tributaries of the Danube between Ratisbonne and Passau. There were other rivers such as the Main, Saale,

Oelsnitz, Lamnitz, Schwesnitz, Grunebach and Perlbach. Fisheries were also situated on lakes, the most important being on the Isar and Ilz.

Pearls from Lake Ilz were reputed to be the finest. By a decree of 1579, they were made the exclusive property of the Bishop of Passau, and whoever contravened this monopoly was to be hanged.

In Saxony and more particularly in Vogtland, fisheries were very active, especially on the rivers Elster, Mulhauser, Freiberger, Mariemeeyer, Trieb, Teil and others. In 1621 the elector Johann Georg I declared them to be a royal privilege and appointed Moritzschmerler as the fishing superintendent.

Austrian Pearls

The province of Bohemia in Austria, where the Moldau, its tributaries, and the blue Danube flow, has produced some fine pearls. In ancient times, Austria was divided into large kingdoms, and fisheries depended on the rulers as main buyers. In 1791, at Prague, Count Adolf Schwarzenberg owned a fabulous collection of shells and pearls which had come exclusively from his own land.

Danish and Norwegian Pearls

The best-known fisheries of Denmark were in Koloing Fjord in Veile province, Jutland. In Norway it was the district of Nadenas and its numerous waterways, Stavanger where the Gon flows, Narim and Quasim where pearls were found. The provinces of Lister, Mandal and Christiansand are strewn with streams, once rich in pearls.

The main waterways containing pearls in Norway and Denmark were discovered by a German named Schmerler. In 1734, Charles VI of Denmark asked the King of Saxony to send him a fisherman for Vogtland to search the waterways of his country. Thus Schmerler was sent to Copenhagen. The report which he made was so precise and his estimates so promising that the King and Queen invited him to the palace, where he was awarded 100 ducats and a pension for life.

Swedish Pearls

According to the writers Olaf Malmer, J. Fischertein, and Gissler, most of the rivers and streams coming down off the mountains in Sweden were extremely rich in mulettes and pearls.

Olaus the Great, Archbishop of Upsala, wrote in 1562 that many fishermen left the island and mountain areas and went to the coastal regions in order to sell their pearls to the women and girls there, where it was fashionable to wear them.

Carl Linne, the celebrated botanist, described the way in which the Swedes fished for mulette in his book 'Lach Lapponica'. Fishing took place only in summer, when the water was low and warm enough. By walking on the river-beds, the fishermen could see the mulettes. When the water was deeper they dived from a boat made from birch wood. When it was sunny, the river-bed could be seen clearly, but in cloudy weather it was hard to see. To correct this, the boat's hull was painted white to reflect the daylight on to the river-bed. The fishermen hung over the sides, each one holding a long stick which ended in a grip, allowing him to bring any shells to the surface as the boat drifted along.

A good pearl was rarely found, even after opening a hundred mussels, but sometimes about twenty small pearls, scarcely larger than grains of sand could be found in a single shell. The large pearls were often reddish brown and occasionally white and round.

It has been stated that a mulette aged seven years always contained a pearl, and that when eighteen years old, one or two would have a pearl attached to the shell.

Almost all the European countries can be said to have had rivers which contained pearls. Finland with the lakes near Kolk; Hungary, and of course Russia with a whole host of streams, lakes and rivers too numerous to mention.

Some of the shellfish on the European coasts occasionally produced pearls. Indeed, it is not uncommon to find them in mussels and oysters, but they are dull and lifeless and consequently have no commercial value. However, in the Mediterranean, some *Pinna mobilis* are found near the coasts of Provence, Corsica, Sardinia and in the Adriatic; and pearls from these regions are sometimes quite large and have a good colour.

CHAPTER 2
The European
Fine Pearl Market

Pearls were, and still are, fished by a variety of peoples on most continents. But throughout the 19th century up to the last World War, there were only two markets of world importance, London and, above all, Paris. These two cities acted as the centres of pearl dealing the whole world over.

Paris

Between the First and Second World Wars, Paris was the principal world market for fine pearls. There were a number of reasons for this: it had a diversity of population; it was a city of exile and welcome for many foreigners; a furnace of ceaseless creativity in the worlds of philosophy, literature and art; furthermore it was appreciated as such throughout the world.

It is for art that the pearl has provided many masterpieces, and enhanced the reputation of the pearl dealer. When one considers that no two pearls are alike, the sorting and setting of them in bracelets and necklaces could only be carried out by an artist's hands. We can all admire the works which bear the creator's mark: Boucheron, Cartier, Chaumet, Mauboussin, Mellerio, Tiffany, Van Cleef, Arpels, all prestigious names with a place in the history of art.

Paris, the showpiece of Europe, welcomed the most important and most beautiful stocks of pearls into her vaults. In fact, counting dealers, importers, traders and couriers, there were at that time about 400 people directly involved in the pearl business. From number 2 rue Lafayette to number 74 rue Cadet, each building contained at least one pearl dealer.

Large importing firms had representatives permanently stationed at the production sites. A few financed fishing trips themselves, despite the hazards and risks that such an operation entailed. Other buyers travelled aboard steamships for 15, 30, even 45 days and disembarked at Bahrein, Bombay, Ceylon, Papeete, Panama, and many other places.

The two largest dealers in Paris were Bienenfeld and Leonard Rosenthal, who was commonly known as the 'Pearl King'.

The traditional centre of the pearl trade in Paris, rue Lafayette, seen here where it crosses rue Cadet.

Politics played a unique role. Russia, because of the Russian war, followed by the Bolshevik revolution of 1917, was a great source of supplies. Paris welcomed thousands of White Russians, many of whom had saved their jewels. They were soon forced to sell these in order to buy homes or continue their long exile in America. Then Soviet officials, learning that Paris was the pearl capital, regularly came to sell their fabulous booty.

Consignees were also very numerous. Most were Hindus, living in Paris, who regularly received merchandise sent by their families and friends in Bombay. The firms of Shroff, Cooper and Shah were well known.

Foreign dealers were in evidence. The most renowned came from Bahrein and was called Alireza. He owned a huge flat on the Champs-Elysees where he lodged his entire retinue, without which he never moved. Furthermore, he had an office in the rue Lafayette directed by a Hindu called Kharas. Twice a year, after each fishing trip, Mr. Alireza came for two or three weeks to the capital, where his arrival was always expected. Accompanied by an employee who carried a case in each hand, chained to his wrists, he went to the office to hand over his treasure. It is with a certain amount of emotion that the older generation like to tell the tale of how this man honoured them with visits. When his stay was over, he left the unsold pearls in his office. They always found a buyer after his departure.

The pearl lapidaries or skinners too, contributed to the high reputation of Paris. When a large pearl was discovered, it was handed to them alone to make it as beautiful as possible. Their renown was world wide and the names Goujon, Duparc, Pitre, Thillier and Payen are still remembered.

This is a story told by one of them. A small importer had bought a pear-shaped pearl in Australia, weighing 143 grains. Its shape and size were exceptional, but from one angle, a blackish area could be seen which lowered its value considerably. All the dealers knew of it and would not offer fair prices. Chance had it that the lapidary and importer were together when a broker sold it yet again for a derisory price. The lapidary picked up the pearl, scrutinised it and told his friend that he was sure that the dark layer was hiding another pearl. He could not guess the size or shape, but it would be of higher quality. His arguments were so convincing that he obtained permission to work on it.

He began without delay and after several days, under the black stain, a white dull layer appeared which was like chalk. The pearl was worthless. Depressed, he put it into a box, wondering how to break the news to his friend, who might as a result be in financial difficulties. The day came when he had to return the pearl, and not wishing to admit that he had been mistaken, he was in a bad mood. Many pearls of the same type and origin, although not as large, had been transformed by his work, but not this one. In desperation he sat down to work again. The first blow of the scraper cracked the material and revealed the pearl which lay underneath.

A few hours later, he handed over the most beautiful pearl that he had ever seen. It weighed 41 grains, was perfectly round and extremely beautiful. The next day it was sold for a very high price to a passing Italian jeweller.

The sheer dynamism of the Parisian business world maintained a constant and regular supply of goods. The clientèle was so numerous and different that dealers had to specialise in order to meet the demand. Some made only necklaces in bright or creamy-pink colours, others in white and whitish-pink, others sold only single pearls. So it was very difficult for an importer, coming back from a long trip, to know the individual requirements of each one. He would use the services of one or two brokers who kept in close contact with the dealers, manufacturers and retailers, and knew where to get the best price for a 'choker' from India, a set of two matching pearls from Tahiti or a strange button-shaped pearl from Australia. They acted as intermediaries between buyer and seller, whose anonymity was jealously guarded until the deal was finished. Their role gave the market a dynamic dimension which the telephone never replaced.

In Paris in the *Belle Epoque* (pre-1914) , there was a particularly high standard of living, and a steady concentration of dealers, offering an unlimited choice of pearls and marvellous necklaces, drew a large number of foreign buyers.

The Americans took the most beautiful pearls, small or large, which had to be perfect in shape, with a bright pinkish-white colour and of high quality. The Germans and Dutch liked small pearls of good shape with clear colours, but of lesser quality. Small pearls with perfect shape and colour suited the Swiss; their perfectionism was reflected in their purchases.

For Scandinavians it was small and medium sizes, round and oval, very white and dull (freshwater types). At the other end of the scale, the Spanish loved large and very large pearls, round or otherwise, of mediocre quality and creamy-pink colour. The Italians liked the same colours as the Spanish, but preferred slightly smaller pearls of higher quality. Small ones of reasonable to high quality in warm colours, even ochre, attracted the Portuguese.

France had an important interior market. This was partially maintained by a custom which dictated that a godfather would buy a pearl or pearls each year of a girl's life, to be made up as a necklace to present to her on her first communion. In rich families, before the marriage, the father-in-law always gave the bride a pearl necklace. French women have always adored pearls, which must not be too big, too small, too creamy or too white; in short the most difficult pearls to find.

The world crisis of 1930 dealt a fatal blow to Paris business. From one day to another, the price of merchandise fell by 80 per cent. An important number of dealers went bankrupt. When business came good again, only about thirty firms were left, and their financial power was not sufficient to support the Gulf fishermen, who swiftly found less dangerous and better-paid jobs with the oil companies. The consignees received no more goods and foreign buyers began to leave the capital. The arrival of the cultured pearl on the market was also very prejudicial to the real pearl market.

Finally the 1939-45 war made this wonderful profession disappear. Today, only the Gourdji firm deals mainly in fine pearls. The decline of the pearl industry was not the only reason for the liquidation of many businesses. During that period, many pearl dealers turned their attention to coloured stones, diamonds and cultured pearls, so linked with fine jewellery, Paris remains an important centre for the profession.

I am certain that with the help of public aid, Paris could quickly rediscover its pre-war international position. The dealers, craftsmen and lapidaries are still there with their creativity, their good taste and their savoir-faire. Massive production would attract a great deal of foreign buyers with the undoubted advantages that this entails; creation of new jobs and influx of foreign currency which France needs so badly.

The Pearl King

The most influential man in the business of pearls between the Wars was Leonard Rosenthal. He was the son of a merchant in Vladicaucasus, who had a shop selling all sorts of products such as porcelain, crystal and pottery, as well as corn, wine and coffee.

One year, the harvests in Northern Russia were very bad and the demand for buckwheat was more and more intense. His father sent him to find supplies at whatever cost. He was only fourteen years old, but after travelling around he accomplished his mission with success. In this way, he entered the business world.

At fifteen he went to see some Russian friends in Paris in the rue Boulle, and was offered his first job, in the Baccarat crystal shops of the rue Paradis. For a month's work, he received the modest wage of two golden louis, and with this capital he launched himself into the second-hand trade by attending various sales. Soon he came into contact with people in the business and gained a real passion for pearls, of which he quickly became a true connoisseur.

Later on, when he had established his pearl business, he decided to deal directly with the Arabs in the Persian Gulf and sent his brother, Victor, to Bahrein. For three years, Victor managed to buy some important sets but the Arabs, ever fearful of foreigners, did not show him the finest pearls. To gain their confidence, he decided to capture their imagination and changed his capital into pieces of silver. Thus, at the start of a fishing trip, he disembarked at Bahrein with fifty mules loaded with chests, which crossed the town to his home.

Astonished, the Arabs believed him to be the richest man in the world and did not hesitate to show him their finest pearls. So the Rosenthal firm was the first to show incomparable pearls in Paris.

Leonard Rosenthal was not merely an astute businessman; he was also a planner and innovator. 'Too often', he said, 'we are distracted by personal problems and ignore thousands of ways of refreshing our minds, if only for a few moments. Who among us, if he so wishes, cannot find time to read a few pages of a good author, to listen to some music or to slow down to watch one of the many street spectacles.'

In 1925, he bought the Dufayel Hotel and had it demolished, to build in its place a block sheltered from the Champs-Elysees. His idea was to decentralise commerce from the heart of Paris and to move it to one of the most famous avenues in the world. From this first success, his company soon bought twenty-six buildings, which were all turned into business premises.

He wanted to communicate and share his knowledge with both influential and humble people. But is not a book one of the best media? So he became an author. Two of his best-sellers on the pearl business are 'In the Pearl Kingdom' and 'In the Gem Garden'. His message also lived on through his son Jean, a companion of the liberation and one time President of the Syndical Chamber; then through his grandsons, Jacques and Huberts, pioneers of Tahitian cultured pearls.

When the 1939-45 war and the collapse came, he had to leave France and for the time being had lost everything. His business genius soon enabled him to make a new fortune in America, however, but he always told his friends that his heart was still in Paris.

London

The pearl market in London worked in much the same way as the one in Paris. The shipping firms were very important because of the British presence at the start of the century in the regions of production such as India, Burma, Australia and many other countries.

The shippers therefore had a permanent stock of varied pearls. The most important were Pittat Leveson Ltd, E.W. Hopkins Ltd and B. Warwick & Co Ltd. They sold most of their goods to manufacturers who made necklaces, but their best clients by far were the French who had gained a world-wide reputation for this sort of work.

Dealers were also very active and their buyers searched the whole world for pearls. Between Paris and London there was constant rivalry for merchandise on production sites. The most active firms were Whitehorn Bros, Alfred Drayson Ltd, Jerwood and Ward, J. Tanburm Ltd, and the Australian Pearl Co Ltd.

At the time, English banks played an important role in the development of the London market. Owing to their deep involvement in the pearl trade, their services were used by many buyers and sellers. Their considerable efficiency and reliability protected each other against all sorts of swindles and embezzlement. They were used as impartial go-betweens. Here are two examples:

The buyer who finished his purchasing in Bombay had his goods delivered to a central bank in London and did not pay the sellers until the goods had arrived safely.

A seller living in a country where the political situation was somewhat risky, could send his goods to a bank with instructions that he was to be sent only 50 to 70 per cent of the total value. This gave him some insurance so that he would not be bankrupt if, for political reasons, he had to leave a country in which he had been working for years and might otherwise have been financially ruined. Many people owed their safety and peace of mind to this system.

During the inter-war period, 30 per cent of the European pearl market is thought to have passed through London. The interior English market was also very important.

One cannot think of the London trade without evoking the name of Louis Kornitzer (1873-1946), author of four books about his life as a pearl dealer, including 'Pearls and Men', published in 1935.

This great specialist wrote with much humanity and many flashes of humour about his first steps in the trade as well as his later encounters with other dealers, and despite the years that have passed, his writings still evoke distant memories of the early faltering steps of many of us still in the pearl business.

When a boy, Louis Kornitzer declared that he wanted to be a tram conductor. 'You shall certainly be nothing of the sort,' his grandmother told him firmly. 'You will be a pearl merchant like your grandfather, and his father before him, may they rest in peace.'

His instruction began at the age of four, almost as far back as his memory could take him. He was seated at a high infant's chair in his parents' workroom in front of a desk covered with green felt, and given a pair of corn tongs and a stack of seed pearls to play with.

He commented in his book that he thought of pearls as living things to talk to, and they seemed to answer. Although he had an affection for the bright ones, he loved even more those that had lost their sheen and gone blind through no fault of their own.

He was never compelled to play with the tongs and pearls, but there were rules to be obeyed. He could not go to the work table with buttery fingers; he had to keep his nose dry while there; and he had to put the seed pearls back in their little boxes, the blind ones going into a separate box. Most of all, he was never to move any of the tools from their accustomed places.

One day his mother asked him if he could separate the white, pink and off-coloured pearls. 'That's easy,' he told her, but when he scamped the work, she took the pearls, jumbled them together and announced reproachfully, 'I see I must do this myself'. It so shattered the young Kornitzer that he begged for another chance and did a better job of sorting. Soon, during his early training, he discovered the pearl scales and their tiny weights, but was not allowed to touch them. It was a great moment when he was first permitted to handle this wonder himself, instead of enjoying only 'the occult fervour of distant joy'.

His mother taught him the language of the scales by tipping out the weights one by one as he sang out, 'Fifty carats, and a half carat, and a quarter carat, and a sixteenth carat, and a sixty-fourth carat,' while he turned over each small weight with his tongs. Although his mother said that calling out 'carat' every time was tiresome, he thought that it robbed the weights of their rightful titles and the announcer himself of his importance.

The weight used universally today, of course, is the metric carat, in decimal points.

Describing the buying of pearls, Kornitzer declared that they were usually dirty, so his parents always wrapped their purchases in a linen cloth with powdered soap which was boiled in water for a while in a small copper kettle over a spirit lamp. When cool, the pearls were washed in methylated spirits so that they shone and sparkled.

The pearls accumulated after buying, selling and cleaning would be graded for size, colour and quality and stored in small metal boxes. When the boxes were filled to over-flowing, the work of grading and collating stopped and many days of stringing followed. Young Kornitzer loved watching his mother's white hands and keen eyes at this work. She made her own needles from nickel wire and chose the finest silk thread.

The threaded needles were laid ready and the seed pearls arranged on the table 'like companies of soldiers going into action'. At zero hour, the first needle would stab unerringly through its tiny heart and the next and the next so quickly that in a moment the three-inch (7.5-cm) needles resembled a trapeze full of flesh-tinted acrobats. A rapid movement of his mother's wrist, and the pearls slid down the silken thread one after another.

Eight-inch (20-cm) lengths containing hundreds of pearls were made up, and a hundred of these lengths were assembled into large bunches with the threads at each end gathered together with blue silk or golden thread and tasselled.

A linen docket attached to each bunch gave the gross weight and the net weight of the pearls. Kornitzer wrote that his family called the bunch *eine Masche* and the French *une masse*. In England the many supplies of pearls provided in this style from India were called 'Bombay bunches'.

Most of the families' bunches went to Italian merchants, but others to Spain and the great markets in Algiers and Morocco, Persia, Afghanistan and China. A small and unusual part of the trade was in selling otherwise useless hopelessly blind pearls to the Chinese for crushing and use in medicine.

Kornitzer wrote that part of the rue Lafayette in Paris, from the Gare du Nord to within a few steps of the Grand Opera House, became the centre of the pearl trade from the last quarter of the 19th century. He described the scene of his day in that street, as in Hatton Garden in London and Maiden Lane in New York, when groups of men 'for the most part sallow-complexioned, beak-nosed and falcon-eyed' stood in groups on the pavement or in the gutter in practically any weather buying and selling pearls.

You could tell which were the dealers because they were haggard, pale and worried. The sleek, complacent and joking ones were the brokers, who touted for business and knew, or ought to have known, the needs of all the dealers.

Louis Kornitzer was not only a famous dealer, but a sage and exceptional linguist for whom contact with other colourful characters, who came to London from Europe, the East and Russia, was a constant delight.

Queen Alexandra wore a great many pearl necklaces and helped to make pearls the fashion for many years in high society. In present times, Princess Diana's love of pearls has had a similar influence.

From 1945 to 1960, London became the largest supplier of pearls in all the European markets in a somewhat unexpected way, which was unenviable and rather sad. In 1945 the Labour Party came to power and voted large taxes on inheritances. As we French know, the English are very attached to their homes and gardens. Many of them would have been unable to keep their property if they had not sold the jewellery and pearls which had been in their families for generations. Most of these valuable pieces went abroad. Although the British State may have become wealthier, the national treasures were impoverished and the whole nation was the loser.

CHAPTER 3
Testimony of
Times Past

At the great exhibition of 1900 which took place in Paris, Jacques Bienenfeld arrived in the capital after finishing an apprenticeship with a Viennese jeweller. He was soon enchanted by the life and splendour of Paris. He went into business in a small shop in the rue Châteaudun and specialised in pearl dealing. He had a true passion for pearls. After the First World War, he moved to 62 rue Lafayette, built up a large company and drew buyers to Paris from all over the world.

This man built up a fleet of ships equipped with the most sophisticated diving materials of the time and organised fishing trips to Venezuela and Colombia. As a leader of men, he possessed great ability in choosing his partners and in delegating his power. Thus he was able to open offices in New York, Bahrein and London. When the catches came in, he sent his best buyers to Panama, Papeete and to the Philippines.

The merchandise arrived in Paris in a raw state and was polished and pierced in his own workshops which employed twenty four people. For the latter operation he had invented a piercing machine and placed the patent with Boettcher, the manufacturers.

Jacques Bienenfeld told his close friend: 'I am able to work like a slave and live like a prince. I make plans at night and am not happy until I can put them into effect the next day.'

London had become a more important base for buying and rivalled his offices at 62 rue Lafayette and 9 and 14 rue Cadet, so he planned to unite the whole Parisian pearl market in one place in order that foreign buyers would have no trouble in finding all the goods they needed. But for many reasons, this project was never realised.

Between 1924 and 1932, he published a journal called 'The Pearl', which had no other purpose than to inform the trade of any new laws affecting countries they traded with, to defend or help colleagues in difficulty, and lastly to promote the pearl in the widest possible way. Other subjects dealt with were art, jewellery, diamonds, emeralds, rubies, sapphires and anything else which affected the business of pearl dealing.

This man had a very strong sense of family loyalty and one of his preoccupations was to have his family around him. A cousin called David replaced him at the head of the company after his death. David was a connoisseur of pearls as well as a careful businessman. He had two sons, but fate took them into other occupations. Thus, shortly after his death, the Jacques Bienenfeld company ceased trading.

Thanks to the kindness of Lili Bienenfeld, I was allowed to consult the bound copies of all the journals 'The Pearl' that were published and permitted to reproduce the most significant articles on the great period of pearls throughout the world. I think of this as homage to this great family for work they did for almost 50 years for the good of the whole pearl business. Here are the extracts:

A Fine Act of Integrity - At the start of 1917 my Moscow representative entrusted Mr. Ovtchinikoff with a string of large pearls which was worth 100,000 francs at the time. Mr. Ovtchinikoff was a dealer well known to Parisians. Before the war he came to Paris quite often with emeralds and imitation pearls from Siberia. His fine Slavonic head was well known. He was the official supplier to the Tsar himself.

Everyone knows the events which overtook Russia.

My representative had to leave the country because of the revolution. The string of pearls remained in the hands of Mr. Ovtchinikoff. The new authorities in Russia made Mr. Ovtchinikoff undergo the same fate as many of his colleagues. He lost a fortune and underwent many hardships. He was even sent to Siberia.

One could therefore imagine my surprise at seeing him again, aged and drawn by his suffering. He had managed to escape via Japan and America. He returned the string of pearls, which I had long given up for lost. Despite his age, Mr. Ovtchinikoff, totally ruined, is now obliged to earn his living as a broker.

I owe it to him, to make known this fine act of integrity. - Jacques Bienenfeld.

Legion of Honour - October 1925 - M. Durafour, Minister of Work, could not make a better choice than to award M. Jean Goujon with the cross of the Legion d'Honneur.

Ever since the government decided to honour our profession, this distinction was expected.

All our congratulations go to M. Jean Goujon.

No one can mention pearls without naming Goujon.

His *savoir-faire*, modesty and integrity brought goodwill to our market; even when abroad, his personality spread the good reputation of the French artist.

Tales from 'The Pearl'

Tales from 'The Pearl' - After a brutal turn, the bus stopped. John Smith, alias Joseph Goldsmith, got up on his tired legs and stepped off.

The sun was not strong enough to heat the air. Mechanically, Smith buttoned up his fur coat and absent-mindedly made his way to the office. He was a tall and well built man. His curly beard, thick lips and strong gaze all had the unmistakable mark of the East. His gait was steady despite his age and nothing in his appearance gave any hint of past struggles. He had fallen low on several occasions and had raised himself up each time, but then he was young and had few doubts in life.

He knew how to say 'no' and only really liked those who needed his help. But now he was old. Those he had helped before, were themselves ruined. But his friends could not believe that he had fallen so far and still hoped he would succeed. He was embarrassed by his old jacket, which the decrepit state of his suits had forced him to wear. Without worrying about the road ahead, he felt some beads of sweat run down his forehead. When he could not find his handkerchief in its usual place, he fumbled in the pockets and felt something hard. 'Another moth ball,' he groaned unhappily. He had some difficulty fishing it out because it had slipped through the lining.

After a moment he brought it out and was just about to hurl it away when he stopped and staggered to one side, his hand closed and pushed it back into his pocket. He was unable to shout out, but instinctively steadied himself against a wall. When he had recovered, he continued on his way. He mused. Twenty years ago he had bought a set of pearls in India, from which the largest and most valuable one had disappeared. All number of searches had been in vain. He had not been insured, relying on his luck. Now, today he had found it. Once again he had been saved in the nick of time by his lucky star.

A passer-by bumped into him and he realised that he was in Hatton Garden.

Instead of going to the office, he went into a neighbouring firm, through a door marked 'Private', smiling all the way. Instinctively he felt that he should have received the pearl from the Gulf that very day. The other man examined it and without asking the price said, 'Buy it for me, I will pay'. Smith imagined his return home that evening, his arms laden with parcels and said calmly: 'Give me £20 to pay for the cable.' - Alfred Deitz

Curiosities - a Pearl Containing Gold

Curiosities - a Pearl Containing Gold - January 1924 - M. Raphael Dubois in a note read to the Academy of Science by M. Henneguy has just announced the curious discovery which he has made in a fine pearl. In certain rivers which flow down the Central plateau, small mussels are found in which fine pearls are sometimes found of some value. In one of these mussels, the author found a pearl of medium size with a piece of shining yellow metal. Upon chemical examination, it was discovered that a golden plate was forming part of the pearl and a small piece of this could be seen on the surface. The presence of gold in the pearl can be explained by the fact that the rivers and waterfalls of the area often carry pieces of gold.

In the same context, other curious phenomena have occurred. At Meru, an old worker of mother-of-pearl owns a shell which contains a fly. The feet and wings can be seen through the mother-of-pearl.

This announcement by scientist M. Raphael Dubois has encouraged us to open a small museum for any kind of shell which has some point of interest.

Some Experiments on Piercing Pearls to 0.33 mm in 1932

Before Piercing				After Piercing				Percentage of Pearls out of the	
Pearls	Weight	Average	1 X	Pearls	Weight	Average	1 X	Weight	Price at 1 X
100	539,08	5,39	2 905,64	100	535,44	5,35	2 864,60	0,6800	1,4100
100	347,60	3,47	1 206,17	100	344,48	3,44	1 185,01	0,9000	1,7500
100	211,04	2,11	445,29	100	208,76	2,08	434,22	1,0800	2,4900
150	159,24	1,06	168,79	150	156,60	1,04	162,86	1,6600	3,5100

The loss of weight caused by piercing pearls as it is done in Bombay is about 30 per cent less than piercing them to 0.33 mm; the diameter of the hole in pearls pierced in Bombay is not always the same. It remains to be seen if the Hindus will conform to the guidelines of the International Conference of the Associations of Manufacturers, Wholesalers and Retailers of Jewellery, Gold and Silverware, and to the regulations laid down by the Syndical Chamber of Diamond and Pearl Dealers, and Lapidaries. - J.B.

Telegram from Tahiti - 3rd March 1924 - We have just received the
following news from Papeete. In mid-ocean, after midnight, a large schooner has foundered. In the heavy seas, only seventeen passengers were saved, but no Europeans died. The survivors were in rowing-boats for five days without fresh water or maps before being rescued.

Many pearl buyers lost their merchandise and some of the money which they had on them.

When the post arrives in five to six weeks, we will give more details.

News from Tahiti - 4th April 1924 - We have just received the following letter from our correspondent:

Papeete 10.3.24.

I left Papeete on board the best schooner, 'Monica', on 22nd February in the morning to travel to Tuamotou and Gambiers to buy pearls and mother-of-pearl.

By 27th February, in reasonable weather, we reached the island Anaa. After taking on several tonnes of copra, we left the aforesaid island on 28th February for Herchetue, 185 miles to the South East.

On 19th February at 6.30 a.m., while travelling at four knots, the boat sunk in less than a minute.

We just had time to leave the schooner and to cling on to pieses of the wreck, wearing only pyjamas and underwear. (Seventeen members of the company.)

After three hours we were able to free and bale out a boat. We put up a sail, saved a compass, a few paddles, a mast and rudder, two cases of beer, one of salmon, two of beef and two of orange; but we did not have a drop of fresh water, or any light, and we drifted helplessly throughout the night. We rowed for four and a half days and with the help of the wind and rain we arrived at the island of Mehetia, totally exhausted after 200 miles.

Nobody was able to save any personal possessions. We were met at Mehetia by the schooner 'Kivi' of the Naval Company and were taken back to Tahiti on 6th March.

Telegram from Bombay - July-August 1924 - At our own request, we have received the following news telegrams:

'For the moment, the market is stable; the monsoon is not far off, and we hope for business soon; the exchange variations are a small hindrance and news from the Paris market is not good enough to provoke any change; nevertheless the Arabs are buying.'

Venezuela - July- August 1924 - The government has just announced the opening of the fishing season for the 1st October, with an increase in the fishing charges. - C.A.

Colombia - July-August 1924 - The Colombian fishing grounds were closed on 30th June and the season ended in a fiasco for all the fishermen; they have all lost money. The Colombian government has imposed such a heavy tax on each diver that even production costs have not been covered.

The date when fishing will start again is unknown. - M.B.

India, Calcutta - 18th March 1925 - The fishing season for pearl oysters, which opened in Ceylon on 27th February has been adversely affected by bad weather. It is not infrequent for boats to be confined to port for several days without leaving. Pearl merchants drawn to Marachchikade, where there are several fisheries, in the hope of seeing a large number of oysters put up for auction each night, have been disappointed. Apart from bad weather, another factor has emerged which is hindering the oyster catch: difficulties have arisen between the Ceylon government and the authorities of Madras province, where the best divers come from, and the settlement of the question of the divers' departure has taken some time. Meanwhile, only 200,000 or 300,000 oysters have been caught instead of a million.

The sanitary conditions of the camp set up by the Ceylon authorities are good and provisions are kept at equivalent prices to those in Colombo.

Prices reached in the auctions range from 38 to 40 rupees for 1,000 oysters; this average is somewhat high because of bids from small traders who generally buy one or two thousand oysters in the hope of finding some pearls. This raises the price for dealers who take more important lots of 20,000 to 30,000 oysters. - Communications from the Office National du Commerce Exterieur.

At Paris - September 1925 - News from Bombay and Bahrein is very encouraging: there is great rivalry between buyers and prices are steady. There is still business going on in Paris but very little speculating; everyone could be said to be on their guard. They are all awaiting the results of the new fishery in the Persian Gulf.

As prices in Bombay are about the same as the previous year and since production is low and buyers numerous, the next arrivals at Paris will be sold at a better price than the present one. Emerald prices are holding steady.

Many people are coming from Holland and Belgium to buy fine old pearls at retail prices. Because of the exhibition and bad weather, we left Paris later than usual this year; and the return of dealers and resumption of business have been slow. News from the American continents is better. - L.P.

Pearls from Madagascar - 5th May 1924 - Pearl dealers in France usually offer very inferior pearls under the name: Pearls from Madagascar. They are genuinely pearls from Madagascar, but only those of poor quality.

Sometimes very pretty pearls are found in Madagascar with a fine orient, but the Hindus who fish on the Great Island coast, send them to Colombo and Bombay, where they are exported under the name: Pearls from India. They arrive in France, saddled with a huge bill.

With the present importance of the pearl market and the large value of these luxury items, measures must be taken to ensure that pearls from Madagascar arrive at the Metropolis by a direct route. - The Jewelers' Circular.

The Financial Situation in Paris - May 1925 - We will give foreign details later on.

As for the Paris market, it has strengthened since April. It is true that speculating has halted for the most part, because of fears about sudden tax changes, few dealers dare buy in stocks of pearls, but small deals have been made leading to no lowering of prices.

Pearls which were bought in India between December and January only came on to the market in March, and they have cost 20 per cent more than those in the previous batch.

So it may be quite possible to buy the new merchandise with fewer shillings, since the Hindu prices are so high that the new arrivals are not competing against the old stock.

Bombay has no merchandise; new production cannot arrive for three or four months and since the Hindus are keen to buy, there is a great battle on in the Gulf.

Indeed, the present calm is the result of everyone restricting his purchases to the minimum, simply through fears of taxes, but the demand continues.

In London business is being done through retailers because of the influence of visitors to the Exhibition.

In Paris, there is an increase in demand caused by the arrival of foreigners. If only government would create some stability, business would pick up its former trend.

The Situation in Bombay - M. Ibrahim, the well-known friend and representative of M. Alireza, has just arrived in Paris.

We went to ask him about the situation in Bombay and the intentions of M. Alireza, because he is usually the latter's precursor, and we wanted to know how soon we would have the pleasure of seeing him.

M. Ibrahim replied that M. Alireza would only arrive - and these are his own words - when 'the market was a lot warmer and exciting'.

When we asked what prices were like in Bombay, we were told: the same as in Bahrein, where merchandise cost 15 to 20 per cent more than in the previous year.

When we remarked that business was quiet, he told us that it was not important to the Arabs, who had no bills of exchange to pay. Was he criticising our commercial system? One can never tell how much scorn an Arab is putting into his words.

He added that the Arabs all work with their resources. They do not sign bills of exchange, they prefer to keep their pearls than have money in their treasure chests. They will sell when the prices are right. Furthermore, the Arabs are convinced that the price of pearls will never fall; it is merely a matter of time.

We report this brief interview in full. - 'La Perle'

Celyon on - January 1924 - Although the pearl oysters on the beds in Ceylon are said to be rapidly multiplying, we will have to wait for six years before they are mature enough to be gathered.

The last successful fishing spree was in 1904.

On 1st January 1900, fishing rights were sold to the firm of Ceylonese pearl fishermen for 20 years, at a price of 310,000 rupees a year; but this was rescinded when there was no fishing in 1909, 1910 and 1911. The pearl beds are believed to extend all along the North West coast from Negombo and Ceylon to Manaar, and the most important beds are well known, although most of them have not produced pearls.

An official inspection of the Ceylon pearl beds has just taken place and a new bed of great importance has just been discovered in an excellent state; the young oysters are being protected against attacks from rays and other fish which feed on these molluscs.

Ceylon - January 1924 - Pearl fishing in Ceylon has been prohibited for 14 years, but there are hopes that it will recommence in 1925 or at least 1926.

The main markets for these pearls are Paris and London, and it is also worth noting that the boom in 1912 which doubled pearl prices from January to April did not result from the Bombay dealers' hoarding of pearls, but in the halt of fishing in Ceylon and the Persian Gulf.

In Bombay in 1913, a powerful syndicate was formed, in which a lot of French capital was invested. But the Balkan war, and the threatening World War made European bankers more and more prudent and they refused to advance money on consignments for Paris and London. An Indian bank which intervened to try and stabilise the market was the cause of a banking crisis in Bombay. At present, the market is very quiet and no further activity is expected until fishing resumes in Ceylon. G. Kung.

Pearl Fisheries in Ceylon - 10th April 1925 - The following note has been received from the French consulate in Colombo, concerning pearl fisheries in Ceylon, whose new season began on 26th February.

Visitors are warned that no pearls other than those obtained from pearl oysters collected during the fishing season can be taken to the fishing camp in Marichchukaddi without the permission of the camp superintendent. This permission was not bound to any payments.

It must be noted that this order which forbids pearl importing without a licence, is meant to prevent the introduction of cultured or artificial pearls into the camp.

Pearl Fisheries in Ceylon - 1925 - We have received the following
message from the French Chamber of Commerce in Bombay, which completes
information which had already been received.

The French consul in Ceylon wanted us to know that the Ceylon pearl
fisheries, which had been closed down for several years, will re-open on 26th
February. We publish below a list of rules about pearl fishing published on 19th
December 1924.

Pearl Fishing in Ceylon 1925:

1 Thirty million oysters are thought to be present on the following beds:
Twynam's, Paar, Penya, Karai, and West Cheval.

2 The fishing base will be at Marichchukadi, on the west coast, about 25 miles
south of Mamear. Sites have been arranged for the construction of pearl and
other shops and the right to occupy these sites for the 1925 fishing season will be
put up for auction by a government agent on Monday 23rd February at 9.00
a.m. Places for 'toddis' to wash and keep the oysters will be auctioned on the
same day.

3 The base will be open to visitors from Tuesday 24th February. Sites for
temporary accommodation will be let by the government agent for the
Northern Provinces, who will be the base superintendent. Visitors will be able to
buy the necessary wooden boards and beams from local suppliers.

4 A rest house with ten bedrooms is being built for the use of well-to-do visitors.
People who require rooms should warn the government agent well in advance,
and should bring their own camp bed and sleeping materials etc.

5 Fishing will begin on about 26th February. No one without a special licence
will be allowed to take out boats or dive in the vicinity of the beds. These licences
will be available from the government agent or his representatives in various
ports throughout India and Ceylon. The number of boat licences available will
be 125, and those for divers will not exceed 1500, not including 500 Arab divers
from the Persian Gulf. All boats and divers must be at Marichchukadi by
Tuesday 24th February.

6 For the buyers' convenience, deposits of at least 250 rupees will be accepted
by the Colonial Treasury or the Government Treasury in Ceylon, and the
purchase of oysters can be made from these deposits. People wishing to make
large purchases of oysters are asked to leave the funds at the Colonial Treasury
in Colombo.

7 A medical service and measure of law and order have been organised, and
drinking water has been laid on.

8 Opening ceremonies etc.

9 Visitors wishing to go to Marichchukadi can travel there
  a. Directly by sea from Paumben (Madras Province)
  b. By rail from Manaar (in Ceylon), then by road to South Bon, then by
    sea to Marichchukadi.
  c. Or by sea from Colombo (115 miles) if the steamships are available.

Any enquiries about travelling from Paumben or South Bon to Marichchukadi, can be sent to the Madura Co. Ltd. or to Mr. P.M.S. Mohammed Meera Sachi and Mr. P.R.M.K. Mohammed Abdul Raanan Marai Kayar at Paumben.

10 Quarantine etc.

11 All correspondence on the subject of fisheries should be sent to The Government Agent, Northern Province, Saffira, Ceylon. The Secretary General's Office, The Colonial Secretary, Cecil Clementi, Colombo.

PS Fisheries will be paid for by the Ceylon Government. A third of the oysters will be given to the divers as their share.

P.P.S. The remaining two-thirds will be sold daily by the government agent in appropriate lots. Dealers wishing to rent shops are informed that they will be let on 23rd February, and that they (or their representatives) must arrive at the camp by 22nd February 1925. - Ceylon Government Gazette.

The Persian Gulf Route - 1928 - One of the greatest routes in the world

has been developing recently. It goes from the Mediterranean to the Persian Gulf, passing via Syria and Baghdad, and thus crossing countries under French and British control.

Although Syria was recently in a state of fluctuation, which the newspapers reported, tranquillity returned a year ago, and peace now reigns there. But the situation south of Syria and Baghdad is less calm, where Great Britain encountered great difficulties with King Hedjaz. The fluctuations in this part of the Asian continent are felt to be a reaction of Islam and the East against Europe, and symptoms of this are demonstrations by Turkish nationalists with Moustapha Kemal, troubles in India, and the war in China.

Few regions have been as affected by the Great War as this one, stretching between Egypt and Persia. Frontiers remain indistinct and it must be hoped that not only will there be a decision on the geographical and political status of this corner of the world, but also a calmness which will open up communication routes from the Mediterannean to the Persian Gulf and improve relations between Europe and Asia. - Relinal.

Departure for the Persian Gulf - 1928 - The fishing season and buying

period have begun in the Persian Gulf. Mr. Alireza and Mr. David Bienenfeld will be on hand in eleven days. The days have long passed since two to three months were needed for this trip. If our government manages to get permission to fly over Arab territory, it will be possible to travel from Paris to the Persian Gulf via Beirut in four days, or if the Turks allow people to fly over their country, the exiting Paris - Bucharest line could be used and one would be in Bahrein in 4-5 days.

The photograph which we are showing confirms the popularity and general esteem which Mr. Alireza enjoys.

This man is extremely polite and very mild mannered. He adds courteous words to all his actions, and knows how to arrange his business transactions in such a refined way, that at his home, it is more like an ambassador's meeting. If he is ever forced to refuse a client something, he does it so delicately that no offence is given.

Mr. Alireza never strayed from his natural idealism and his faith is always apparent. At prayer time - whoever he is with at the time - nothing prevents Mr. Alireza from accomplishing his religious duty. He merely asks for permission to interrupt the conversation for a moment and kneels down in prayer.

Let us add that Mr. Alireza gives most of his profits to schools, which he has set up in Arabia, where 1,200 pupils are being taught at his expense.

It is not surprising that such a man enjoys great popularity in his own country. He is equally popular in Paris and every time that he leaves our capital a crowd of friends gather at the station to wish him goodbye.

From the Government of Bahrein - 25th June 1930 - Translation of Proclamation No. 1889-17 from 1348.

The following matters are raised for public notice:

1 The import and transport, sale, possession or handling of cultured pearls in Bahrein are forbidden under pain of imprisonment.

2 Any help given to anyone committing the above offences will carry the same penalty.

3 All people are required to denounce instantly to the police or to a government agent any contravention of the above law, and in case of failure to do this, they will be liable to all the punishment of paragraph 1.

4 The sale of unpierced bleached pearls in Bahrein is prohibited and liable to the same penalties. Pearl working is allowed.

5 The import and use of diving equipment is prohibited in Bahrein. Any person importing such equipment will have it confiscated. - C. Darlymple Belgrave, Financial Councillor to the Bahrein Government.

Departure from the Persian Gulf in 1929 - We are showing a photograph below of Mr. David Bienenfeld, leaving for the Persian Gulf. At the station, we had the pleasure of meeting Mr. Mohamedali Zair Alireza, who had come from London to greet his old friend and colleague, Mr. Bienenfeld.

On this occasion, Mr. Alireza was happy to give 'The Pearl' representative his impressions on the pearl markets of Bombay and Bahrein. We reprint his words here: 'In reality there are no more pearls in Bombay or Bahrein, everything is in London or Paris. The Arabs have sold everything. According to news which I have just received from over there, there is great competition. Everyone has money and accordingly the rivalry is heating up. Because of this, I foresee an increase of 10 to 15 per cent. I can also tell you that the catch this year will not reach Europe until the second half of January.'

When we asked why Mr. Alireza stays in London rather than Paris, he answered 'Customs and financial formalities make business in France very difficult. Before the arrival of the tax on business profits, speculation still existed in Paris, that is to say selling between dealers, which facilitated selection and natural sorting by quality, size and colour. The 2 per cent tax has stopped these business deals, but I am keeping on my Paris office and Allah will help me to deal once more with Parisian businessmen.' - La Perle.

N.B. We are told that the pleasant buyer Mr. Saul Pack left at the same time as Mr. David Bienenfeld. Buying in the Gulf has begun six to eight weeks earlier this year than in previous years.

Extract from a letter from the Persian Gulf - 25th October 1930 -

There is very little merchandise because the fishing entrepreneurs have heard about the world crisis and do not want to spend too much. Only 5,000 boats have gone out this year instead of the usual 15,000. On the other hand, the Arabs who have bought pearls are hanging on to them, and are speculating on a rising market.

Most of the pearls have been bought by the Hindu Gaimnal and the Arab Hilal. They had not bought anything for two years, but they were attracted by the prices which were considerably lower than those of 1929 at the start of the season. They will not let any merchandise go except at a large profit. Gaimnal is just as big a speculator as banker and Hilal is extremely rich.

According to what Said Omar says, a man who knows all the fishing deals, the 1930 production will only be one third of the previous year's catch.

Up to now neither I nor Mr. X have found an interesting pearl. The small production has altered the situation considerably.

We both came in the hope of finding something worthwhile, but the scarcity of the merchandise and the arrival of Hindu and Arab buyers, drawn by the early low prices, have resulted in there being nothing for sale at prices other than last year's.

There are several lots in the hands of the fishing entrepreneurs, but now that the season is almost over, they will not sell them for six to eight months, because only the new season will make them do business.

In my opinion, you will find Paris or London cheaper than out here. I await your instructions under these circumstances.   Signed, David Bienenfeld.

In the Persian Gulf - 1st October 1931 - Extract from a letter sent to me

by the Bienenfeld firm about the present situation in the Persian Gulf.

In Europe one feels that a buyer backed up by resources can find bargains out here and impose his own price. This is a grave error, and the rash man who opposes current opinion would do well to leave, because no one can equal the Arabs in making other people dance to their tune, even when they want to sell.

Their stubborness and haggling try the nerve and the patience of an inexperienced European.

This year, there were few goods for sale, and the battle centred on a few lots and very few pearls. The native dealers who bought them from the fishermen (one wonders where they find the money) always fix it so that they are not in a hurry. We will see what will happen after the end of the fishing season: for the moment all prices are holding up.

When the time comes to go to Bombay, which is the main market for Arab dealers to dump pearls which are left unsold, we will see if prices fall, or if they will try to get the best prices possible.

It is difficult to guess their intentions, because these people have no pressing needs and know, thanks to their vast experience, that prices always rise in the end.

Furthermore, so few boats have gone fishing this year that, following instructions, I doubt whether I will be able to buy anything remarkable although competition is less tough because of the absence of certain Europeans. - Adam Freund.

In the Persian Gulf - 12th December 1931 - Extract from a letter sent by the Jacques Bienenfeld firm about the present situation in the Persian Gulf.

Since my last letter, I have nothing remarkable to report. However, prices have become more stable than they were at the start of the season, because of the lack of merchandise available. The fishing entrepreneurs had not had enough money to equip their boats and when they realised that, contrary to expectations, there were enough buyers, it was no longer possible to send out further boats, because of a lack both of time and of money - money was very scarce! So, the season ended with only one-third of the boats which had gone fishing in 1930.

With some rare exceptions, no dealer can do any classing of pearls, as was possible in 1928-29. One or two Arabs have kept batches of pearls from last year, but they will not sell them for a small profit, even if it means holding on to them for several years.

Small pieces of merchandise of four grains, and large pearls, have increased 15-20 per cent in value from the prices offered at the start of the season, and a lot have already been sold to the Indian market; not a single pearl is left from last year in these categories.

As for pink pearls, there is a struggle between speculators and fishing entrepreneurs: everyone tries to discourage anyone else, and whoever has managed to buy pearls of this quality holds on to them in the hope of making a big profit.

The fishing season this year finished a lot later than normal because of the circumstances which I have just underlined. - Adam Freund.

Editor's Note: In our view, this year's production is about a quarter or a fifth of the reduced 1930 total.

In the Persian Gulf - October 1932 - The representative of the Jacques Bienenfeld company telegraphs us this information from Bahrein: This year, production in the Persian Gulf fell to 14 lacs of rupees, about £110,000, of which 85 per cent has already been sold.

At the start of the season, prices were slightly lower than those of 1931, but in July they became firmer and even surpassed those of last year.

Some fishing entrepreneurs refused to equip their boats because the pearl price was not covering their expenses. There are very few beautiful pearls.

Merchandise of mediocre and inferior quality, sent from Venezuela in large quantities to Bombay, has helped satisfy demand, so that despite the scarcity of local production, the price of the inferior merchandise has not been raised.

FAMOUS PEARLS

Pearls have always fascinated men and women to such an extent that some have gained a name and a history. But sometimes it is extremely difficult to tell the difference between historical fact and fables or legends.

The Pearls of Cleopatra

Cleopatra's pearls are undoubtedly the most famous in the world because of the marvellous anecdote which is told about them (see Chapter 1).

The only report which we have about these pearls, comes from Pliny (naturalist and historian who was alive in 23 BC). He describes them as being pear-shaped and reckons their value to be 16 million *sesterces*. History tells how Lucius Plautus prevented the queen from dissolving the second pearl. After Cleopatra's death, the pearl was brought to Rome and, on the orders of Augustus, it was cut in two and made into ear-rings for the statue of Venus which was in the Pantheon temple.

Guillaume Bude, the French philogist and humanist (1467 -1540), mentions the halves of this pearl in his work (1514) on money and the prosperity of nations. He reckoned their value at 250,000 golden *ecus*.

La Peregrina or Incomparable Pearl

The fabulous pearl from South America called La Peregrina belonged to Philip II of Spain (1527-1598) and weighed 134 grains. The Garalasso of Vega who saw it in Seville in 1597, tells how it was discovered by a black diver in Panama in 1560 and thanks to this, he gained his freedom. But another story says that it was caught off Venezuela, in 1574, then given to the King by Don Diego de Ternes.

Jacques de Treco, court jeweller, estimated the value at between 30,000 and 100,000 ducats. He explained the disparity in the figures because there was nothing with which to compare such a beautiful pearl.

Catherine de Medici owned the most beautiful pearls in Europe - two pear-shaped pearls weighing 92 and 96 grains, which were given to her by Francis I.

Mary Stuart, Queen of Scots, had beautiful pearls which were coveted by her mother-in-law, Catherine de Medici, who commanded Bodutel de la Forest, the then Ambassador at the English Court, to get them for her. But they were acquired by Queen Elizabeth I of England in 1568.

Some of these pearls can be seen in The Louvre, in the portrait of Mary, painted by Paul Delaroche.

The Pearls of Georgibus of Calais

One of the most important pearls ever imported into Europe was brought from India in 1620 by François Georgibus of Calais. It was pear-shaped, with a very fine orient and did not weigh less than 126 carats. Georgibus sold it to Philip IV of Spain for 80,000 ducats. As it was impossible to find another like it, it was used as a button on the royal cloak.

The story is told that once the deal had been made, the King asked how he had dared put such a high value on a single pearl. Francois Georgibus replied that he knew, somewhere in the world, there would be a King of Spain.

The Pearl of Charles II of Spain

A pearl was given to Charles II of Spain by Don Pedro of Aponte, Count of Palmer. It was discovered in 1691, almost 100 years after La Peregrina, and the two pearls were mounted on ear-rings worn by successive queens. But they were destroyed in the fire which ravaged the old Madrid palace in 1734.

The Gresham Pearl

During the reign of Queen Elizabeth I, Sir Thomas Gresham gave a reception for the Spanish ambassador. To impress his guest during dinner and show him the grandeur of England, he reduced a pearl worth £15,000 to powder, mixed it with wine and raised it in a toast to the Queen.

The Pearl of Charles I

According to history, Charles I is said to have worn a beautiful pearl on his right ear. When he was condemned to die, a large crowd came to watch his execution. Those closest to him hoped to get the pearl as soon as the head was severed.

But it was probable that, knowing his fate, the poor King entrusted the pearl to a close friend before his execution.

Jean-Baptiste Tavernier

Jean-Baptiste Tavernier was one of the most remarkable French jewellers ever known. He died in Moscow in 1689 at the age of 84, after completing a business trip.

He was able to obtain recommendations from the French Crown which allowed him to meet the great personalities of the time, who did not hesitate to show off their treasure. So he was able to admire wonderful collections. In 1630 he left for Constantinople and Persia, returning to France in 1632. He left again for India in 1638 and reached the Kingdom of Golconda. After returning in 1642, he went on four more voyages, visiting almost all of Asia. In 1669, he was raised to the nobility by Louis XIV.

In 1676 a book by him 'The Six Voyages of J.B.Tavernier in Turkey, Persia and India,' was published, in which a multitude of detail was given about the pearls of Shah Sofi of Persia, of the Iman of Muscat, of the Grand Mogul, and many others.

To find out the exact weight of pearls described by Tavernier one has to calculate the weight used at the time. He used the Florentine carat, which equals 3.04 grains troy, the troy being the English measure used at that time for precious metals, stones and pearls.

The Most Fabulous Treasure in India

The Gaikwar of Baroda owned what was probably the most fabulous treasure in India. It comprises a belt with 100 rows of pearls ended by a tassel of pearls and emeralds, estimated to be worth several millions of dollars. One can also admire a carpet of pearls, 10½ ft long and 6 ft wide, made up of rows of pearls apart from the edge, 11 in wide and the central motif which are made of diamonds.

Some people say that the carpet was meant to cover the tomb of Mahomet, others say that the great Mahratta Kladarao wanted to give it to a princess, whom he loved.

But the English governor intervened and judged that Baroda province was not rich enough to release such a valuable treasure. So this treasure remained the property of the province. No fortune was big enough to afford to buy it.

The Crown Jewels

We owe one of the most fabulous pearl stories to King François I of France who decreed in 1530, that with every new sovereign, a careful inventory should be taken before they were handed over. Thus the Crown Jewels became the property of the nation. They were guarded by the Crown Jeweller. This title was retained until 1870.

To start the collection, François I donated six of his most beautiful sets of jewellery, which were valued at 270,000 ecus. Because of wars and various plots it is impossible to follow the collection's development exactly but it is thought that it only became significant under the reign of Louis XIV.

In 1791, at the demand of Parliament, an inventory of the jewels was made. Shortly afterwards, Parliament voted that they should be put up for auction. This auction was to have taken place in 1792 in a warehouse near the Place de la Concorde, in the present Maritime Ministry.

The jewels were put on display in rooms which were badly protected and most were stolen before the auction, which was cancelled.

The thieves had no difficulty gaining entry into the building for several reasons. Protection was almost non-existent and when Restout the commander of the guard, complained about the lack of men under his orders he was told by Commander Doucet, 'Guard the doors yourself.'

This version of events seems to contradict the accusation made by a guard at the Tuileries 'M. Restout already sounds like a tyrant; he is sucking dry all the aristocracy in this house; *he* needs guards!'

Because of the ease with which they carried out their haul, the thieves are thought to have had certain accomplices, because after the theft, the political parties accused each other of having mounted the operation.

The theft was carried out by a band of rogues who were very badly organised. They needed three nights to carry out the theft - the 11th, 13th and 15th September. On the last night, emboldened by the ease of the first two nights, they decided to finish off their pilfering with a celebration at the scene of the crime.

They brought food and more than enough wine. Soon, when sharing out the spoils, violent fights broke out which awoke the guards, who went to fetch reinforcements from the Feuillants post in the rue Saint-Honore.

Two thieves were caught. Their confessions allowed almost the whole gang to

PEARLS IN THE FRENCH CROWN JEWELS

Pearl type	Weight in Grains			Francs
	Number	Average	Total	
Round pearls	1		109 1/4	200 000
	3	79	238 1/2	29 000
	11	77 1/2	804 1/2	37 300
	7	64 1/2	450 1/2	19 400
	14	53 3/4	753 1/4	23 100
	43	34 1/2	1488 1/2	16 100
Pear-shaped	2	115 3/8	230 3/4	300 000
	4	99 1/4	397 1/2	64 000
	6	163 1/8	978 3/4	92 000
	8	114 1/4	914 1/4	55 000
	47	42 1/4	1989 3/4	24 600
Ovals	3	27	290 1/2	42 000
	9	72 1/2	654 1/4	20 100
	11	43	473 3/4	5 000
Egg-shaped	1		145 1/4	10 000
Irregular	12	39 1/2	475 1/4	7 300
Buttons	1		198	15 000
	6	66 1/4	398	4 900
Baroque	4	37 1/2	150 3/4	1 500
Necklace pearls	310	21 7/8	6778	29 400
	503	35 3/8	17 919 1/4	995 700

be rounded up. Luckily, most of the jewels were quickly recovered, since the thieves were swift to reveal the hiding place. Hints and information given to the police by large jewellery firms which had been offered stolen goods, enabled them to recover most of the collection.

Among pieces which were lost was a blue diamond said to be from the Fleece of Gold, which was sold in England. When it had been worked by skilled craftsmen, it was given the name of its prestigious owner: Hope.

Pearls from the collection were valued at 995,700 francs at the time.

Napoleon I and III increased the Crown Jewels, but after the fall of the latter, by a decree on 10th December 1886, the jewels were auctioned off at the Pavillion de Flore on 12th March 1887. Thus a part of the French national heritage disappeared.

The Regent

The Regent Pearl was sold to Fabergé in St. Petersburg from the estate of Princess Youssoupoff.

Originally, this pearl of 336.9 grains was mounted on a tiara worn by Marie-Louise, Empress of France. Then, on the orders of Napoleon III, it was detached from the tiara and inserted in a brooch by the jeweller Lemounier in 1853, and this was how it went to Russia.

The Queen Pearl (La Pellegrina)

The Queen Pearl was listed in an inventory of 1791, but disappeared after the theft and has an unusual history. It is said to have been acquired in 1669 by a dealer called Bazi. In 1691, it was described as being totally round, unpierced, and weighing 110 grains. Among the pearls stolen in 1792, there was a golden box containing an unpierced pearl of rare quality. On this box were the words 'The Queen Pearl.'

In 1818, G. Fischer de Waldheim, vice-president of the Imperial Medical-Surgical Academy of Russia, published a book about La Pellegrina, a pearl weighing 110 grains, perfectly round, unpierced, of incomparable beauty, and belonging to the Zozima Brothers of Moscow. They kept it in a golden box whose lid was made of convex crystal, and which itself was enclosed in a silver box.

In 1827, Z.P. Zozima died at a very old age. But a few months previously, some of the finest pieces of his collection had been stolen by one of his Greek compatriots. La Pellegrina was among those items.

In 1840, a German Johann Georg Kohl, upon his return from Russia, tells a strange story about a pearl from Moscow. A rich dealer in Moscow, whose name is unknown, and feeling his old age, left his business in the hands of his children and retired to a monastery where he lived the simplest of lives. The only object which he had kept with him was a pearl in a precious casket. Enormous sums had been offered by great dealers, but he had always turned them down.

He only showed his pearl on rare occasions to people who had been recommended to him. Each time, the pearl presentation was the object of a small ceremony. When all the guests had arrived, the old man excused himself to go and fetch a box from his cell. On his return, he covered the table with white satin, took the pearl from the box and rolled it gently on the table. It was perfectly round, unpierced with no flaws, and was exceptionally beautiful.

No one was allowed to touch it and the silence in the room was only broken by admiring murmurs.

One day, the old man fell ill. He took the pearl in his hand and never put it down. When he died, it was very difficult to recover the pearl because he was gripping it so tightly.

The similarities in descriptions leads us to believe that La Pellegrina was The Queen Pearl.

The (Freshwater) Queen Pearl

A round freshwater pearl is also called The Queen Pearl. It weighs about 100 grains, and belongs to the Evans collection, which is now the property of Pennsylvania University. Discovered by Jacob Quackenbuch in Motch Brook in 1857 it forms a real part of American history. He sold it for 1,500 dollars to Charles Tiffany, who sent it to Paris where it was bought by a great jeweller who released it to be given to the Empress Eugenie.

In 1870, on account of the revolution, the Empress had to flee Paris and was helped by a young dentist from Philadelphia. As a token of her gratitude, she made him a present of a magnificent pearl, and this is how The Queen Pearl returned to the United States.

At the time, Charles Tiffany was accused of paying too little (1,500 dollars) for a pearl weighing 100 grains. He replied by saying that it may have seemed a small amount to someone outside the profession, but one had to take into account the fact that it was one of the first pearls found in Motch Brook and there was still hope that many others would be discovered. If that happened, what would the price then become for a 100 grain round pearl?

The Hope Pearl

At the start of the last century, the banker Henry Philip Hope bought an important collection of jewels, comprising one exceptional pearl.

In 1839 in the jewel catalogue of the Hope collection, the pearl was described as follows: An Eastern pearl, pear- shaped, irregular, its weight is 1,800 grains; it measures 5 cm (2 in) in height by 11.42 cm (5 in) in circumference at the widest points and 8.25 cm (3.25 in) at the narrowest. The bronze colour at the base becomes lighter towards the top where there is a lively white colour.

The top of the 'pear' was attached to the shell. To hide this defect and to give the pearl good proportions, this part was covered by a gold crown strewn with rubies, diamonds and emeralds.

In 1886 in an auction at Christie's, it was sold to Garrard and Co. of London. It is now in the Smithsonian Institution, Washington, USA.

The Southern Cross

The most famous Australian pearl, the Southern Cross, was discovered by a man called Clark. It is made up of nine pearls of the same size fused together. The cross is formed by seven pearls in a straight line, and the two cross-pieces by two pearls - one on the left and one on the right of the main section. Clark handed his find over to his boss, Kelley. This superstitious man thought that it was a message from heaven and hurriedly buried it. After 18 months, when nothing unlucky had happened, he went to fetch the cross, which on all the evidence, did not seem at all maleficent.

A few days later, he showed it to one of his friends who unfortunately dropped it and a few days later, hurt his hand seriously.

The cross was stuck back together, then sent to London to be examined by experts, so it is said. Another story by a pearler who saw who saw the Southern Cross around 1882 to 1883, just after it was found, wrote later that it was in three pieces and still needed an extra pearl to make a shapely cross. A suitable one was brought from the pearling fleet based on Cossack and fixed with diamond cement into a convenient hollow provided by Nature on the side of the centre pearl. Although they knew what had happened, none of the experts was able to find the break. It is now the property of an Australian syndicate.

The Pearl of Asia

The largest pearl in the world is the Pearl of Asia. It weighs 605 carats or 2,420 grains, and is mounted on a group of golden branches and leaves, enhanced by blocks of jade and a large cabochon of pink quartz. Its very white colour leads us to believe that it came from a *Pinctada maxima*.

It is said to have been the property of the Emperor of China at one time, but today is safely guarded in a bank vault, rolled up in blue silk cloth, in a golden box, protected by a leather and velvet case, which is itself placed in a silver box.

Pearls of China

In 1860, European troops besieged the Summer Palace in Peking and pillaged it. A report says that after the soldiers had passed through the Treasury, the floor was covered in jewels and fabulous gold and silver objects. Many of the pearls brought back by the soldiers supplied the London and Paris markets for some time.

A number of these pearls were dark cream in colour. Many of them came from the coasts of Burma. Unfortunately they were pierced lengthwise, because the Chinese used them as buttons, sewn on to their clothes.

The Pearls of Elizabeth, Empress of Austria

Empress Elizabeth of Austria was better known on the cinema screen as Sissi, and her pearls have a very strange story.

After the suicide of her son, the Archduke Rudolf, the Empress started to

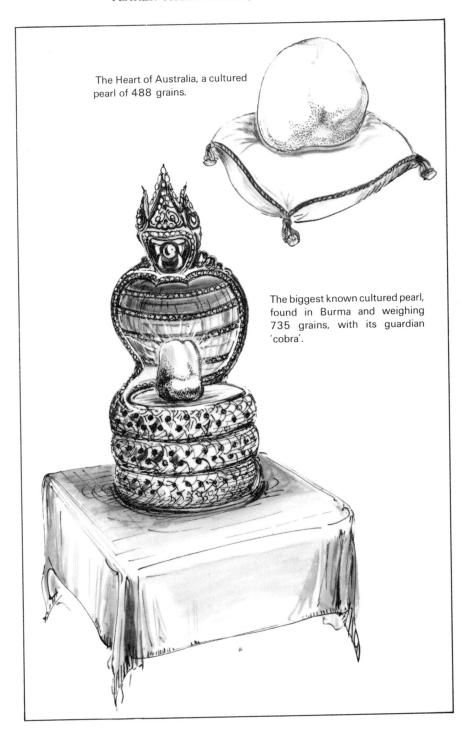

The Heart of Australia, a cultured pearl of 488 grains.

The biggest known cultured pearl, found in Burma and weighing 735 grains, with its guardian 'cobra'.

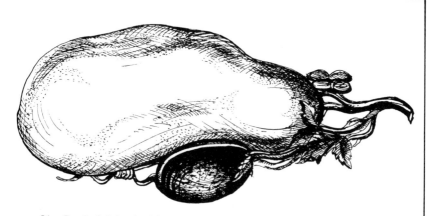

The Pearl of Asia, the biggest known natural pearl in the world, which weighs 2,420 grains. It is mounted with gold stalks, leaves and tendrils and pieces of jade and rose quartz.

The baroque Hope Pearl, weighing 1,800 grains. It is mounted in a jewelled crown to form a pendant. The colour is bronze at the bottom merging into white at the top.

The Arco Valley Pearl, weighing over 2,300 grains, has been in the same family since 1700. It is supposed at one time to have been offered to Marco Polo by the Emperor of China.

travel in Europe, to soothe her grief in the excitement of travel. She always took with her a small box containing her favourite jewels, amongst which was a magnificent pearl necklace.

One day, she told a Hungarian gentleman that her necklace did not have the same sparkle as before. He told her that there was a secret way to keep the pearls looking young. He said that the Romans, great admirers of pearls, used to dip them into the sea from time to time, to keep their brilliance and life.

The Empress was impressed by this tale, and ordered a wooden box to be made with small holes. She then went to her villa, Achilleon in Corfu. In the presence of a lady-in-waiting and with the help of one of the fishermen, she immersed the small weighted box in the sea, and it contained her precious necklace.

A short time afterwards, when travelling to Geneva, the Empress was assassinated by the Italian anarchist Luchesi. The necklace was forgotten after this tragic deal.

Kaiser Wilhelm II, who inherited the villa, knew about the story and had searches carried out in vain. Since then, teams of amateur divers have periodically searched the Bay of Corfu.

The Arco Valley Pearl

The Arco Valley Pearl which has been in one family since 1700, can only be handed down to male descendants. A legend says that the day when it is lost or sold the dynasty will end.

According to the Duke of Arco, the pearl was given to Marco Polo by the Emperor of China.

Weighing 230.15 grains, it is the second largest pearl in the world, only the Pearl of Asia surpassing it in weight. Its form is irregular, and its colour mainly white, but pinkish-brown at the base. It measures 75 mm high by 52.5 mm wide (3 by 2.1 in).

Madame Nordica's Pearl

Worth mentioning also is the pearl of Madame Nordica - the 175 grain *Haliotis* pearl; the Holy Sepulchre pearl given by King Victor Emmanuel II and set in a crown by the jeweller Augusto Castellani in 1868; the black pearl of Count Battyani; and the collection of Morgan Tiffany made up uniquely of pearls from oysters and shellfish in America.

Famous pearls do not only belong to the past. It may be that tomorrow, on the chance of one dive, a man may draw a pearl from a humble mollusc, so beautiful that only a poet can describe its beauty. Indeed, in almost all the places which I have visited, there are still isolated fishermen who fish for oysters and pearls. Their annual production is very small, but what does it matter? What is important is that they are still there, guardians of the old traditions, and ready to pass them on to children and grandchildren, so that the past and experience are never lost.

Celebrated Cultured Pearls

I know of only two celebrated cultured pearls and I hope that any other exceptional ones are announced and recorded so that the knowledge of them is not lost because they were acquired by anonymous buyers.

Hopefully, the owners of these two, the Burmese government and the Swiss firm of Golay Buschel, will be followed by others and any other remarkable cultured pearls will receive the merit they deserve.

Golay Buschel's pearl, which was shown at the Basle Fair in 1984, weighs 122 carats and is named the Heart of Australia. It came from the Southern Seas and is slightly baroque, but of fine colour and lustre.

In 1977, the Burmese fisheries produced a huge cultured pearl, the largest known to date. It weighs 183.75 carats. Regarded as one of the treasures of Burma, it is displayed with a 'guardian' made from Burmese gem minerals - a jade cobra in the form of Naja, decorated with over 280 grammes of fine gold and set with 1502 facetted rubies and two rubies cut en cabochon.

Collections of Pearls

Among our friends, relations or those close to us, there are hardly any who do not own, either shown in a shop window or guarded in some drawer, a fairly precious collection of objects, of which they are proud.

When I was recently invited to a friend's house, I was delighted to admire the pearls which he had collected according to his taste. There were all shapes, colours and origins. They were mounted on stands, and further back on small racks were the mother-of-pearl shells from which they had been taken.

My friend had spent ten years building up his collection. Its value did not exceed 30,000 francs (say £3,000), a modest sum compared to the cost of even minor collections of works of art, miniatures or jewels. But in the course of the conversation which followed, we were surprised to find how little the guests present knew about pearls, their source, the necessary techniques for catching and working them, and how the explanations which we as professionals offered, provoked a great deal of curiosity. The dinner which followed was livened up by many questions about the past, present and future of pearls in the world.

Pearls are not only precious for their market value or even the aesthetic effect which they produce; they are a source of fascination which arouses such wonder at their presence at the heart of shellfish as well as at the ingenuity of men in catching them.

PART TWO
PEARL SHELLFISH AND THE FORMATION OF PEARLS

CHAPTER 4
Pearl Oysters

Although regarded by some people as a mineral likened to gems, the pearl is an organic product secreted by a living creature. It results from the pathological reaction of a shellfish organ against the accidental introduction of a foreign body.

Oyster Varieties

It is wrong to call all pearl shellfish 'oysters'. Indeed most pearl types are from the *Pintadine* family, whereas true oysters commonly called 'plates' or 'Portuguese' in fact belong to two other families respectively. Nevertheless to conform to everyday usage, we will continue to call them oysters.

Certain oysters are very well known for their shell. This is often the most interesting part of the animal from the financial point of view. In certain regions, fishermen search for the oyster more for its mother-of-pearl than for its pearls. Mother-of-pearl was used extensively in the button industry and represented the main source of the fishermen's income until the 1950's, when the market collapsed. The pearl was a bonus, a piece of good luck for the fishermen.

Oysters can be split into two large families. In the first group are:

Pinctada martensi fucata, China and Japan
Pinctada radiata, Persian Gulf
Pinctada vulgaris, India and Ceylon
Pinctada fucata, Australia and New Guinea
Pinctada maculata, Polynesia.

The varieties of oyster in this family have no interest to fishers other than in the pearls which they might contain, because their shell is very thin and valueless.

The second family includes the large oysters which contain the biggest pearls:

> *Pinctada maxima*, Philippines, New Guinea, Australia, Indonesia, Burma.
> *Pinctada margaritifera*, Polynesia, Red Sea.

These are fished both for their mother-of-pearl and their pearls. Contrary to the general opinion, the flesh of the *Pinctada* is not edible.

The Anatomy of the Oyster

The oyster, like every other animal, possesses a heart, stomach, and mouth. It breathes through its gills and feeds itself with micro-organisms, phytoplankton and zooplankton, filtered from the sea water. There are male and female oysters, although there is no exterior sign to tell them apart. The oyster can change sex between two reproductive cycles.

The longest that an oyster lives is about thirty years, but few live as long as this, because there are many predators, such as sponges and lithophages (small bivalves which weaken the shell and make it more vulnerable to fish, balista, rays and other enemies). An oyster's age can be determined by the grooves in its hinge, just as one tells a tree's age from the rings in its trunk.

When an oyster starts to breed, it sets off a chain reaction with neighbouring oysters. Eggs and semen mix at the mercy of the currents. The fertilised eggs remain in a plankton state for 20 to 30 days. By the 45th day, the oyster reaches a diameter of 10 mm (0.5 in). It has a foot which allows it to move. When it finds a suitable place, an organ situated in its foot secretes a fibrous material, the byssus, which holds it in place. The oysters attach themselves to suitable anchor points at depths of 15 to 20 metres (50 to 65 ft). It seems that the light plays an important part in their choice.

The part of the animal which is most interesting is the mantle. It is a fold of epithelial material that envelopes the animal. The halves of the mantle are joined together at the hinge. The outer edge is split into two parts; one covers the periostracum, the edge and crust of the shell, the other covers the mother-of-pearl, which it produces through its epithelial cells. All pearls, whether natural or cultured, depend on this end part of the mantle. So it is vital to be able to tell them apart to understand the process of pearl secretion.

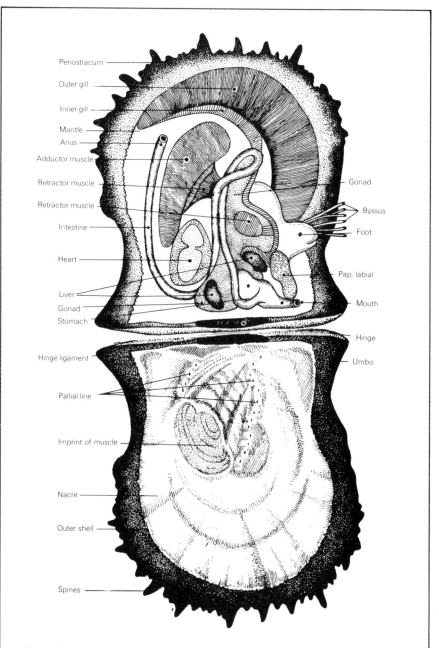

The anatomy of an oyster. The part of most interest to the pearler is the mantle.

CHAPTER 5
The Birth of the Pearl and its Chemical Composition

As we now know, the pearl is the result of an anomaly, of an accident. It results from a freak of nature which is easy to imagine. A fish, searching for food, passes near to an oyster and, finding nothing, moves off elsewhere by using its tail. This movement causes a cloud of sand, from which several grains lodge in the oyster. The oyster can get rid of most of these, but those which bury themselves in its flesh with a few epithelial cells will be changed into pearls.

Movement of the sea-bed, storms, flooding which causes strong currents and land subsidence, algae and small animals all disturb the calm of the sea depths and cause the conditions under which pearls are produced.

Cestodes are worm larvae which become lodged in oyster tissues and then form pearls. It was the scientist Kelaart in 1859, who discovered that oysters in Ceylon were infested with these cestodes. He even proposed to infect certain oyster-beds so that the worms would improve the pearl production. In 1894, Seurat confirmed the presence of cestodes in the *Pinctada margaritifera* of Tahiti. The researcher Hornell stated that pearls in the *Pinctadas* originated from several types of larva from various creatures.

In the Red Sea, when the rains were heavy, fishermen stated that rays came to search for food in great numbers in the chalky water. The following year, a great many pearls were discovered in these areas. The explanation for this phenomenon was discovered only at the turn of the century, by a scientist who noticed that ray excrement contained a parasite (accarus) which, once free in the water, attached itself to the flesh of the oyster. In order to get rid of these parasitic larvae, the cell tissues secrete material which encases the parasite, but which may not eventually become a pearl. Divers often find brownish cell clusters in oysters, but no pearl.

For a pearl to be formed, the larva must be surrounded by epithelial cells, which are the only ones to secrete the pearly material. It is not known why some larvae become pearls and others do not, but it is likely that, when it enters the oyster's flesh, the larva drags with it a certain quantity of cells which forms a pearly bag.

The same principle applies to grains of sand and other matter which gathers in the oyster.

Sometimes the origin of the pearl is a cyst which, for some unknown reason, turns into a pearl. In this case, the pearl bag takes a long time to form. If the pearl is cut in half, a kernel of semi-organic black material can be clearly seen, which results from the decomposition of the cyst after it is surrounded by the pearly material.

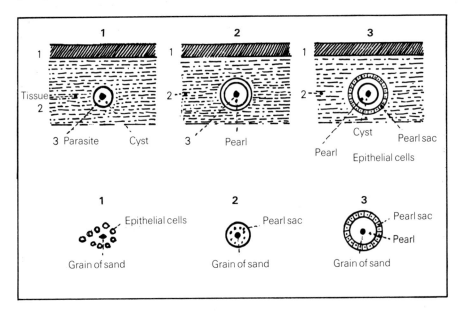

The chemical composition of a pearl can vary according to its place of origin. In certain cases the quantity of organic material or of water is different. But these variations are very minor and the following figures are fairly accurate.

Calcium carbonate = aragonite,	91.72%
Organic material = conchiolin,	5.94%
Water	2.23%
Other substances	0.11%

Aragonite is made up of microscopic crystals arranged irregularly which reflect light on the pearl's surface. Conchiolin is the organic bond between these crystals. Water is essential - every organic material contains it. Other substances are mineral salts for the most part. The name 'aragonite' was given to the calcium carbonate contained in pearls because its chemical composition is very similar to a type of limestone found in the province of Aragon in Spain.

'Conchiolin' is a Greek word meaning 'shell' and has the same root as the word 'conchology', the science of the study of shells.

Differences between Pearls and Mother-of-Pearl

From a chemical point of view, the differences between pearl and mother-of-pearl are very minor and only the proportions of their components vary.

	Pearl	Mother-of-Pearl
Calcium carbonate	91.72%	84.57%
Organic materials	5.94%	11.76%
Water	2.23%	3.17%
Various other substances	0.11%·	0.50%

The figures are variable to some extent because the components of pearls or mother-of-pearl are affected by the food, the salinity, the water temperature and the region where the oyster-beds are found. To obtain figures that are absolutely precise, one would have to make two or three graphs of comparison for each area of production.

Calcium carbonate will form in three ways: 1 Irregular shape; 2 Triclinic crystal system - calcite; and 3 Orthorhombic crystal system - aragonite.

The horny outside of a shell is made of conchiolin, which is also the material used to cement the crystals of calcite and aragonite together. The animal first deposits a layer of albuminous material on the inside of the shell. Then the epithelial cells in the mantle exude drops of calcium carbonate which crystallise differently according to where they are deposited. The layers nearest the inside of the shell are of calcite, stacked in columnar form as can be seen from the diagram.

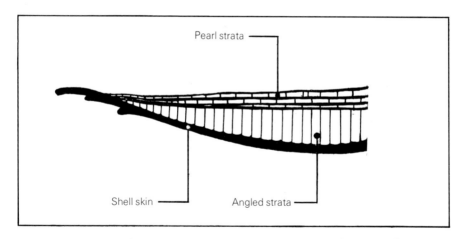

The calcium carbonate exuded from the epithelial cells, as shown in the diagram on p.111, top, crystallise differently according to where they are deposited. In mother-of-pearl, so-called angled strata of calcite are formed on the shell and the pearly aragonite crystals on top of this. The crystals are bonded to each other in both cases by aragonite.

Over these, the calcium carbonate exuded becomes aragonite in thin layers. As each drop grows it expands until the pressure against previously deposited layers flattens it, forcing it to grow sideways. Eventually it meets surrounding exudations and crystallises. The result is like a pattern of six-sided floor tiles because the crystals are normally twinned and have pseudo-hexagonal instead of rhomboid shapes. The process continues layer upon layer, the thickness of each being around 0.25 to 0.50 micron (a micron = 0.01mm or about 0.004in).

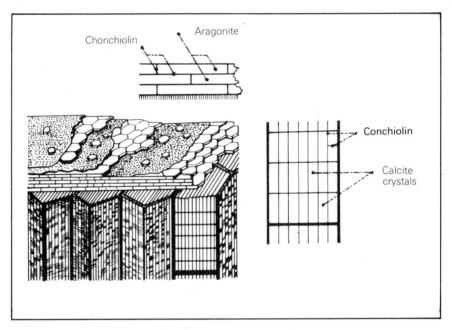

A closer, three-dimensional view of the structure shown in the previous diagram. The lower calcite crystals are angled because they form in the triclinic crystal system in which no axes are at right angles. The aragonite crystals of the pearly layer at the top are orthorhombic but are twinned so that they form hexagons. The conchiolin layers are shown in the brick-like diagrams.

In a pearl, only aragonite is formed, in concentric layers. The aragonite crystals have their optical axes at right angles to their main surfaces, so that all the optic axes in the pearl are radial. This is important not only in the creation of the pearl's lustre and orient but in determining the differences between a natural and a cultured pearl.

The aragonite layers are not continuous, but have irregular edges where a layer is not complete, as shown in the drawing of an electron microscope photograph, which looks rather like a fingerprint. This is the cause of the

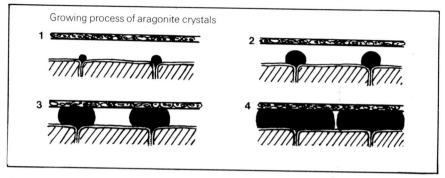

Growing process of aragonite crystals

Stages in the formation of calcium carbonate crystals. 1 Epithelial cells exude the mineral in liquid form. 2 They grow into droplets. 3 When they reach a barrier, they become flattened. 4 As more liquid is exuded, the drops contact each other and at this point they solidify into six-sided aragonite crystals.

roughness of a natural or cultured pearl when rubbed on the teeth, compared with the smooth artificial pearl.

Comparing a pearl and a ball of mother-of-pearl, it will be seen that the pearl has a pearly lustre over all its surface, whereas the ball of mother-of-pearl has this in only two places. This is because their structures are totally different. The ball of mother-of-pearl has been cut from a piece of mother-of-pearl which has relatively flat layers, whereas the pearl has been formed in a sac (bag) in which the pearly material has formed around a nucleus, either naturally or artificially lodged in the flesh of the oyster.

The mother-of-pearl secreted by the mantle's exterior is deposited in thin

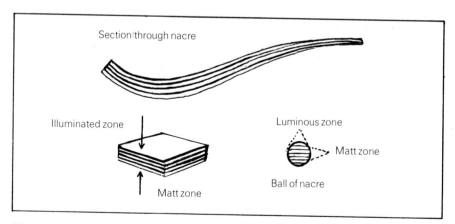

Section through nacre

Illuminated zone

Matt zone

Luminous zone

Matt zone

Ball of nacre

The nacre, which comes from inside the shell, has a laminated structure. If a bead were cut from it, it would have two luminous spots opposite each other and a band of matt material around it, as shown on the right.

layers throughout the oyster's life. This is how one can determine the oyster's age by counting the number of layers. These deposits are released in two stages. Firstly the mantle secretes a fine net of organic matter (conchiolin) which is like the mesh of a fishing net: then the chinks of this mesh are filled with calcium carbonate crystals (aragonite). The crystals all face the same way, which explains why light is reflected by them in only two directions.

Merely looking at a piece of mother-of-pearl, polished on every side, is more eloquent than any description.

The passage of the light through the fine layers of mother-of-pearl, and its distortion by the aragonite crystals, produces a radiance which is called the mother-of-pearl's 'water'; the finer the layers of the mother-of-pearl, the more beautiful the water.

As for the pearl, its formation results from the same process, except that the conchiolin mesh and the aragonite crystals are secreted around a natural or artificial nucleus by the pearl sac (bag) whose internal wall is coated with epithelial cells.

The pearl layers are placed one on top of the other, rather like the layers of an onion. According to the water, and the time of year, these layers can vary in size and there can be differences of several hundredths of millimetres on the same pearl. In the cold season, the oyster's metabolism slows down and the pearly secretions are much finer than those of the summer. This explains why, in the northern hemisphere, cultured pearls are harvested in winter, and in the southern hemisphere in summer, because an important criterion of pearl estimation depends on the fineness of the layers, called the 'orient'.

The Orient of the Pearl

A pearl's orient is one of the most difficult properties to define. It results from the distortion of the light through the aragonite crystals, which gives the impression that one is looking at a shining ball whose contours are translucent. The finer the pearly layers, the greater the orient that the pearl will possess. For example, black pearls, freshwater pearls and Australian pearls have no orient because their layers are too thick or too deeply coloured, but they can have a certain gloss. Pearls from the Persian Gulf, Ceylon, China, Japan and Burma have both orient and gloss.

If a pearl is cut across the middle and a cross-section examined under an electron microscope, a multitude of aragonite crystals will be seen in very thin layers, reminiscent of a tree trunk sawn across to reveal the growth rings. Because the layers are translucent, light can penetrate the layers of a pearl's surface to varying depths and can be reflected from and refracted by different layers.

The light that returns to the eye after it has been so altered produces the beautiful effect known as the orient. When the layers are thin and pure, the orient is at its best because more layers are penetrated. Thick, denser layers, on the other hand, result in poor orient.

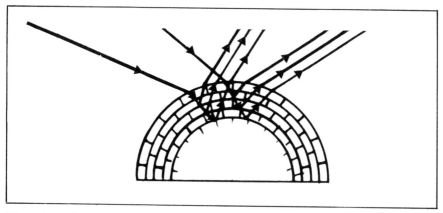

The orient that gives a pearl its beauty is caused by light being reflected and refracted by several layers of aragonite at the same time. If the layers are thin, more are penetrated and the orient is better.

The orient, which is a phenomenon of light reflected from inside the material, must not be confused with the lustre, which is only the reflection of light from the surface. The most beautiful white pearls are those which, because of their structure, combine these two optical phenomena.

When light is reflected from a smooth surface, as depicted on the left of the diagram, the lustre is good, but when the surface is rough, it is poor. The edges of layers on the surface of a pearl may affect the colour, because these tiny edges can break up a wave front of white light and produce spectral colour by interference.

Pearl working demands the total or partial suppression of certain layers of pearl matter. The structure of the pearl then undergoes a change which involves a change in the reflection of light. The skill of the lapidary or pearl-skinner is to carry out this work as finely as possible so that the change is imperceptible.

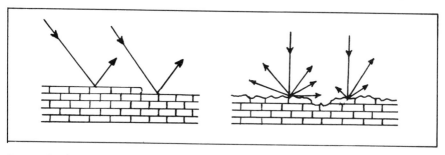

Lustre is different from orient as it is a surface effect. When the pearl surface has a multitude of stepped aragonite layers, the lustre is good, as on the left. If the surface is abraded, any light reflected is diffused and the lustre is bad.

The Colour of Pearls

There are pearls of many colours. If the reasons for this are known, they are only very general, and any conclusions drawn from observation of a particular environment are imprecise. The same oyster-bed can produce white pearls, cream pearls and pearls of two colours.

Four main factors play a role in the colour of a pearl.

1 The presence of mineral salts in the water, due to the type of marine soil. Iron gives a light brown colour; azurite a blue colour; smithsonite a grey colour. Pearls which are cream, and even gold contain a large percentage of magnesium carbonate, iron oxide and aluminium. White pearls have a small percentage of magnesium carbonate and almost no iron oxide or aluminium.

2 The degree of salinity. Water that is very salt produces cream pearls.

3 The amount of plankton. Water rich in plankton gives the pearl a light green tint, as can be seen in Australian pearls.

4 The water temperature. Warm water increases the metabolism of the animal and the pearl layers are thicker, so that, whatever the colour, the pearls are rather dull.

When white light is reflected from two different surfaces very close together, the two reflected waves can be out of phase, which causes interference, so that some of the colours comprising the white light are cancelled and others are enhanced, resulting in some muted rainbow colours. The effect of the edges of aragonite layers, mentioned earlier, is similar. Interference colours are commonly seen when a rain puddle has a film of oil on it.

To summarise colour in pearls, it can range from white through various tints to black, which is the absence of all colour. There are two main causes:

1 The effects of ambient light falling on the surface and being altered.

2 Chromatophores in the pearl strata.

The causes of certain colours are as follows:

Pink: the result of light interference from the inside of the pearl strata.

White, silver: the result of the reflection of light inside the pearl strata.

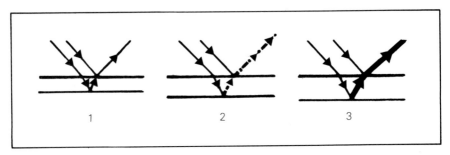

Colour can result from different effects. Light reflected from the surface and also penetrating the layers will produce different colours. 1 White and silver by reflection. 2 Pink by refraction. 3 Another colour such as blue by illuminating coloured matter between the nucleus and pearl strata.

Yellow, salmon pink, black: the result of chromatophore in albumin in the pearl strata.

Blue: the result of coloured material between the nucleus and the pearl strata.

With all these different factors, pearls can have thousands of reflections and colours, and every woman will be able to find a beautiful colour in her pearl.

Differences in Shape and Flaws

Differences in shape occur by accident. When it is in the oyster, a pearl often changes its shape. Thus, a round pearl can easily change into a pear shape, an oval, irregular or button shape, with the help of certain devices such as:

1 If a small pearl attaches itself to a larger pearl. The pearl sac surrounds both pearls and continues to secrete layers of pearl.

2 A pearl reaches a certain weight, slides towards the bottom of the sac and is impeded by a muscle or an organ, and then exerts pressure over a large area. The mother-of-pearl is deposited in liquid form and the pressure exerted by the pearl prevents regular deposits.

3 It sometimes occurs that organic matter is secreted at the same time as mineral matter, and as it decomposes this creates internal blisters.

4 Water temperature and salinity are also factors which can affect the regular secretion of the pearl sac.

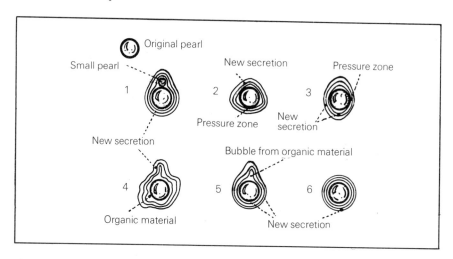

A pearl can change in shape during its formation, even after being round. It may become joined to a smaller pearl as at 1. If it is subject to uneven pressure, it may take another shape as in 2 and 3. Adjoining foreign matter can make it baroque as in 4, cause a blister on it as in 5, or a surface defect as in 6.

When these four main factors are all present, they can produce pearls of many shapes.

The pearl sac is in a state of constant change because it grows with the pearl that it is producing. It undergoes pressure and tearing. Any anomaly will affect it and will upset regular secretions. This explains why there are often flaws in pearls. I agree with the old Japanese saying: 'The most beautiful women have beauty spots. The same thing applies to pearls.'

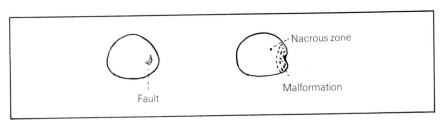

Durability of Pearls

Pearls are quite soft in comparison with most gems, yet they can be durable, on the evidence of survival of many historic pearls over several centuries. The mineralogist and gemmologist traditionally use an old scale of 'scratch hardness' devised in 1822 by a German mineralogist, Friedrich Mohs. He listed ten minerals and numbered them. A mineral will be scratched by those with higher numbers and will scratch those with lower ones.

It must be understood that the numbers are not degrees or quantities of hardness, merely numbers. In other words, there is only a small difference in scratch hardness between (1) talc and (2) gypsum, and varying differences between other neighbours. Between (9) sapphire and (10) diamond, the difference is extreme, more than the whole of the rest of the scale, because a diamond is about a hundred times more resistant to scratching than a sapphire.

Number 7 is very important for gems because dust in the air and on clothing comprises small particles of sand, which are (7) quartz, and will scratch gems with lower Mohs' numbers. Here is the full scale:

1 Talc 2 Gypsum 3 Calcite 4 Fluorspar 5 Apatite

6 Orthoclase feldspar 7 Quartz 8 Topaz 9 Sapphire

10 Diamond

Emerald's number is 7 1/2, jade 6 1/2, and opal, moonstone and turquoise, which are considered soft in mineral terms, are 6. The organic gems are much less hard, coral is 4 1/2 and pearl only 3 1/2. However pearls will not be ruined or broken even if dropped on a cement floor because of the cushioning effect of calcium carbonate well amalgamated by gelatinous conchiolin, which absorbs some of the impact. The thicker the layer of nacre, the better the protection. It is encouraging to know that a slight mark can be effaced by polishing.

CHAPTER 6
Unusual Pearls

Oysters do not produce pearls only. Depending on the parasites which attack them, and the way in which they react, various pearl formations are produced. Among these are found:

Baroque pearls   Blisters   Blister pearls   Concretions

Very large baroque pearls can reach sizes of 30 to 40 mm (1.2 to 1.6 in) in height by 20 to 25 mm (0.8 to 1 in). They are caused by a foreign body which is either animal or vegetable.

The foreign body, usually a small crab or algae, enters the oyster itself, not merely penetrating under the mantle as is the case when blister pearls are formed. As soon as the foreign body enters the oyster, the process of rejection begins. The oyster surrounds the animal with a material which neutralises the irritation.

When pearly material is deposited on the foreign body, it is inflated, in its liquid form, by the various gases from the animal or vegetable decomposition.

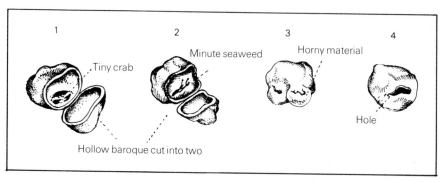

Whole blister pearls are formed by organic material being encapsulated in pearl layers and then decomposing and creating a gas. In 1 and 2, the blister is shown cut across. Sometimes the gas splits the blister as in 4.

For this reason, the French trade calls baroques 'soufflures' - puff balls. Baroque pearls are not very significant as pearls. The pearly material is released irregularly, and the thickness of the layers on a blister can vary by several millimetres.

On some baroques, a great amount of disorder can be seen in the process of secretion. The pearly material is either displaced by black horny material or by living animal matter which soon decompose to leave a hole, which is later filled with special cement when mounted on a piece of jewellery.

Natural blisters were once mounted in gold with diamonds and used as hat pins. When possible, jewellers created figures of Venus and other gods, with the blisters as the bodies. Such jewels are often very valuable, a good example being the Canning Jewel.

The Formation of a Blister and its Origins

Blisters are swellings which appear on the inside surface of the oyster shell and which are convex in their shape.

The most common are those caused by small crabs, which find an ideal hiding place under the oyster's mantle. When they die, the oysters cover them with mother-of-pearl, which, as it is in a liquid state, is blown up by the gas coming from the decomposing corpse. This explains the bulging appearance of such a blister.

Blisters are formed in the same way from pieces of decaying vegetation.

Some blisters are strangely flattened; these are made by the oyster accelerating its secretion of mother-of-pearl in order to defend itself against attacks from shellfish and worms penetrating its shell.

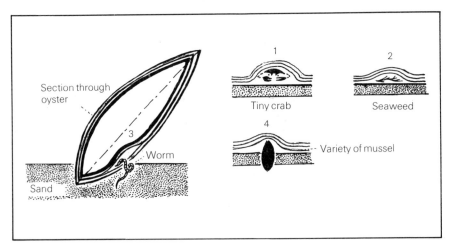

A blister can be formed on the shell by organic material penetrating the shell as in 3 and 4, or by entering when the oyster gapes and being trapped next to the shell as in 1 and 2.

The Formation of a Blister Pearl

Pearl and mother-of-pearl are secreted by the epithelial cells of the oyster, but under different conditions. The pearl is formed inside a pearl sac in the very flesh of the oyster. The *inner* walls of this sac deposit concentric layers of pearl. But mother-of-pearl is deposited on the inner walls of the shell on the *outer* side of the mantle.

The oyster has no means of defence other than to close its halves at the approach of any danger, or to eject foreign bodies and pearls formed around them.

Such movements sometimes tear the pearl sac and expel the pearl which is irritating the oyster. Either the pearl falls out of the shell and is lost for ever or, if its weight and position may be such, it slides underneath the mantle. The pearl will then gradually be covered by layers of nacrous material parallel to the mother-of-pearl and cemented to the shell as the oyster grows.

The pearl has become a blister pearl.

In old oysters, pearls are often found which are totally encased in mother-of-pearl. Only faint swellings reveal the presence of such pearls. Pearls that are too firmly embedded in the mother-of-pearl are irrecoverable.

Divers are well aware of the potential danger of an oyster closing on some part of the anatomy, but whenever they find an old oyster, they are careful to keep it shut for another reason - so that it does not release its pearl before they reach the surface.

The Recovery of a Blister Pearl

A pearl ejected from the centre of the oyster, even if it has been firmly cemented to the mother-of-pearl, is still fairly valuable. It must be removed very carefully from the shell so that the layers of mother-of-pearl remain. If they were detached, the pearl might well be too small or too baroque in its shape.

Blister pearls always have a side of mother-of-pearl where they were attached to the shell. (Sketch on page 120, top).

The value of blister pearls is always less than that of complete pearls of the same size. But they are not cheap. The exceptional size of some of them enables designers to create jewels of great beauty.

The Recovery of a Pearl from a Blister Pearl

Sometimes when an oyster is recovered from the ocean, it has hardly begun the process of cementing a blister pearl. At that stage, when the pearl is covered by only a few layers of mother-of-pearl, the layers merely have to be delicately removed to recover the original pearl.

The Hindus, great admirers of pearls, to which they attribute virtuous properties, have gained a world-wide reputation for their work in this field, for which they use special tools whose use is a closely-guarded secret.

The most difficult part of the operation is to estimate whether the value of the recovered pearl will compensate by its brilliance, beauty and colour for the loss

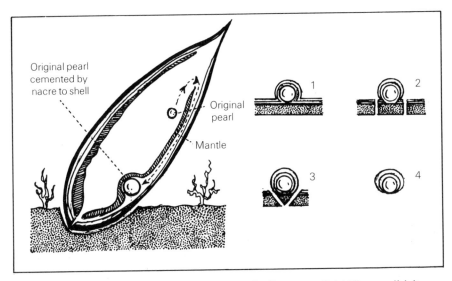

A blister pearl attached to the shell may be hollow or solid. When solid, it may have been caused by a pearl being expelled from the body of the oyster, trapped under the mantle and then cemented to the mother-of-pearl inside the shell. When cut out, it will have an eccentric layer of nacre.

of the blister pearl which, thanks to its size, was already quite valuable.
Shown below are the four main stages of recovery of such a pearl.

Pearl Concretions

Pearl concretions are caused by the amalgamation of a number of small natural pearls in the mantle of the oyster.

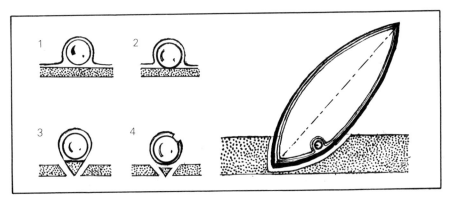

Occasionally a pearl cemented to the shell already has an adequate layer of nacre. In this case, it can be cut out of the shell as shown, and the cone of shell removed as well as extraneous skins from the pearl.

After a storm, a swirl of water, or perhaps a fish passing by, the oyster absorbs a great deal of sand or other material. It will then begin to form pearls round all the grains that remain. Soon, because of their number (often several dozen), the pearls touch each other. The pearl secretions then overflow and bind the pearls together, imprisoning them all in a mass of pearly material. As the pearly material is in a liquid state, the process is easy to imagine.

Pearl concretions are always baroque in shape and rarely of much value. Their use is the same as that of baroque pearls or blisters.

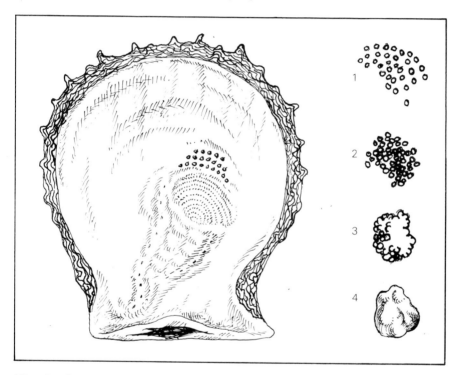

Tiny foreign secretions can cause tiny blister pearls to be formed. As they grow, these can become joined into a single baroque mass.

CHAPTER 7
Pearl Shellfish Other Than Oysters

Very many molluscs produce pearls. It would be lengthy and fastidious to name them all, so only the most important are mentioned, those that count as gems. The pearl material varies according to the organism which secretes it.

Haliotis

One of the best known is the *Haliotis*, part of the gastropod family. They are found in temperate waters as well as tropical waters. In cold water they measure 10 to 15 cm (4 to 6 in) in length, but in warm water they can reach lengths of 20 to 25 cm (8 to 10 in). The inside of the shell is covered with grey mother-of-pearl and is opalescent and spotted with dark layers of horny organic material.

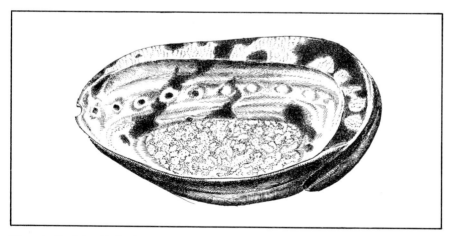

The shell of the Haliotis, sometimes called an 'ear-shell' because of its shape or 'aurora shell' because of its irridescent colours, which are distinct from mother-of- pearl. It is used for making buttons, ornaments and papier-maché .

This shellfish lies in shallow water. When there is a strong tide and the sea is ebbing, specimens can be found embedded in rocky crevasses.

It has always been sought for the flesh of its large foot, which when cooked carefully, constitutes a dish which is appreciated in many parts of the world. Among tropical species the shells can be 2 to 3 mm (0.08 to 0.12 in) thick and are used for button making and fancy goods.

The pearls are often baroque, weighing several dozen grains, and have an unusual iridescence, comparable to that of the black opal.

Pinna

Known by mankind since ancient times, *Pinna* live mainly in the Mediterranean near the coasts of Provence, Italy, and off Corsica from Porto-Vecchio to Bonifacio, as well as the coasts of Sardinia, Greece and Italy. They are also found along the coasts of North Africa and at certain points of the Red Sea.

Fishing for this shellfish was very active in ancient times, and in the same areas fishermen would find *Murex*, which have a gland containing a purple liquid used for dyeing wool, *Pinna*, whose flesh was eaten, and byssus, with which they made precious clothing.

The fishing methods were very different. On the African coast and the Red Sea, the same technique was used as for oyster fishing. On the European coasts, fishermen used a long pole from a boat, at the end of which there was a two-pronged fork. The base of the shellfish, which is a lot narrower than the central part, is planted several centimetres down in the sand, and it is therefore simple to pass the fork around the base and lift the shellfish from the sea-bed to the surface.

Another technique used consists of lowering a looped cord on to the shell, tightening it, and pulling it to the surface. This type of fishing demanded great dexterity, but had the advantage of allowing molluscs to be caught in relatively deep water.

Pinna pearls do not have the onion-like layered formation of the *Pintadines*, but instead they have a fibrous prismatic structure, which gives the surface a honeycomb texture.

Pinna pearls are not very valuable except as objects of curiosity. They contain a large percentage of water and in time many of them dehydrate and crack, thus losing any value. Their colouring is also very varied; white, brown, yellow and reddish brown are all found.

Tridacna

Better known by the name 'stoop', *Tridacna* are found in many tropical regions. Three main varieties are worth noting: *Tridacna gigas*, *Squamosa* and *Hipopus maculatus*. They are usually fished in shallow water, found on beaches or more frequently embedded in blocks of madrepore.

Tridacna pearls have the same structure as *Strombus* pearls which makes them very difficult to tell apart. Only the colour of the *Tridacna* pearl, which is usually pale pink, gives any indication.

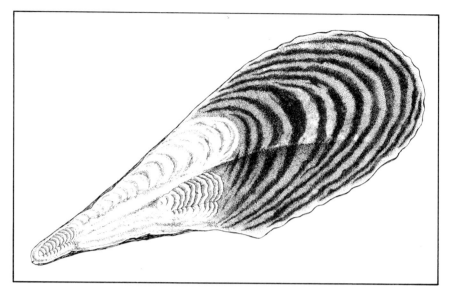

The Pinna, which has a wedge-shaped shell with a thin dark lining of nacre and occasionally produces black pearls of lower quality.

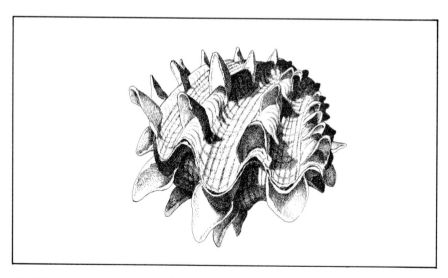

The Tridacna shell, which is found in three main varieties. The Tridacna gigas is more popularly known as the giant clam, the largest known shell, which has been used for church fonts. A diver trapped by one faces almost certain death. Occasionally such shells produce pearls that are always symmetrical and sometimes have a pleasant sheen from some directions, but are not valuable.

Strombus Gigas

Fairly common on the coasts of the 400 Bahama Islands, the shellfish *Strombus gigas*, or great conch, can be found by walking along the reefs at low tide or in shallow water. It is collected by divers using long poles from boats.

Unlike that of oysters, its flesh it delicious and is much appreciated by the island inhabitants. The shell is a light pink and is sought for cameo manufacturing.

The pearls are normally embedded in the mollusc's flesh. There is a small channel leading to the outside of the shell, which sometimes enables the animal to eject a pearl by rippling its muscles. Pearls from this shellfish are often small, oblong and semi-baroque. Their colour is also variable and there are often white and pale yellow patches mixed with pink, although they are known as pink-pearl. It is very easy to confuse them with pink coral. The colour is also reminiscent of certain pink opalines.

Close examination reveals that from certain angles the pink-pearl reflects light rather like a sapphire. By watching the point of light through a magnifying-glass, one sees that they are closely grouped and look like small sparks. The specific gravity of coral is 2.69 whereas that of pink-pearl is 2.85, which is one way of identifying them.

The Unionides

Almost all freshwater bivalves belong to the *Unionide* family and are more commonly called 'mussels' or 'mulettes'. Their shells are oval, regular, and symmetrical; the outside is usually dark brown and the inside is smooth white mother-of-pearl, sometimes with traces of light brown. They are found fairly extensively in rivers and also lakes in Europe, Russia, China, Japan and America, having a great ability to adapt to local conditions.

In France, two distinct varieties are found: the *Anodonte* in lakes and ponds, and the *Unio* in streams and rivers. In the first variety, the shell is brown, smooth and can reach 14 to 16 cm (5.5 to 6.25 in) in length. In the second the shell is dented, thick and irregular and 12 cm (4.75 in) is its maximum size. Its black colour makes it easily confused with pebbles, a case of Nature imitating Nature.

Unionides have a strange way of reproducing which is worth noting. The eggs are laid in Spring but instead of being carried by the current, they are kept in the gills. The fertilised eggs turn into larvae in this cavity. Occasionally some will escape because of the movement of the shell. They live in the water until they meet a fish, such as a gudgeon, carp, or bleak. The larva enters the gills of the fish and clings on with its hooks until it becomes encased in a swelling. It then feeds on the blood of its host. After about two months, when its gestation is over, it frees itself and finds a hollow to begin its adult life.

Unionide pearls are usually white and milky; some have blue, brown, green and red glints. In the trade, they are often called 'fantasy colours', to distinguish them. Their prices are normally less than those of sea pearls, but a few have almost equalled them.

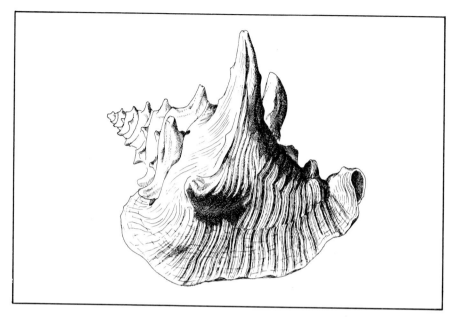

Strombus gigas, the great conch of the West Indies, one of the largest shells, which can weigh up to 2.5 kg (5 pounds). It produces non-nacreous pearls of a pinkish colour, but its main use is for Italian shell cameos and for making porcelain.

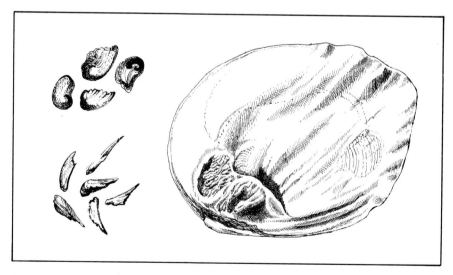

The Unionides comprise a large family of molluscs which produces freshwater pearls. On the left are some irregular pearls from them, the lower ones known as 'dog's teeth'.

Pearls - Magical Virtues

Since ancient times, pearls have exerted an aesthetic fascination on men and women as objects of jewellery, but they were also known for their supposed magical and therapeutic properties.

King Solomon is said (Proverbs 10 to 22) to have dictated that the gems possessed curative properties. Some of them give protection from fever and other ills, others bring wealth and love. It is regrettable that the great King could not give us any details about the nature of these gems, but pearls would certainly have figured in his account.

That pearls are endowed with curative properties is a magical belief which is fairly widespread. This is shown by their incorporation into various statues which are supposed to be able to cure all sorts of illness or bring good luck.

It is obvious that pearls bring wealth because their original value can increase. A pearl's value also increases when one finds a matching pearl, and when they can be set in a necklace with similar pearls.

As for love, a pearl is the most beautiful gift that a man can give to a woman. Furthermore, if one believes in its aphrodisiac qualities, once dissolved is it not the ideal philtre to make a neglected wife love one?

In the Saiminki and the Yoyakusuwa, two very famous works from the Far East, the use of powdered pearls is recommended for stomach disorders, eye or rheumatic pain and to stop haemorrhages; it is said to be a general tonic and an aphrodisiac, and should be mixed with other products such as bear liver, opium, camphor of Borneo, various plants and so one. In another work of natural history, (Lishicuin, 1596) from China, fresh pearls are said to be used to combat eye and liver infections.

The Hindus give pearls different virtues according to their colour. Golden ones are supposed to bring wealth and good luck, those with a honey-coloured tint prevent clairvoyance, white ones bring fame, blue ones bring good luck and flawed pearls bring misfortune. In an essay on gems, written by Buodhabhatta, pearls are said to be worn by those wishing to become prosperous.

Another essay on pearls, dating from 1240, written by the physician Narahari who came from Kashmir, states that pearls cure eye sores, and they are an antidote for poison, states of depression, and finally are an excellent tonic.

In 1881 Prince Sousindo Mohun, Maharajah of Tagore, gave an amazing list of the therapeutic virtues of powdered burnt pearl. It strengthens both body and soul, he said; when mixed with a sorbet it purifies the blood and prevents any kind of haemorrhages; it stops the devil entering one's spirit, removes unpleasant tastes from one's mouth and was said to cure stomach, intestine and heart troubles.

Powdered burnt pearl mixed with water, then dried and taken as snuff, cures headaches, cataracts, lachrymal and ulcer pains. Used as a toothpaste, it strengthens the gums and makes the teeth very white. When rubbed into the skin with other medical powders it cures all skin complaints, stops any bleeding and helps cicatrisation. Taken orally it is a marvellous serum.

Beautiful Ago Bay, off the coast of Mie Prefecture, southern Honshu, Japan, where cultured pearl rafts are anchored off the coast of the Pacific. The rafts are towed some 300 miles south to warmer waters during the winter so that the oysters in the baskets below them do not hibernate.To the left of the rafts in the centre can be seen the newer ball float method of holding the baskets of oysters.

In the early days of pearling, women divers in loincloths dived for the oysters. Then Mikimoto introduced white suits, partly for religious reasons, but also to scare away sharks and other predators. Some 'amahs', as the women divers were called, are still diving in the Mikimoto national outdoor museum.

Australia once had a thriving pearling industry based on Broome, on the north of Western Australia on the Great Sandy Desert coast. Here some pearlers of the Australian Pearling Company are cleaning shells.

In order to prevent too great an effect on the brain, he stated that each dose of powdered pearl should be less than 20 grains and should be mixed with powdered mother-of-pearl or burnt Basud powder.

Millions of Hindus prepare a mixture of lime, burnt powdered pearl and boiled areca nuts, which they wrap in a betel leaf and chew for hours. They attribute to the mixture the power to purify their breath, assist their digestion and stimulate their nervous system.

The Arabs also use powdered pearl as a curative; Whitelow Ainslie wrote in 1825 that physicians from those countries believed that pearls would cure eye complaints, nervous trembling, depression, haemorrhages and heart palpitations.

The European countries were also interested in powdered pearl. In the 13th century a German monk, Albert Magnus, recommended it for troubles of both heart and mind, but also for dysentry and haemorrhages.

At the same time, Spanish physicians recommended its use for people suffering from palpitations, melancholy and shyness for, mixed with certain herbs, it purified the blood, strengthened nerves and improved eyesight.

In the 17th century, Anselin de Boot, who worked at the court of Emperor Rudolf II of the Hapsburgs, revealed in one of his many works, the recipe for *Aqua Perlata*, which according to him was excellent for regaining one's strength. Here are the ingredients and method of preparation. First of all the pearls are dissolved in vinegar, lemon juice, vitriol or sulphur. To this is added the juice from a freshly squeezed lemon and a great deal of sugar. To 4 oz (100 g) of this solution, 1 oz (25 g) of the following products were added: rosewater, essence of strawberries, borage or melissa, and 2 oz (50 g) of cinnamon. The solution must then be mixed as thoroughly as possible. De Boot further recommended that the recipe should be prepared very carefully, in particular that the pan should be covered when the pearls were dissolving, in order to stop the essence evaporating. A scientific analysis of this drink reveals that it could actually cure heavy fevers. Indeed, it contains a great amount of vitamin C and some calcium.

The English philosopher, Francis Bacon (born 1561), gave us a simplified version of *Aqua Perlata*, which consists of dissolving pearls in lemon juice. Powdered pearl was used extensively by many people mixed with the appropriate medicinal herbs. One cannot deny that it is good for our bodies, because its components include calcium, organic materials containing amino acids, plus a small quantity of mineral salts.

Hindus and Chinese have always been great consumers of powdered pearl. Calcium is essential for the body. The make-up of our bones depends on it; it also prevents the blood from becoming too oxygenated and maintains a certain degree of alkalinity in the body. It seems certain to me that if some laboratory researcher inquired into the proporties of powdered pearls, he would discover, or rather rediscover, an effective remedy for many illnesses.

PART THREE
CULTURED
PEARLS

From
Natural Pearls
to Cultured
Pearls

From the 20th century the use of diving suits in the fisheries, which allowed divers to collect vast numbers of oysters, threatened to devastate the oyster-beds and endanger the survival of every species of pearl oyster. But fortunately at the same time conditions for pearl 'production' were totally revolutionised by the development of cultured pearls. Before then and as far back as one can go, we only knew about concretions which were formed spontaneously and quite by chance in the oyster or other shellfish.

The discovery of one such pearl was a very lucrative find, for which hundreds and even thousands of oysters were sacrificed. It is thought that only three out of every 1,000 oysters found produced a pearl of any value. The development at the turn of the century of the process of cultured pearls - the first experiments in which were made many years ago - now allows systematic control over a phenomenon which used to be entirely fortuitous. From then on, large-scale production of pearls has been possible, because *every* oyster at a farm was destined to produce a pearl.

The cultured pearl struggled against the suspicion and mistrust of dealers and great jewellers who considered only natural pearls to be of any value, and for whom the idea of an implanted pearl seemed false and artificial, since this was wholly incompatible with the tradition of their profession. But, in a matter of a few decades, as natural pearls became rarer and rarer and the cultured pearl products were perfected, the cultured pearl received its 'patent of nobility' from the most famous jewellers.

It must not be forgotten that whether natural or cultured, the pearl is still one of Nature's creations. It is the result of chance, which man can almost provoke by his skill, but is different from the objects which are fashioned and treated in factories.

Cultured pearls have shapes and colours independent of any human wish. We can only set in motion a natural organic process and watch over its evolution, but we cannot substitute anything in its place.

CHAPTER 8
The Origins of the Cultured Pearl Industry

Archaic Procedures and their Limits

The first attempts to make cultured pearls which are known to us date from the second century B.C. A Greek writer Apollomius of Tyre tells how the Arabs of the Red Sea tried to make pearls. They spread oil on the sea to calm the waves, then they dived to collect the oysters. When they brought these to dry land, they cut the oysters' flesh and a white milky liquid flowed out, which was collected in various mussels. When it dried, this liquid became as hard and shiny as real pearls.

From this brief description it is difficult to tell the precise process that was used. Nevertheless, it seems unlikely that such events could have occurred as they have no foundation in fact.

In China, the first attempts at producing cultured pearls go back to the 13th century and are attributed to Yu Shun Yang, born at Sou Tcheou Fou. Not far from there, in the village of Chung-Kwan-O, a temple was dedicated to his memory, and every year families who grew pearls gave a large festival in honour of their founder. Moreover, they were bound to give a sum of money for the upkeep of the temple. In the Canton region, this art was also practised by many craftsmen. The manufacturing technique was fairly simple in principle. It consisted of delicately opening the mussel *Dipsas plicatus*, with a piece of bamboo, pushing back the flesh which covered the interior shell and implanting a half sphere of mother-of-pearl, a ball of damp mud with some camphor oil, or a lead or tin figure representing the god Buddha in a seated position.

The treated mussels were then placed in cages and put in canals, streams, pools or lakes. In a short time the mantle regained its former position and covered the implanted object with a layer of mother-of-pearl which became thicker the longer the shell remained in the water.

In order to facilitate the rapid secretion of pearl layers, several processes were used. The first was to pour a powder of fish scales into the mussels. Then, to increase their growth, balls of honey, ginseng powder and other medical roots were dropped into the water.

Several thousand Chinese worked at making cultured pearls. Every year, millions of pearls and Buddhas were sold still attached to the shell. Then with the help of a small saw, the figures and pearls were detached, the lead, mother-of-pearl or mud withdrawn, replaced by wax and sealed by a very fine layer of mother-of-pearl.

The first European to become interested in cultured pearls was the Swedish botanist Carl Linne. In a letter of 13th December 1748 to the Swiss anatomist Von Haller, he revealed that he was able to produce pearls in five to six-year old mussels. It appears that the King of Sweden bought his process which then became a royal monopoly. Pearls produced by Linne's process, which was based on a Chinese method, did not give the expected results and the experiments were soon abandoned. The British Museum has a few specimen pearls produced by Linne.

Between 1844 and 1859 Kelaart made several experiments with cultured pearls in Ceylon and California; here again, his method was derived from the Chinese technique.

In 1884, Bouchon - Brandely did some experiments on the *Pinctada margaritiferae* of Tahiti. His very original method was to pierce the shell in several places, then to pass a ball of mother-of-pearl into the oyster on a copper wire, blocking up the holes with pieces of wood. The oysters were returned to the water and a few months later there would be a new layer of mother-of-pearl on these balls. But once again, the pearls obtained were of very poor quality and the reaction of the copper to salt water was one of the main reasons for the experiment's failure.

Establishment of the Present Technique

The invention of round cultured pearls as manufactured today is the work of the Japanese Tatsuhei Mise, who obtained his first round pearl in 1904. Another Japanese named Nishikawa must have obtained his first cultured pearl at about the same time, as they both obtained their licences within five months of each other in 1907. Both these Japanese discovered, almost simultaneously, that a

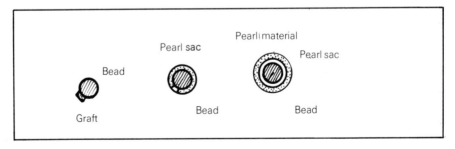

The three stages in the formation of a cultured pearl. On the left is the bead with the graft; next the sac that is formed around the bead by the oyster; and on the right the bead covered with nacre by the sac.

graft of epithelial membrane and a piece of mother-of-pearl had to be inserted if a round pearl and not merely a ball of mother-of-pearl was to be obtained.

Mikimoto obtained his licence in 1914. His method was to cover a piece of mother-of-pearl with epithelial tissues, but this technique is no longer used because it is too slow and delicate. Moreover, it often involves the death of the oyster in question.

Cultured pearls are produced nowadays by the Mise-Nishikawa method. A graft of epithelial membrane is taken from the oyster, then inserted with a piece of mother-of-pearl in the gonad of the same or of another oyster. The cells of the graft develop around the mother-of-pearl and thus form the pearl bag which, once complete, secretes the pearl material around the core.

The Mikimoto Legend

It is hard to talk about cultured pearls without mentioning, however briefly, the long life of Mikimoto. He was born in 1858 in the port of Toba. His first name was Kichimatsu; this name seemed predestined because Kichi means luck and Matsu means pine-tree, which is a symbol of prosperity in Japan.

His parents were modest people who were vegetable and noodle dealers, and Mikimoto made his entry into the business world by selling these products.

He soon became interested in the fishermen in Ago Bay, who dealt in natural pearls, and began trading as a pearl buyer. His taste for perfection led him to select the finest pearls; thus in 1887 at an exhibition in Tokyo, the Empress noticed his pearls and he was awarded a prize.

Because of the great demand for natural pearls Mikimoto was certain that the oyster-beds would soon be exhausted. So he decided to 'grow' pearls. He met the scientist Yoshikichi Mizukuri, a specialist in marine matters, who told him that experiments of this nature were already under way but no interesting results had yet been obtained. Mikimoto began his research and, for several years, he employed a whole village to collect the mother oysters necessaary for his experiments.

At the outset, Mikimoto tried to manufacture pearls by using the Chinese method of fixing fragments of mother-of-pearl on to the oyster's shell. It was only in 1893 that he obtained his first pearls, which are now called 'mabes'. Mikimoto then set up a base on the island of Tatoku, 3 km (about 2 m) from the coast of Shinnei-Mura, and began a massive production of mabes. Between 1893 and 1916 he had to struggle against all sorts of setbacks and it was not until 23 years later, in January 1916, that he solved the problem of round pearl production.

In 1900, the terrible 'red tide' - Akashio in Japanese - a lethal proliferation of plankton which asphyxiates most molluscs, destroyed nearly all his oysters. This red tide returned in 1905, but Mikimoto was able to combat it more effectively. He employed all available divers and increased their wages by 50 per cent so that they worked continuously to clear his oyster-beds. By doing this he managed to save one-sixth of his oysters.

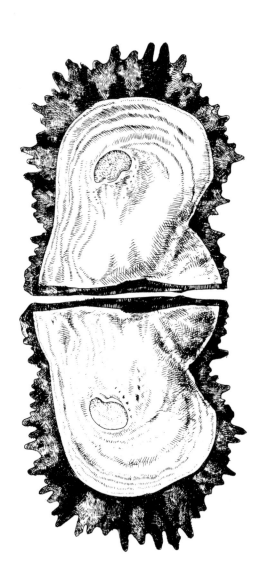

The oyster favoured for pearl culture, the Pinctada martensi or Pinctada fucata. They are not edible oysters.

After the last war, at the age of 85, Mikimoto reorganised his farm and in 1951, he had about 20 million cultured pearls in his grounds. He died in 1954 at the age of 97 on the island that he loved so much. This was one of his dearest wishes.

If, as we have just seen, and contrary to what many people believe, Mikimoto was not the inventor of the cultured pearl, it is nevertheless thanks to his qualities as an excellent technician and an able businessman that the cultured pearl has gained its present world-wide reputation. Indeed after his death his company produced 500 necklaces daily for export throughout the world. These necklaces were first-rate pieces of work in the homogeneity of their colour and the impeccable quality of each pearl which formed them. At that time, Mikimoto was competing against natural pearls - and to offer perfection was the only way to win.

Nowadays, necklaces can be found in every quality and at all prices. This is a good development because, however rich a woman is, she can beautify herself with a pearl necklace. It is the dream that Mikimoto pursued throughout his life.

On top of one of the rafts, which are made from cryptomeria poles lashed together to form an open grid about 30 metres (100 ft) long by 10 to 13 metres (30 to 40 ft) wide, below which the oyster cages are suspended. The rafts are mounted on tarred barrels as floats, keeping them 30 to 45 cm (12 to 18 in) above the surface. The wire cages are suspended by ropes and usually contain 12 to 20 oysters.

CHAPTER 9
Cultured Pearl Manufacture and its Technique

For even one pearl to be formed, hundreds of men and women have toiled and watched over its gestation.

A short time before the oysters begin mating, the oyster farmer places collectors in the water and, a few weeks later, thousands of oysters will have been collected. The young oysters are removed and placed in nurseries on large trays, protected from predators by small-mesh nets. The oysters are kept like that for two years, continually watched and regularly cleaned. Then they are sold to a farmer who keeps them in his farm for a year so that they can acclimatise to the water which will be their new home.

Then the oysters are placed in a more pleasant environment to undergo the grafting and to survive the operation. But before the grafts can be taken, the farmer has to check that his rafts, boats, and the whole infra-structure of his farm are in good working order. This is a big job if one thinks of the number of cables, chains, bamboo poles, ropes and baskets which have to be repaired or replaced. Food and lodgings for his employees have to be prepared because for the next two to three months they will transform a peaceful farm into a hive of human activity.

The purchase of the cores relates to the size of the pearls that the farmer wishes to obtain. But the larger the core, the greater the percentage of mortality after the graft has been taken, and this explains the high price of large pearls. Farmers generally specialise in certain sizes - some produce pearls of 2 to 5 mm diameter, others 5 to 7 mm and larger.

When all the checks have been made the real work can begin. One group is in charge of supplying the grafters with oysters; once the graft has been taken, another group returns the oysters to the baskets, which are re-attached to the rafts. The oysters stay there for 1 to 3 years and are carefully watched so that the corpses of those which did not survive the grafting operation can be removed before they contaminate the water, and so that various predators can be chased away. Algae and other vegetation is also removed before they become attached to the shells and harm the oysters.

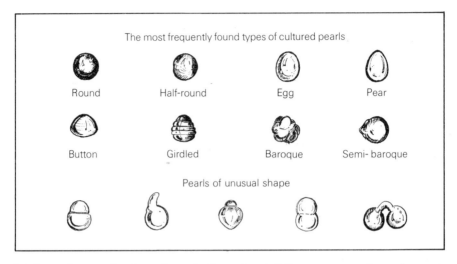

The most frequently found types of cultured pearls

Round · Half-round · Egg · Pear

Button · Girdled · Baroque · Semi- baroque

Pearls of unusual shape

Various shapes of cultured pearls. From top left they are: round, semi-round, egg, pear, button, girdled, baroque and semi-baroque. The bottom row shows shapes classified as fantasy.

Grafted oysters do not stay in the water more than three years, for the following reasons.

The longer a pearl stays in the water, the greater the risk that it will become baroque and that natural elements will disturb the harmony of its development, and thus the greater the risks that the pearl farmer will run. One must not forget that the quality and size of a pearl are not only dependent on the time that the oyster is immersed or the size of the core, but also on the nature of the oyster. From a core of 3 mm the gain in one year can be anything from 3.5 to 5 mm.

The quantity of plankton and the water temperature of the culture beds have also to be closely watched. If the water is too cold or there are insufficient plankton, the rafts are moved into better positions. If the water is too hot, the baskets must be lowered even further.

At last the harvest arrives. The farm buzzes with activity. Boats are manoeuvred to and from ; the sea, churned up in the wake of the boats, seems to be celebrating the birth of the pearls.

Once the harvest is over, the farmer entrusts the cultured pearls to a co-operative which handles the sale to necklace manufacturers. The sale is done by auction and only the Japanese are allowed to buy, but foreigners can make deals on the side. This is in order to keep the Japanese work-force.

In this context 'manufacturers' are people who work with the raw pearls, in Japanese, the Amage. The first stage is to pierce the pearls, then to soak them in a solution of oxygenated water, so that organic impurities between the core and the pearl material will be dissolved. Thus the pearls become pure and slightly bleached. When the pearls are dried, they lose the green tinge that freshly collected pearls always have.

The merchandise is then sieved, and pearls of the same size are sorted by colour, then by quality. Then, one by one, they are placed in grooves, ready to be threaded. Once threaded, the necklaces or chokers are arranged according to size and quality.

To put a value on the production is not easy. This explains the differences in price between various manufacturers, depending on the quality of the end result of the pearl production process.

Foreign buyers deal with the manufacturers, and so large numbers of pearls find their way to the markets of Paris, Bombay, London and New York.

All too often the cultured pearl is considered to be an insignificant product, because it has been 'grown'. But this attitude overlooks the years of care and effort which have been necessary to obtain that precious object - the pearl.

Instrument Used for Operating on Oysters

Operating on oysters is carried out in Japan by women, and in the Pacific by men. The distance and tough working conditions in the second case are the only reasons for this variance.

It takes two years to learn just the grafting techniques and even longer to obtain beautiful cultured pearls. It is worth noting that percentages of baroque, pear, round and button pearls can vary from one operator to another; the technique is within the capability of many, but the highest degree of creativity is reserved to an elite.

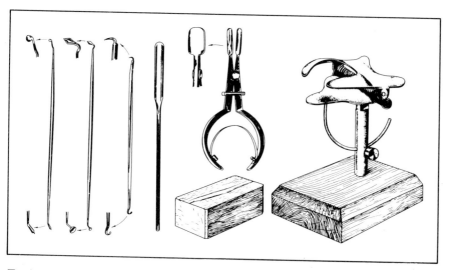

Tools used by workers on a cultured pearl farm. That on the right is for holding the shell. Its level can be adjusted. In the centre is a pair of tongs and on the left, surgical implements.

According to the size of the core, an oyster is capable of secreting two to three pearls at the same time. The gonad, the sexual organ of the oyster, is quite important in this context.

Siting a Cultured Pearl Farm

When choosing a site for a farm, many variable factors have to be taken into consideration. The relief of the region - mountains, reefs, or other natural features - must protect the farm from wind, currents and storms. However, the proximity of any river, which could cause the desalination of the water following heavy rainfall, should be avoided. The most favourable depth of water appears to be 6 to 15 metres (20 to 50 ft).

A constant regularity of temperature is very important. The type of sea-bed, whether rocky or sandy, and the presence of gentle currents to bring food and oxygen to the oysters are of prime necessity and must be taken into account if the farm is to have a chance of success. But over hundreds of kilometres, there are few sites which satisfy all these conditions.

A raft moored near a loading station. The barrels which form its floats can be seen at the end. Rafts are towed to various places according to the season. Baskets can be lowered if the water temperature should drop or if the salinity of the water should change because of heavy rains. Oysters are normally brought up and cleaned of marine growths and moss at least four times a year.

The Preparation of Oysters

Before a graft is taken, the oysters are starved for several days. This period of fasting allows:

1 The gonad - the sexual gland of the oyster which receives the core and the graft - to become empty.

2 The oyster's metabolism to slow down, which diminishes the risk of rejection.

3 The oyster to open up voluntarily, so that small wooden chocks can be placed between the shells without any harm to the animal.

After the operation, oysters, still wedged open, are rested for several days to reduce the risk of their rejecting beads.

The Cores

The cores are made from the following shells: *Amblema, Quadrula, Fleurobema and Megalonaia*. These are types of freshwater mussels which come mainly from Mississipi. Their special quality is that they have a specific gravity similar to that of a pearl. Their hardness gives the best results, and their thickness allows cores of 2 to 12 mm in diameter to be taken. The neutrality of the colour - vital for producing beautiful cultured pearls - is also very satisfactory. In fact if the core had any colour whatsoever it might be transparent through the pearl layers and would substantially affect the final cultured pearl.

The shell is cut into thin sheets, then cubes, which are rounded in a tumbler, revolving barrels with progressively finer abrasives. The balls obtained are placed between two steel discs in which grooves have been cut. One of these turns, taking the cores with it, so giving them identical diameters and an immaculate polish.

A number of experiments have been made with other shellfish but the bad colouring of the cores, or their unsuitability for the industrial process, led to these being abandoned.

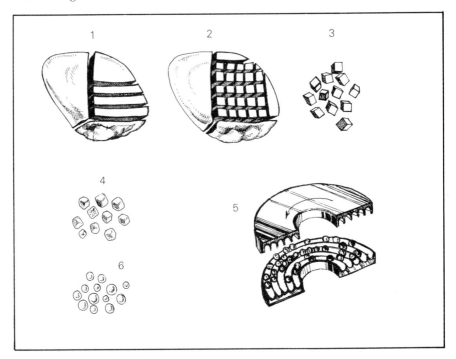

Stages in making beads from the shell of the Mississippi mussel, from which cubes are sawn. They are partly rounded by tumbling and finished between grooved steel discs, as shown, using finer and finer abrasives.

The Amah

Before full mastery of oyster farming with *Pinctada martensi*, it was the Amah (Japanese female diver) who brought the mother oysters from the sea-beds. They were linked by a rope to a round tub with a glass bottom, allowing them to locate the oysters from the surface.

This type of fishing is still carried out, not for the *Pinctada* but for the many other shellfish which are dear to the Japanese palate.

In earlier pearl culture in Japan, the women divers wore special costumes and were known as Amahs.

Operating on the Oysters

The operation which has to be carried out to obtain the cultivated pearl occurs in three stages.

1 Preparation of the graft.
2 Attaching the graft.
3 Inserting the core.

The preparation of the graft is essential for the success of a cultured pearl. This is why the removal must be carried out with the same care and meticulousness as a delicate surgical operation. The graft is taken from the retractile edge of the mantle of a living oyster.

The oyster is carefully opened with a sharp knife, the blade being inserted between the two valves, cutting the adducent muscle which is attached to both shells. At this stage of the operation absolutely no harm must be done to the mantle.

A strip about 7 cm (2.8 in) long and 3 to 4 cm (1.2 to 1.6 in) wide is cut from the edge of the mantle. This strip of living tissue is carefully laid out on a block of damp wood and any mucus wiped off with a sponge.

The scalpel separates this strip of the outer edge from the mantle which contains black, thick areas and which does not secrete pearl material. The remaining tissue is trimmed down to make a long narrow strip of about 2 to 3 mm. Then it is cut crossways into small squares. The size of the squares is calculated in accordance with the diameter of the cores being used. Each graft must be big enough to cover about one third of the core.

The grafts taken are attached to an apparatus which is plunged into a vessel of seawater maintained at a moderate temperature of 17 to 22C (63 to 72F). Grafts can live for about two hours in contact with seawater.

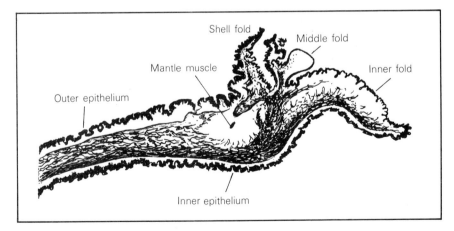

Cross-section of the mantle of an oyster. Successful pearl culture depends to a great extent on the place where the graft is removed from the mantle. The most common place is from the lower layers.

Several methods are used for this operation. The most common is for the graft to be taken from the lower layers of the mantle. The strip of mantle is removed immediately, using either scissors or a scalpel to cut the tissue from the molluscs shell. The strip is then withdrawn with the help of forceps and placed on the block of damp wood. The productive mother-of-pearl cells are placed face down on the block while the strip is cleaned of mucus, and then it is turned over and cleaned again.

It must be stressed that, to produce pearls, the cells producing mother-of-pearl must be in direct contact with the core in the oyster's body. As these cells are found only on the outer layer of the mantle their positioning on the wooden block at the moment of their removal must be very precise. Grafts prepared in this way are inserted before the core, and are positioned above it.

Another method is to place the strip of tissue with the mother-of-pearl cells face down against the block of wood. In this case the core is first inserted into the oyster's body, then the graft.

The gonad is definitely the organ in which the implant of the graft and core is best tolerated by the oyster and in which the graft finds the best conditions to develop.

The insertion of the nucleus is also a meticulous operation. The oyster is held partially open by a wooden chock and placed on an apparatus which holds it steady at the operators' eye-level. With the chosen valve (side of the oyster) on top and the grafts ready, the operator carefully moves the mantle folds with the help of a spatula, to reveal the foot and body of the animal. A clamp is used to hold the foot and to prevent any muscular contraction.

An incision is made in the epithelium of the foot with a flat stylet, so that a narrow passage is opened up in that mass of tissue.

The graft is inserted into this passage to the required position, then the core is inserted into the oyster directly above the graft. The foot is then gently massaged with the back of the stylet to close the wound and the mucus released greatly assists in forming a scab. The foot is freed from the clamp, the wooden chock withdrawn from the two valves and the operation is over.

If a second nucleus is to be inserted, the wooden chocks are left between both valves and the oyster turned over so that the lower valve is on top. The folds of the mantle are moved once again, and the viscera exposed. The foot is immobilised and the epithelium covering the viscera is pierced by a stylet. The graft, then the core are inserted into the gonad. For this second operation, care must be taken not to perforate or damage any vital organs (especially the liver).

Some very skilled technicians are able to insert a third core when the oyster is in the same position; but this operation demands a level of delicate skill which few can attain.

One year's apprenticeship is necessary before acquiring a satisfactory technique for such operations. During this period, apprentices practise inserting marbles and cutting out grafts. A good technician can insert about 30 cores an hour.

The Recovery of Pearls

The pearls' recovery is the moment of truth awaited by producers of cultured pearls throughout the world. However large their businesses, this, for them, is the most important moment because they will reap the results of years of careful work spent looking after the oysters which they have watched, hatched and coddled.

After the siting of a farm, the producer has to wait for 2 to 3 years before the first harvest. Then, if grafts are inserted every year, an annual production will be obtained. In Japan, most of the oysters are opened from December to January each year, and the pearls sold then to manufacturers.

Piercing, chemical treatment, classifying and stringing the pearls takes them about two months. For these reasons it is pointless for a buyer to go to Kobe or Tokyo before the end of March to the beginning of April.

In both hemispheres, when the farms are situated near the equator where there are no real seasons, certain producers graft and harvest twice a year. This has two advantages - firstly it reduces the risks that bad weather could cause for the rafts, and secondly, it halves the necessary outlay needed for this stage of pearl production.

The prices of *Pinctada maxima* and *margaritifera* are so high that the pearl's extraction is carried out like a true surgical operation. The oysters are split open; the gonad and pearl bag are cut by a scalpel and the pearl and kechi then removed. If the technician believes that the oyster has survived the three years of gestation without any problems, he will place another nucleus in the position of the extracted pearl and the oyster will be kept for another two years. About a third of the oysters are 're-cycled' in this way.

During the harvest, apart from cultured pearls, blisters, kechis and occasionally natural pearls are found. This is because oysters which have been operated on cannot be sheltered indefinitely from the various parasites which cause the formation of natural pearls.

When certain oysters are no longer in any condition to undergo a grafting operation, the farmer sometimes attaches cores on to the inner surface of their shells so that mabes or blisters can still be produced.

Pearl Layers in Cultured Pearls

It is often thought that the longer a pearl remains in the body of the oyster, the thicker will be the layers of pearl-material. This is broadly correct, but should not be taken as an absolute rule. In fact the most important and least forseeable factor is the very nature of oyster and how it reacts to the grafting operation.

We also know that the colder the water, the slower the metabolism of the oyster, but it must not be forgotten that the oyster is a unique animal with its own behaviour. As with every living species, there are strong and weak, large and small ones; diseases which we do not know about can affect groups or individual oysters. By trying to imagine what can happen to an oyster during the period of its pearl's gestation, one can find a thousand explanations for the disparity in the size of pearls harvested from the same raft.

The most striking example is that of the large pearls produced in Australia and Burma. We know that the grafts are added to cores of 7 to 8 mm (0.27 to 0.31 in) in diameter, and the grafted oysters remain in the same place on the same raft for three consecutive years. At harvest time it is confirmed that some pearls have a diameter of 8 to 9 mm (0.31 to 0.35 in), while others measure 14 to 16 mm (0.55 to 0.62 in).

Because of their size Japanese oysters cannot take cores larger than 9 mm (0.35 in). The skill with which the Japanese can find mother oysters and their high degree of technical skill, enables them to produce not the largest pearls possible, but to adapt to world demand which, because of different fashions in various countries, needs pearls of many diameters.

Oysters in Japan remain on average one to two years in the water after the grafting operation. From about 5,000 oysters operated on with cores of 6 mm (0.23 in) pearls will be recovered with a diameter of 6.2 to 6.5 mm (0.24 to 0.25 in) and even some of 8 mm (0.31 in).

Treatment of Pearls

Drying This is a very important operation; it removes the small tint of green colour peculiar to all freshly harvested pearls (the Hindus used to leave the pearls in the sun on the terraces of their houses to dry out properly).

Bleaching Some pearls have a certain colour because of the shellfish which secrete them and the conditions of their gestation. In cases of an excessive secretion of organic material, the pearls produced can have an unpleasant colour due to dehydration.

The popular colour of pearls depends on individual tastes, but also on different nations and fashions. It is a general rule that white is the most universally appreciated colour.

In about 1922, a Japanese called Fujido, having learnt that the Italians used oxygenated water to change the colour of brown coral, tried to use the same technique on pearls. This consisted of plunging pierced pearls into a solution of diluted oxygenated water, contained in a glass beaker which was exposed to the

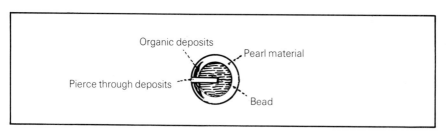

A cultured pearl with a blemished area, on the left, caused by organic deposits. It is pierced from this side for mounting.

sun for a long while. In this way he succeeded in improving a great number of pearls.

He is said to have made a fortune in a few years, because at that time it was simple to collect vast quantities of 'stained' pearls, thrown away at the sea-side by the pearl farmers of the village Koshiga who thought they were valueless.

In time the bleaching technique became fairly widespread. Nowadays most Japanese companies possess large drying rooms where and sun drying has been replaced by electric lamps, and with treatment in oxygenated water and carefully guarded proportions of benzol, ether, alcohol and so on.

Dyeing After bleaching, there are often irregular patches of colour on the pearls. It is therefore necessary to dye them to gain a more harmonious colour. Although it is not legal to dye pearls without specifying it on the invoice - obligatory for pearls which are dyed black - for white pearls it is impossible to distinguish bleached pearls from unbleached pearls, and pearls which have been dyed from those which have not.

Dyeing pearls is more the job of harmonising colours than dyeing in the true sense of the word. When one accepts that a pearl is mainly built up of an accumulation of carbonate layers with a small amount of hard organic material, the dye must penetrate both bodies and fill the space between the carbonate crystals.

One of the dyeing methods is to wash white pearls in pure water, then immerse them for six hours in alcohol at a temperature of 40C (104F), finally they are transferred to a colouring solution at 49C (120F) consisting of 600 cc (21 fl oz) of water for 2 g (0.07 oz) of colouring dye, plus 400 cc (14 fl oz) of alcohol to which is added 0.1 per cent pyridine or iodised potassium, where they remain for 160 hours. The pyridine and iodised potassium help the colouring to dissolve, accelerate the solution's penetration and assist the stabilisation of the colouring dye.

Each firm guards its dyeing secrets very jealously. However, we know that most of them use colourings which are soluble in water or in oil. The colour of black pearls is almost always attained by silver nitrate and other mineral salts.

So that there is no possible confusion between natural black pearls and pearls which are dyed black, the word dyed must, by law, appear on an invoice which might read as follows:

Sold - 1 cultured pearl, dyed black
Sold - 1 string of cultured pearls, dyed black.

Mabes or Compound Pearls

The manufacture of a mabe (a Japanese term) is based on the principle of a blister's formation whose origin is animal or vegetable.

The first operation consists of parting the oyster's mantle, then attaching a specially shaped core to the shell. This sort of operation lasts only a few minutes, during which each oyster can receive up to six cores, three through each valve.

Then the oyster is put back in a basket and re-immersed in the sea, where the mantle gradually regains its position by secreting pearl-material on these foreign bodies.

After a year, when the main harvest is over, the manufacture of the mabe can begin, as follows:

1 Removal of the mabe by cutting it from the shell with a circular saw mounted on a drill.

2 Separation of the mabe from its mother-of-pearl support.

3 Separation of the mabe from the original core, to remove all the organic substances which might exist between the core and the pearl shell and affect its colour.

4 Cleaning the mabe, now a hollow shell, with diluted hydrochloric acid.

5 Removal of the collarette (the flange that is left) so that only the circular section is left.

6 Filling the pearl hemisphere with polyester resin, rubber spray or some other substance (every producer has his own secret material) so that the mabe is as beautiful and as firm as possible.

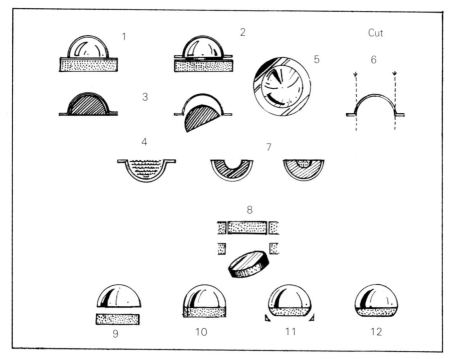

Stages in the making of a mabe (cultured blister) pearl. It is cut out of the shell leaving a rim. The base and bead are removed and the hollow blister pearl is then filled with resin and the rim cut off. A small hemisphere of nacre (7) helps attachment of the base.

7 The insertion of a small mother-of-pearl hemisphere into the centre of the mabe to make the setting strong.

8 Cutting a base of mother-of-pearl and glueing the base to the mabe.

9 Adjustment of both sections.

10 Polishing the finished work.

Mabes are mainly used for ear-rings and rings. The first use is by far the most appropriate because, despite the great care in manufacture, a mabe has the inconvenience of being fragile. The most common diameters are 13 to 16 mm (0.51 to 0.62 in).

This technique offers a lot of possibilities. For example, if the round core were replaced by a pear-shaped one, pear-shaped mabes would be obtained.

Some organic materials are deposited accidentally near the core because of the swelling which it causes under the mantle. Such materials will also be covered by pearl secretion and will begin to rot. The gasses released by this phenomenon blow up the pearl material which is in liquid state at the first stage of its secretion. Thus mabes can be given baroque shapes.

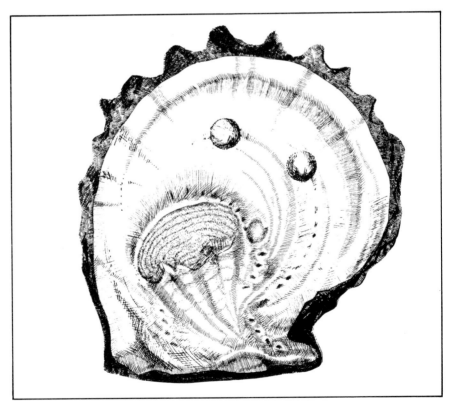

An oyster shell with mabe pearls formed on it. Usually three are placed in each half of the shell.

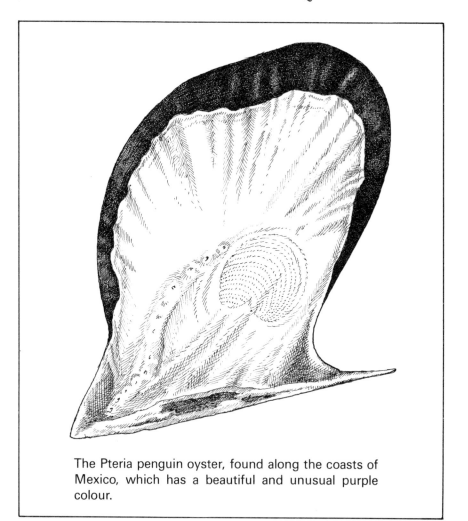

The Pteria penguin oyster, found along the coasts of Mexico, which has a beautiful and unusual purple colour.

The Japanese, Australians and, more recently, the Tahitians currently use this technique although one should really say *re-use* it because its invention is attributed to the Chinese Yu-Shun-Yang, who lived in the 13th century.

Pteria penguin is the scientific name of the shellfish used exclusively for the manufacture of true mabe pearls. The term mabe comes from the name which the Japanese give to this variety of shellfish, but all pearls grown in this way from *Pinctadas fucata, maxims* and *margaritifera* are now called mabe.

This shellfish is very widespread in Southern Japan and even Indonesia. A variety of *Pteria penguin* is found on the coasts of Mexico, which has a very original and beautiful purple mother-of-pearl.

Numerous attempts at growing round pearls have been tried in the shellfish, but the frailty of its constitution has precluded any financially viable result.

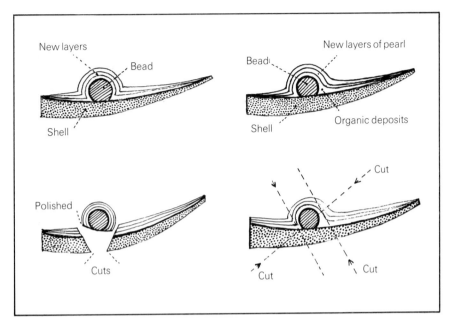

Cultured blister pearls are produced in the same way as mabes on the shell, but a three-quarters round bead is used instead of a hemisphere. It is removed from the shell by cutting in the manner shown, which preserves as much nacre as possible.

Cultured Blister Pearls

Cultured blister pearls must not be confused with mabes, although they are obtained by the same principle. Indeed, instead of attaching a semi-spherical core to the shell of the oyster, a core is attached which is three-quarters of a sphere.

The structure of the pearl is very special. It is midway between a three-quarter cultured pearl which has been cut to remove a flaw but whose original core remains untouched, and a mabe whose original core has been removed.

The growth of a blister pearl results from phenomena which occur when a natural pearl rejected by the oyster slides underneath the mantle and becomes encased in mother-of-pearl.

Such pearls are rarely found on the world market. Because of their cost - although they are easily grown - they give only a small profit. Often, when the mantle secretes new layers of mother-of-pearl, it does not cover the core's base and leaves large deposits of organic material, which when rotted deform the pearl.

The extraction of cultured blister pearls often requires the shell to be cut by a very skilful technician, capable of rounding and then polishing the base of the pearls.

Oyster-Farming at the Service of Pearl Culture

Ever since the technique of growing cultured pearls was mastered, the greatest problem facing growers has been obtaining live oysters. In most cases, production of oysters in the laboratory has proved to be a failure because of the high costs of the process.

Growers turned to the methods of collecting oysters from their natural habitats which, from region to region, give fairly good results. The principle behind this method is, during the mating season, to leave in the water as many obstacles as possible to which the young oysters will attach themselves.

The most usual method is to leave wooden faggots the places where currents should lead the young oysters. Once young oysters are firmly attached to the faggots by the *byssus* they are recovered and placed in baskets underneath a raft not far from dry land so that the oyster farmer can keep a close watch over them.

Depending on the particular species, oysters cannot be operated on until they are three to four years old.

One of the problems of pearl cultivators is to collect the young oysters. This is done by hanging bundles of faggots, like 'witches' brooms', in the water to which the young oysters attach themselves. Here are some bundles being prepared.

Top Left: Each bundle of faggots is enclosed in a net and hung where favourable currents are expected. The young oysters can be seen above travelling in the current.
Bottom Left: Gangs on the shores wash the young oysters before they are transported to the farms.

Below: A faggot raised from the water. The young oysters clinging to it are very small.

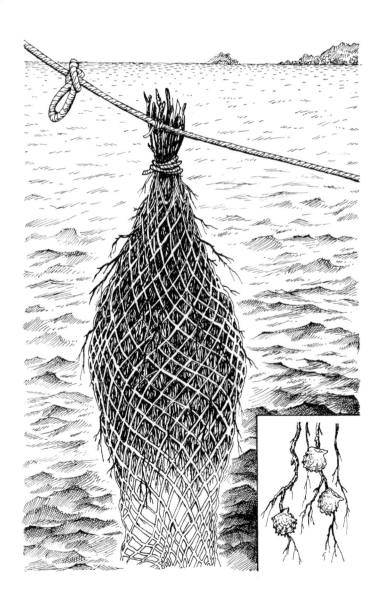

In Japan rafts are being displaced by floats holding baskets of oysters. The baskets below the rafts are hauled up and scrubbed of weed, barnacles and suchlike by hand several times a year. With the float system, a winch on a boat hauls up the baskets and cleans them by high pressure water jets automatically one after the other.

Baskets are hanging from a raft. The young spat are first bred in tanks and transferred in size groups to baskets in the sea when large enough. After three to four years beads are inserted, and after six to eight years cultured pearls are harvested.

In Southern Japan, the country's largest lake, Lake Biwa, covering an area of 2,500 square metres (3,000 square yards), there are beds of fresh water molluscs which produce mainly irregular cultured pearls without cores of various colours. The fisheries are fenced off as seen here. Fresh water pearls are also cultured in the Shanghai district of China.

Many cultured blister pearls are also produced in Lake Biwa. Here is an opened shell showing a number of blister pearls still covered by the mantle.

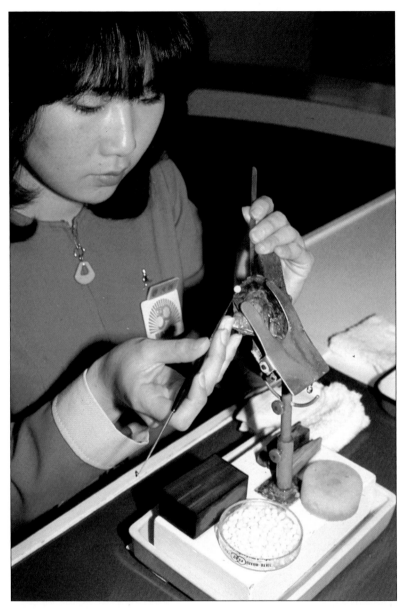

A variety of clips, tongs, scalpels and other surgical tools are used when the beads are inserted. The oyster shell is opened slightly and wedged. The mantle is opened and the adductor muscle pulled to the left. A T-shaped incision is made in the gonad and a small square of mantle and a bead is placed under each side. Small squares of mantle can be seen on the wooden block at the bottom. The bead being inserted is held in the cup-shaped end of a tool.

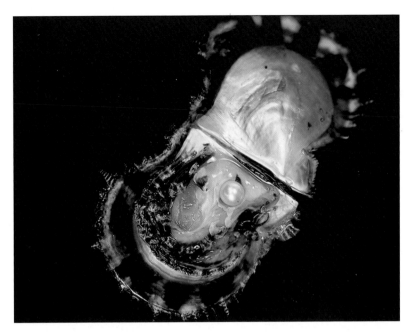

A large well-shaped cultured pearl being recovered from the gonad area of the oyster. To the left is the stomach and the slightly darker zone on the left is the adductor muscle. The less a pearl is moved by the oyster, the less likely it is to be mis-shapen.

A cultured 3/4 blister pearl, from a fresh-water lake. The exposed nucleus can be seen at the base. Curved grooves at the sides, merging at both ends, are typical of such pearls.

CHAPTER 10
Cultured Pearls Throughout the World

The South Sea Pearls

Once the technique for making cultured pearls had been perfected on oysters of the Japanese archipelago, the problem arose of how to spread the process to the large *Pintadines* of the Pacific, which produced the largest natural pearls.

The real pioneers of these large cultured pearls, which are called 'South Seas' are three Japanese: S. Fujita and T. Nishikawa, very experienced technicians, and K. Iwasaki from Mitsubishi, which financed the experiments.

In 1916 they established a base in the Philippines near the Mindanao sea, on the island of Zamboanga. They soon realised that the region was politically unsafe and that piracy was rife. For a time, all work was abandoned.

Their search led them to Indonesia, which was then under Dutch control, and they set up a base on the island of Boeton, south of the Celebes, in 1918.

Their choice was guided by the fact that there were a great number of oysters available and the island was separated from the island of Muna by a narrow channel carrying a constant current of water which cleaned the coral and sandy sea-bed, ensuring that the oysters had a rich and plentiful food supply. But it was not until 1922 that the Jakarta authorities granted exploitation rights to the new company, which was called the Boeton Pearl Cultivation Co.

The adaptation of the grafting techniques on the *Pinctada martensi* and *Pinctada maxima* took a long time, and it was 1927 before the first encouraging results were obtained. Six years later, the company employed some new technicians whose names have remained famous - G. Ishikawa, H. Iwaki, R. Wada Sike. Since the end of the Second World War they have spread the grafting techniques on *Pinctada maxima* which they acquired when working for the Boeton Pearl Cultivation Co, throughout the Pacific.

In 1941 the company was re-organised by the military and ceased all pearl dealing when it became the Boeton Trading Co. It is thought that between 1937 and 1941, the company produced about 200,000 carats of pearls, a relatively small figure in comparison with those obtained by modern large pearl farms, but one must not forget that these were the first ever cultured pearl harvests in the South Seas.

Japan

Of all the pearl-producing countries, Japan is by far the most important. Their lead can be explained in several ways. The first man to perfect the technique of growing cultured pearl was Japanese. The oysters used are the *Pinctada martensi* and *fucata* which are very common on all coasts and can easily be used in oyster farming. The winding contours of the island form natural bays sheltered from both wind and storms.

Most of the farms are found on the west coast of Japan, where they are particularly numerous. After the harvest, every farmer sells his goods by auction, through a co-operative system where only Japanese are allowed to bid, so that treating, classifying and piercing the pearls is carried out by Japanese, thus ensuring employment for a large number of men and women.

Situated at the edge of the inner sea which protects the island of Shinkokv, Kobe is a big centre for cultured pearl dealing. It shares the monopoly for this business with Tokyo. Foreign buyers always came into contact with manufacturers, dealers and brokers from the two towns.

The Japanese, always very sophisticated in their international business dealings, have been able to keep their traditions intact. When dealing with these men, who are in contact with their past as well as the future, the approach of a

Tor Road, one of the best known streets in Kobe, the main market place for cultured pearls in Japan.

possible supplier and the conclusion of a business deal have nothing in common with our Western ways.

A sense of keen observation and patience, as much as the importance of one's money, are essential if one is to be invited into a Japanese home.

Burma

Burma, in South East Asia, is bordered by Pakistan, India, China, Laos and Thailand. The pearl farms are found close to Thailand in the Bay of Mergui. The oyster used is the *Pinctada maxima* which has a gold lip in this area and produces richly-coloured mother-of-pearl with opal-like reflections.

In the 50's the Japanese firm of Tagashima set up a cultured pearl farm which still provides the largest and most beautiful pearls in the world. The *Pinctada maxima* well deserves its name; it is huge in this region. The mother-of-pearl can often weigh 1.5 kg (3.30 lb) and sometimes even 3 kg (6.60 lb), in comparison with 800 g (1.85 lb), which is a good weight for an Australian oyster. This is why such oysters sometimes produce exceptional pearls of 14 to 15 mm and even 18 to 20 mm in diameter. Furthermore, the pearl layers are solid, thick and made of very good material.

The colour of Burmese pearls is incomparable. Some are golden, others are white like silk, and between these two colours, a rich variety of shades can be seen. Creamy pink is the rarest of all and also has the finest orient.

Total production is about 20,000 pearls a year, of which only 10 per cent are round, which explains the rarity and high price of Burmese necklaces.

For some years the farm has been under control of the government, which organises the sale of produce once a year. Pearls are divided into lots of all diameters, shapes and quality. The buyer has to make a sealed bid and then await the count of other bids. The nervous tension is extreme, because a lot of 40,000 US dollars can be lost for a mere dollar. This nullifies all the hopes and hours spent classifying, measuring, and estimating the value of the pearls by the unfortunate buyer, who must reflect that in such circumstances luck is just as important as wisdom and technique.

Australia

In 1955-56 a group of Japanese led by T. Kuribayshi co-operated with Otto Gerdau Co of New York, the well-known mother-of-pearl dealers, and the Australians, Brown, Dureault, Streeter and Male, to establish a pearl farm at Port Augustus. After a few years, this experimental site was abandoned for another one called Kuri Bay.

The first harvest was sold in Melbourne in 1959 to two companies, the Australian Pearl Co Ltd of London, represented by Boris Norman, and Pearsydiam of Geneva, represented by Mr. Morand. The first harvest was very similar in weight to that which came from Burma; about 20 kans.

The farm at Kuri Bay was supplied with mother-of-pearl for the cores of cultured pearls from Broome, about 2400 km (1500 miles) away. The chief

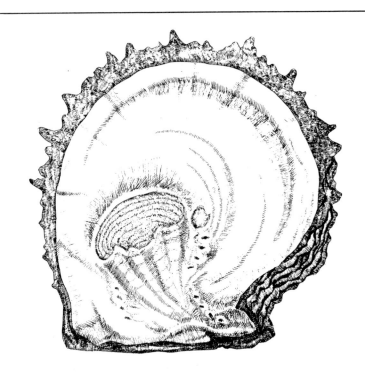

Pinctada maxima, the large pearl oyster found on the Barrier Reef off Australia, in the Mergui archipelago, and in the waters of the Philippines, Malaysia and Indonesia.

technicians, H. Iwaki and Renji Wada, were reputed to be the best in the world at that time.

During the same time in 1959, Cape York Pearling Co obtained permission from the Queensland authorities to grow pearls in a place with the evocative name of Escape River, north of Cape York. This company had business links with the Kakuda Pearl Co of Ise and Cultured Pearl Export Co of Tokyo, represented by J-M. Jerwood.

In order to recover its initial investments as quickly as possible, the company only grew mabes for the first few years, since they were in great demand on the world market. Then it moved successfully to producing round pearls.

Shortly afterwards another company, Nippo Pearls PTV was set up on Friday Island, then others on Horn Island, Packie Island and Goode Island. That is how the great Australian cultured pearl adventure all began.

Australia has two important centres of cultured pearl production. The first is in the Broome area, on the Western coast, to the north of the great sand desert. The oysters do not have a gold lip because of the type of water. Pearls produced often have a metallic sheen, which is very popular with Americans, Japanese and Germans.

The second area is at the tip of Cape York in Queensland, by the Great Barrier Reef. The type of water here creates a gold lip on the shell, and so many of the pearls have to be worked on.

The Australians' main problem is the difficulty of obtaining oysters. Although well-known for the abundance of mother-of-pearl and pearls, the area no longer produces many oysters. Every oyster caught is jealously kept for pearl production.

Once grafting is finished, the oysters are kept for three years in baskets suspended from rafts. During this period they are constantly watched. Oysters which have not withstood the grafting operation are quickly withdrawn, and any parasites are removed as soon as they appear.

The state of the rafts is also closely watched. The wood, chains, ropes and floats are systematically replaced at the first sign of weakness.

At harvest time, every oyster is passed under x-rays to check that it contains a pearl; if not, then the oyster can produce between four and six mabes. The demand for these pearls is fairly small in France and the UK. Luckily, however, Spain absorbs almost all world production.

There are two ways for dealers to obtain Australian pearls: in Tokyo from the large firms with links with Australian producers, which is by far the simpler method, or by going to the farms themselves, which is only possible by small aircraft, then by jeep. The weather is very important for these trips, because even in the slightest storms, the bush runways cannot be used for hours or even days afterwards.

The pearling centre at Cape York in north-eastern Australia. See map on page 50

Tahiti

The first cultured pearl experiments which enjoyed any success were undoubtedly those of Jean Domard, then director of the fishing service. He is the father of the cultured pearl industry in that region. Indeed, in 1962, he brought over Japanese technicians who were then working in Australian farms. This choice was very judicial, because these technicians had been used to working with the large Pintadines, which were very close to the *Margaritifera* species found in Touamotou and Gambiers.

As soon as his idea was launched, more farms were set up by brilliant businessmen with a spirit of adventure and a taste for risk. In alphabetical order one could name: J-C Brouillet, J. Branelec, K. Chaze, B. Reed, J. Rosenthal, J. Tapou, A. Vairaaroa, R. Wan and several others since the first appearance of the French edition of this book in 1983.

The farms were sited on atolls with such splendid names as: Marutea, Takapoto, Ikueru, Manihi, Ame, Aratika and Rangiroa. The difficulties facing them are critical and comparable with those met in Australia, the Philippines, Indonesia and so on.

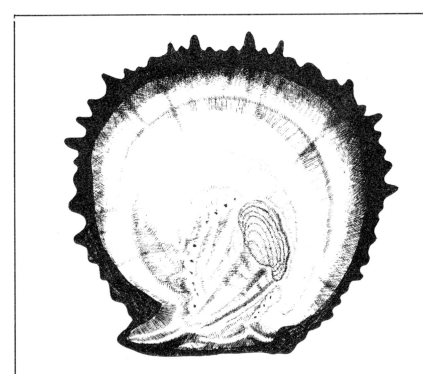

The type of Pinctada margaritifera pearl found in Polynesian waters and used for culture in Tahiti.

The supply of live oysters is a constant worry, but research undertaken on the subject of oyster farming is very promising and leads to the hope that in a few years the farms will have no further problems in procuring oysters.

At present the divers dive for fixed periods in specific zones, under the protection of a co-operative. On board a canoe, they leave early in the morning with only masks, snorkels and flippers. During the day the oysters they collect are kept in baskets or bags hung alongside the canoe. At the end of the day, on their return to the coast, they place the oysters in specially constructed pens until they are sold to the pearl growers.

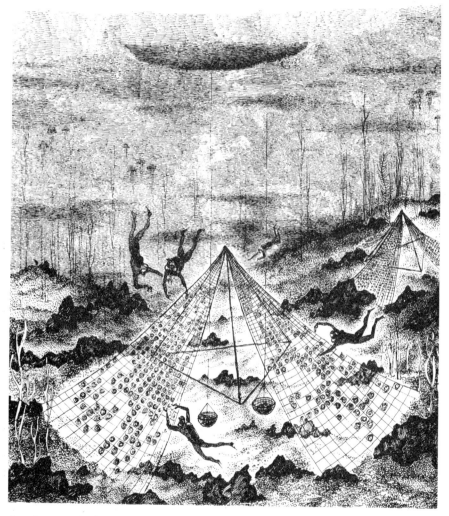

A unique technique of farming is used in Tahiti, employing tents of netting 6 metres (about 20 feet) high, held up by tripods.

When the oysters are too young to be operated on, they are placed in nurseries which have infra-structures of rectangular shape made by metal tubes, from which nylon ropes of about 3 metres (6.75 ft) hang. The young oysters are pierced through their hinges and hung by stainless steel wires through the holes hooked into the rope. About 20 oysters can be kept on each rope.

Each farm has its own nursery. Indeed, a large concentration of oysters in a relatively confined space allows a number of young off-spring to be collected on the farm infra-structure made up from ropes, chains, poles and so forth.

At the time of the grafting operation, which is between June and September, the healthier oysters are selected to produce round pearls. The others, which are often too old, are used for the manufacture of mabes.

In the better-equipped farms, several months after the operation the oysters undergo an x-ray test to determine whether the core has been rejected or if it is still well placed. If the core is in place, the oyster is placed on an infra-structure

The oysters are pierced near one end of the hinge and attached to the netting by galvanised iron wires.

in deeper water, where it remains for at least two years. Oysters which have rejected their cores are used to produce mabes.

The oyster employed is the *Pinctada margaritifera*, the peculiarity of which is its black lip. It produces pearls ranging from whitish grey to pitch black, as well as browns of every variety. It is almost impossible to find pearls with a diameter less than 8 mm (0.32 in).

The price of these pearls is based on that of the South Sea pearls - those of Australia, Burma and the Philippines.

The first harvest of about 1,000 pearls took place in 1965. The pearls were shown to a number of experts and dealers from all over the world, who judged them by their own particular markets and standards and pronounced that they had great potential, but that was all.

Dealers specialising in the sale of artificially-dyed pearls recognised a serious competitor; others, aware that the market for black pearls represented only a small percentage of the world pearl market, believed that the repayment of the cost of setting up a farm would take a long time.

The launch of this new product was the work of an American, Salvador Assael who, through his business genius and sense of publicity, was able to sell Tahitian pearls to the world's greatest jewellers, first of all in his own country, then in Europe. Without this man, the cultured pearl industry would almost certainly not be where it is today.

Many Tahitian producers have no contracts with Japanese firms, so that Tahitian pearls therefore go directly to many places: Papeete, Tokyo, Kobe, Paris, New York, and others.

The creation of the cultured pearl industry also saw the birth of a new method of keeping oysters. A tripod 6 metres (nearly 20 ft) high by 3 metres (nearly 10 ft) at the base is hung with netting to support the oysters. The oysters are pierced in their hinges and attached to the netting by galvanised iron wire. About 1,000 to 1,500 oysters can be kept on each such tripod.

The Philippines

The first man in the Philippines to successfully implant a cultured pearl was a Japanese called Takachima. Expelled from Burma at the start of 1962, he searched for a new site on which to establish a pearl farm. His choice was the Gulf of Davao, in the South East of the Philippines, on the island of Mindanao.

His success sparked off other initiatives. Today, there are seven pearl farms at Davao, Guivan, Surigao, Bantayan, Sambaonga, Bugsuk and Samporna. Total production is about 20,000 pearls a year.

Curiously, these farms are a long way from each other and are situated in places where there is no natural mother-of-pearl. The only region where Pintadines are found in any great quantity is the Mindanao sea. Transporting oysters to various farms often causes problems. Indeed the population on the coasts of the Mindanao sea is Muslim and separatist, whereas the rest of the country is Catholic. Additionally, there are linguistic problems and the great distances that have to be travelled.

This state of affairs makes the purchase of pearl oysters dangerous and costly. Indeed, Muslim divers are used to selling their oysters in lots and are not prepared to remove young oysters or oysters too old to undergo grafting. Transporting them over long distances also causes a high rate of mortality. Finally, the piracy which still exists in these parts takes its toll. A reasonable evaluation of the price of each operable oyster would be about 14 American dollars.

As in all the countries in the northern hemisphere, the harvest takes place in winter-time. Many of the farms have close commercial links with Japanese firms, which explains why it is almost impossible to find a single pearl in Manilla. The South Seas pearl market takes place at Tokyo, so it is here that one has the greatest chance of finding cultured pearls from the Philippines.

The colour of these cultured pearls is very similar to that of Burmese pearls, for example cream and pinkish. Certain jewellers accord a pearl some value only if it is pinkish white, but the public is becoming more and more discriminating and women have realised that a pinkish white necklace does not always give the sheen which they expected, whereas pinkish cream pearls give the neck a resplendent look and an aura of brilliance.

If we go back into the past, to the good old days of the natural pearl, pinkish cream was the colour most favoured by those who wore the pearls.

A Model Farm

Of all the countries where pearls are grown, it seems to be in the Philippines that one encounters the greatest difficulties in setting up and maintaining a farm. Despite - or maybe because of - all the problems one faces in pearl growing, it was in the Philippines that I visited a 'model farm'. It would not be an exaggeration to call it a unique creation, built in two years and just about to produce its first harvests.

The farm was set up by a young Frenchman, Jacques Branellec, who had gained a great deal of experience in Tahiti and had become one of the top technicians. He is also a diver, pilot, navigator, and adventurer in the noble sense of the word, who held all the winning cards for such a venture.

In 1979, he arrived at Manillo where he met a young Philippino called Manuel Cojuangco, a graduate from a good university, who belonged to one of the noblest Philippino families. The enthusiasm, knowledge and combined efforts of both these young men led to a pilot farm being set up in record time on the island of Bugsuk. They had to overcome numerous difficulties, but their desire to succeed was so strong that nothing could stop them.

Since the area had no oysters, the first stocks were imported on the air route which linked Bugsuk to the coasts of the Mindanao, which was fairly rich in *Pinctada maxima*. The stretch of land is Muslim and the partners were Catholic, so they had great difficulty in obtaining the necessary number of oysters. In this region, as in many others, the unfortunate intolerance of religions divides men with such force that they distrust one another with deep conviction.

While this was going on, the infra-structures and buildings of the farm were being constructed. The house for the technicians comprised single and double bedrooms, kitchen, dining-hall and conference room which could also be used for entertainment and was equipped as a video cinema and a library. Other leisure facilities would soon be added because technicians have to live in difficult conditions of distance and isolation from their families, where they have to perform intense and demanding work.

The building for the workers, all Philippinos, was split up when it was realised that the different ethnic races have different languages, customs and eating habits. Each quarter has its own kitchen, dining room, bedrooms and so on.

The other buildings were huts and laboratories. The huts sheltered the biggest equipment, such as the baskets which would contain the grafted oysters and be immersed in water. There were also several kilometres of chains, cables, ropes and all the tools needed for their upkeep. Lastly, the most delicate equipment - the air-compressors and the diving gear - were kept in huts.

There are two types of laboratory. One is for the technicians and is used during the grafting operations. It contains an x-ray machine so that the forming pearl can be seen, as well as a complicated pharmacy for the staff, enabling first aid to be given in cases of cuts and bites from snakes and insects which can be very dangerous in that climate.

There is also a resuscitation machine in case any of the divers has a serious accident. In order to prevent such accidents, the team work with strict discipline for a maximum of three hours at depths of 15 to 30 metres (50 to 100 ft).

The other laboratory is used for research. For this it is equipped with tanks and basins, pumps, retorts, test tubes and all sorts of tubes which are impossible to identify if one is not competent in the fields of oyster farming or marine biology.

Once these buildings had been erected and the farm's supplies had arrived, measures had to be taken to guard against theft or even armed attack which was not infrequent in the region. For this purpose, a network of tracks was built which are patrolled day and night by armed men who are in constant radio contact with guard posts.

The success of this enterprise demanded special talents, and notably the presence of highly competent technicians. A laborious search was undertaken to find the best in the world and to employ them. With oysters at 14 US dollars each, one cannot afford to make mistakes.

As soon as they arrive at the site, the oysters are placed in baskets which are submerged to depths of several metres. Once the grafts have been taken, the oysters are replaced in the baskets and immediately re-immersed. Each day for six weeks the baskets are turned 180 degrees. This operation has more chance of ensuring that the core (the future pearl) remains in the gonad of the oyster. Later on, the baskets are lowered to 15 to 30 metres (50 to 100 ft), which is an exceptional depth compared to that of other areas. This depth discourages pirates and other thieves, and also guarantees a more stable temperature, a more constant degree of salinity and, lastly, avoids all superficial currents.

Every three months the baskets are brought to the surface and the oysters taken out one by one to be cleaned, because their shells can be covered by various animal and vegetable matter. This close watch is kept up for three years to encourage the production of fine pearls.

The first harvest of 6,000 pearls indicates that pearls from the Philippines have a definite future. In fact, because of a lack of shells, Burma and Australia are producing fewer and fewer good quality pearls of a reasonable size.

As at other sites, the problem of oyster supplies is very important. However, close examination has revealed that many small oysters become lodged in the farm's infra-structure. Careful work could allow hundreds to be collected from ropes, posts, platforms, rafts and anything else submerged in the water. If three years of careful attention were given to these young oysters, they would become operable adults.

Not all cultured pearl undertakings on the Pacific coasts are as methodical as this one, which hopes for large-scale production. As a sample, here are the annual harvest records of a small farmer in the tropical South Seas:

mm	Rounds		Pears		Pears 2nd Class		Buttons		Baroques		Pears and Rounds 3rd Class	
	Pearl	Carats	Pearl	Carats	Pearl	Carats	Pearl	Carats	Pearl	Carats	Pearl	Carats
10 and +	95	776.02	59	545.02	54	499.18	132	1030.17	151	1368.49	172	1435.45
9 3/4	48	327.44	21	161.38	16	121.50	48	311.94	40	304.32	95	656.10
9 1/2	114	719.51	39	278.44	50	361.63	56	337.82	84	577.19	125	817.14
9 1/4	67	393.03	33	218.93	49	317.67	55	306.61	47	293.76	110	674.20
9	135	734.58	56	344.35	70	418.63	71	372.55	62	356.58	171	965.34
8 3/4	101	502.73	60	337.01	58	310.45	43	208.56	55	308.56	493	2322.56
											—	
8 1/2	116	533.89	54	280.13	67	337.58	47	204.05	117	528.48	1166	
8 1/4	102	433.67	44	211.40	59	317.57		566				
8 and −	85	326.97	25	102.40	81	314.24	29	113.62				
7 3/4	50	173.53	391		504							
7 1/2 and −	32	102.82										
	945							481				

If one realises that only 10 per cent of round, pear-shaped and button pearls are perfect in colour and quality, the smallness of the table above explains the high price of beautiful pearls.

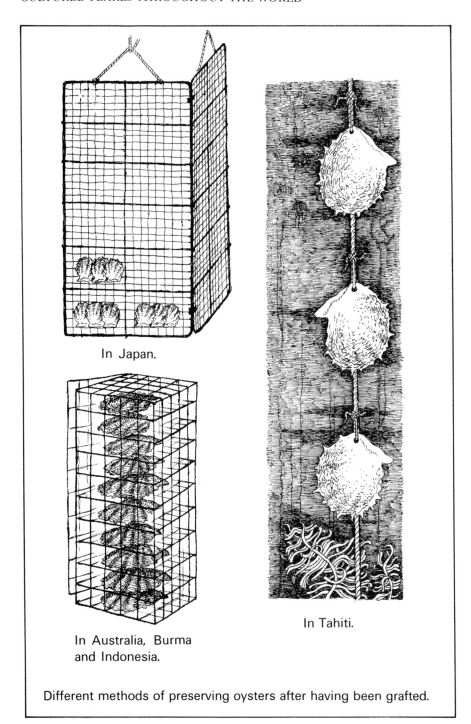

In Japan.

In Australia, Burma
and Indonesia.

In Tahiti.

Different methods of preserving oysters after having been grafted.

CHAPTER 11
Varieties of
Cultured Pearls

There are four main varieties of cultured pearls. They result from the shellfish used and the regions in which they are produced. These are the shellfish concerned:

Pinctada martensi and *Picata fucata* - Japan and, for several years, China.
Pinctada maxima - Pacific, where most farms are found in Australia.
Pinctada margaritifera - Pacific, very plentiful in Touamotou and Gambiers.
Hyriopsis schlegeli and *Cristria plicata* - Japan in Lake Biwa, China, and Korea.
These are the only freshwater shellfish from which pearls are grown.

The Kechi
The first three usually produce a by-product called kechi. This is a Japanese name which designates one of the small baroque pearls extracted from the oyster's gonad at the same time as the cultured pearl.

As we have seen, the grafting operation is carried out in three stages, the incision of the gonad, the introduction of the bead core, and the insertion of the graft. There are then three possibilities for the production of kechi.

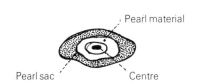

Pearl material

Pearl sac   Centre

One of the small baroque pearls known as kechi, removed from pearls at the same time as the cultivated pearls. They can occur for several reasons.

1 The graft is loaded with epithelial cells, some of which are detached from the gonad, multiply and quickly form a small pearl bag which then creates a pearl of 1 to 2 mm (0.04 to 0.08 in) diameter.

2 The graft is not in close contact with the core. The epithelial cells form a pearl bag around the graft and create a baroque pearl of 3 to 4 mm (0.12 to 0.16 in) across.

3 The oyster manages to expel the core from the gonad, but the smaller graft remains. The same phenomenon occurs as in the previous case.

Pearls which are grown without a core are based on the second example. The same phenomena occur with larger pearls *Pinctada maxima* and *margaritifera*, but the kechi is considerably bigger. When it does not exceed 6 to 7 mm (0.24 to 0.28 in), it is sold as such; when it is bigger, it is sold as a baroque pearl. No trickery is involved; with or without cores, the value of baroque pearls remains the same.

The South Sea Pearls

Since the last world war, the cultured pearl industry has spread throughout the Pacific on the Asian and Australian coasts, but not on the American coastline.

Throughout the world there is a fair number of pearl farms. Some are organised and run by large multi-national companies, producing 40,000 to 50,000 pearls a year. Others are created, financed and run by ambitious, hard-working adventurers, who manage to collect between 3,000 and 10,000 pearls annually.

Living conditions are very hard for the pearl farmers because of the climate, which is often tropical, with two hot and dry or hot and humid seasons. They are remote from everything, on an island or a gulf, often on a piece of land of about 3,000 to 5,000 square metres (2,600 to 4,300 sq yd) which has had to be cleared metre by metre. The isolation is total. The nearest town is usually tens of kilometres away. Access to these farms can only be gained by sea or land, by using a track built by the farmers themselves. This can be used only for six months in a year, because after the first drops of rain it turns into a mud bath which will dry out only after several days of hot sunshine.

Keeping a farm going in such conditions is an act of valour. The slightest accident can reduce years of hard work to nothing at all. If a strong wind breaks the fastening of a raft, it will soon become dislodged and the oysters will be dragged to the bottom by their own weight and quickly die, covered in sand. If a motor boat breaks down, there is no point in sending out an SOS - there is nobody in the vicinity; the only possibility is to make a quick repair so that the boat does not become a cork on the ocean or break up on the reefs. The slightest illness or injury can become dramatic unless sufficient medication is available. Everything has to be provided in duplicate or triplicate, because anything could happen.

Men able to live in such conditions are exceptional. They are often self-taught and learn to become mechanics, blacksmiths, hunters, cooks, doctors and electricians. Let us pay them tribute and thank them for allowing us to enjoy the marvellous South Sea pearls.

Cultured pearls from the South Seas are generally larger than 10 mm (0.4 in). In general one can say that Australian pearls are white with a silvery tint; those from Burma and Indonesia go from pinkish cream to cream; and those of Toumatou are from light grey to jet black in appearance.

Black Pearls

Most black pearls are produced by the *Pinctada margaritifera*, which is in plentiful supply in the Archipelagos of Touamotou, Gambiers and the Marquises Islands. Other regions of the world, from the Red Sea, Panama, and Fiji to Mexico, also produce black pearls, but to a lesser extent. The precise reasons for this peculiarity are probably due to the presence of mineral salts in the water, as well as the type of plankton which the oysters eat, but also to the nature of the species.

Depending on the region from which they originate, pearls have reflections and shades of a different hue, but the most beautiful are certainly those from Touamotou.

Black Cultured Pearls

With the extension of farms into the South Pacific, the development of the cultured pearl industry in Tahiti has seen the birth of a cultured pearl that is coloured naturally from grey to black. The diameter of these pearls is rarely less than 8 mm (0.32 in).

Cultured pearls dyed black must not be confused with cultured pearls which are naturally black. Indeed, in the cultured pearl business Nature provides too many pearls whose colours are uncommercial, such as too creamy and even faintly yellow. Man uses dyeing techniques, generally employing mineral salts, to produce artificially black cultured pearls.

To identify such pearls, if one does not have an expert on hand, the safest way is to ask advice from the Chamber of Commerce laboratory in London or Paris, the Gemological Institute's laboratories in the USA, or a qualified gem laboratory in other countries.

Biwa Pearls

The *Hyriopsis schlegeli* is a mollusc which lives in freshwater and more especially in Lake Biwa in Japan. Adults measure about 24 by 13 cm (9.5 by 5.2 in) and are 6 cm (2.4 in) thick. The outside of the shell is covered in a dark brown corneous material, and the mother-of-pearl inside is speckled with brownish patches.

The animal breathes through gills; its food is made up of plankton and phytoplankton. The young shellfish stabilises in about 1 to 2 metres (3 to 6.5 ft) depth of water. As they grow, they descend even deeper. Most specimens are found at about 5 metres (16 ft).

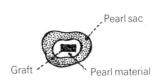

A Biwa pearl, which is cultivated round a piece of mantle instead of a bead. They are also called non-nucleated pearls.

In 1928 a Japanese named Masayo Fusia began growing pearls in the freshwater Lake Biwa, near the village of Smima. Consequently the lake's name is used for freshwater cultured pearls.

Lake Biwa is the largest lake in all Japan. It covers about 2,500 square metres (3,000 sq yd) and its maximum depth is 9 metres (30 ft); its bottom is made up of rocks and mud. In the shallower parts of the lake, stretches of mixed mud and sand are found, which form an ideal bed for the development of the bivalves.

Hyriopsis schlegeli and another variety, *Cristaria spatiosa* are used for growing cultured pearls. The same principle is used as that for sea pearls, but its application is slightly different because of the type of shellfish used.

The complexity of the mollusc's digestive system and more particularly the numerous twists and turns of its intestine make the introduction of a core impossible without damaging this organ. Several days after the operation, about half the molluscs die. Those which survive produce pearls of which only 10 per cent are marketable. With such a poor yield, it was impossible to create pearl farms. A new method was then tried, growing coreless pearls or, strictly speaking, ones with an organic core.

After opening the mollusc, the mantle is delicately separated from the shell, then a strip of flesh about 40 mm (1.6 in) by 5 mm (0.2 in) is removed by a knife from the outer face of the mantle. This strip is cut into squares of 5 mm (0.2 in). The mantle is replaced against the shell and the small pieces of flesh are inserted into the gonad with the utmost precision, so that the intestine is not harmed. This completes the operation. Unlike oyster grafting, no core is introduced. The graft itself takes on the role of the core.

Then the molluscs are replaced in water for about three years. The pearls obtained are fundamentally different from sea pearls because they have no inorganic core. Despite this, by law they cannot be classed the same as natural pearls, because they result from human intervention. The diameter is rarely greater than 6 mm (0.24 in) and their shapes are baroque in nine cases out of ten.

When seen under x-rays, a Biwa pearl contains hollows left by the decomposition of the graft.

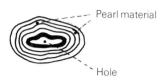

A Biwa pearl may have a hollow centre owing to decomposition of the graft.

Contrary to what happens to sea oysters in Japan, the *Hyriopsis* are not killed as soon as their pearls have been collected. After the pearls are carefully extracted from the cavities where they have grown, the shellfish is put back in the water for about five years, without a new graft being inserted. Since the pearl bag has healed over, the pearly cells of its inner walls continue to secrete pearl material. This explains why second generation pearls are a lot denser than the first generation. Occasionally, if the mollusc is tough enough, it may be replaced in the water to produce a third generation of pearls.

One operates on the *Hyriopsis* when it is about three years old, and it lives to the age of 25 to 30 years. As there are about five years between each harvest, the *Hypiosis* is sacrificed at the age of 18 years. Its shell is thrown back into the lake after the flesh has been removed. By gradually dissolving in the water, the shell provides a reasonable amount of calcium which is indispensable for the growth of future generations.

The colours of Biwa pearls are very varied, ranging from pinkish cream to dark brown. After some treatment in oxygenated water, many become lighter and turn pinkish white.

Growing pearls with a core has not been totally abandoned, but it is reserved for the production of large pearls from 9 to 14 mm (0.36 to 0.55 in) diameter. The core is often pierced in order to fix it in the mollusc.

Most of the produce of Japan, China and Korea is sold to the Middle East or to the United States. The Chinese and Koreans have also been important producers of coreless cultured pearls for some years.

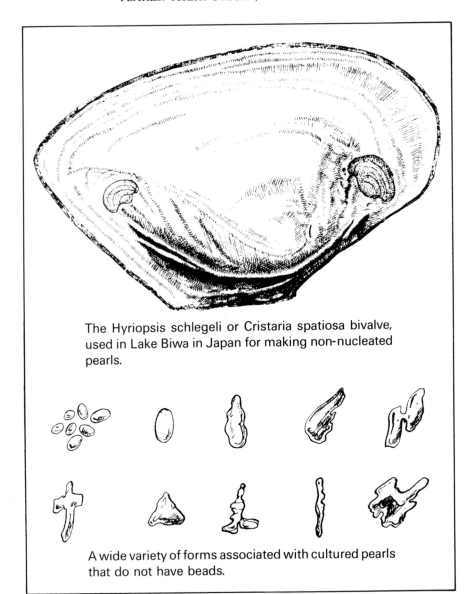

The Hyriopsis schlegeli or Cristaria spatiosa bivalve, used in Lake Biwa in Japan for making non-nucleated pearls.

A wide variety of forms associated with cultured pearls that do not have beads.

CHAPTER 12
Imitation Pearls

Imitation Pearls

Man has always striven to imitate that which is beautiful and it is only natural that the pearl, that fascinating creation, delicate and soft to the touch and gaze, has not escaped this general rule.

It appears that the first people to succeed in this domain were the Venetians. In the 16th century, they had already mastered the process of glass making, and possessed the secret of the manufacture of iridescent glass. To create artificial pearls they blew small bubbles of glass which were then filled with a sort of wax, to reinforce their strength.

The most beautiful imitation pearls were made with essence of orient, a substance derived from fish scales, with which glass beads were coated. The substance was fortuitously discovered at the end of the 17th century by an ingenious Frenchman called Jacquin. This is how it occurred: Jacquin was in the kitchen when his serving woman was scaling bleak (a type of fish) in a basin. He noticed that the water had mother-of-pearl reflections and, watching more closely, saw that they were produced by the thin skin which covered the scales dissolving in the water. He decided to filter the water to recover the pearly substance and mix it with a varnish of his own making. The product was baptised 'essence d'orient'.

Essence of Orient

With time, techniques improve and secrets are revealed; thus there are improved methods for the production of essence of orient. One of their processes consists of washing 2 kg (4.4 lb) of scales in water which has ammonia added to stop their rotting. After the first wash, with the help of a churn holding 6 litres (1.3 gallons) of water, they are ground for 30 to 40 minutes, with ammonia constantly being added. The liquid is left to decant for several days, then it is washed and decanted once again, so that a totally clear solution is obtained.

The pearl paste which is recovered is mixed with an equal volume of alcohol and stored in a cool place in a corked bottle. After several days the liquid is filtered, the paste is again mixed with an equal volume of alcohol and the process repeated. This operation is designed to dehydrate the paste which, when it has the same consistency as syrup, is carefully mixed and boiled with gelatine.

Demand for this prodigious product has never stopped increasing. When one considers that about 2,000 bleak are needed to make 1 litre (1.8 pints) of essence, the fish supply is far too small to supply such a demand. When the Germans, Italians and then the Americans launched themselves into the manufacture of essence of orient, they turned with great success to other species of fish such as shad, herring and certain members of the salmon family.

Hollow Pearls and Full Pearls

With essence of orient, two distinct types of pearl are made: hollow pearls and full pearls. Hollow pearls are made from bubbles of glass into which a drop of essence of orient is placed. Then they are rolled about so that the liquid is evenly spread over the inside. After the essence is dry, the beads that will be threaded for necklaces after final piercing are filled with wax. Those destined for earrings, pendants and hair-pins are filled with paraffin wax.

Full pearls are made from an opaline type of glass ball or a ball of mother-of-pearl. In cheap manufacturing, a plastic ball is used. Each ball is stuck on a brass stem which is fixed to a cork mat holding 100 to 150 balls, depending on their size. The mats are turned over and briefly dipped into essence of orient. Then the mat is placed in a dryer. This operation is repeated until the desired colour and brilliance have been obtained.

Then each pearl is taken off its metal stem and the small globule left by substances running after successive dippings is carefully cut off. The pearls are classified by size and colour and those pierced right through are strung on necklaces, chokers or neck-chains. Those with one hole are used for rings, earrings and brooches.

Imitation pearls are easily recognisable if examined with attention. The exterior of hollow pearls is a smooth layer of glass, perhaps with several scratches. The polished surface can always be identified under artificial light.

In the case of full pearls, touching lightly is often enough. As the pearl or necklace slips through one's hands, it gives the impression of something greasy or soapy. When examined under a lens, the outer areas of the hole often reveal the varnish curling or coming away at the edges.

In both cases, if there is the slightest doubt, gently rub the pearl against a tooth; the imitation will slide, whereas the natural or cultivated pearl will jar and grate. This 'old wives' method' is infallible and experiments should be carried out to gain experience in it.

Certain imitation pearls have been made with varnish based on lead salt.

They are dangerous to wear. Their sale has been banned in France for many years and was reinforced by a later decree dated July 24, 1967, which stressed that even keeping imitation pearls which have a lead salt varnish was prohibited.

Finally one should know that in selling and advertising, the word 'pearl' means only natural pearls.

The International Confederation of Gems, Jewellery and Gold, Diamond and Pearl Dealers (CIBJO) has put forward proposals which apply to all of Europe as well as to the United States, India and Japan. The UK has been a member of CIBJO for many years and regularly new countries join. The proposals are adopted in various ways by different countries, in the UK normally under the Trading Standards regulations as established by court of law decisions.

Here are the relevant sections on imitation pearls.

B.2.3 Imitation Pearls - Imitation pearls are artificial products manufactured by man, imitating the appearance, colour and effect of natural or cultured pearls but possessing neither their physical nor chemical properties nor their composition.

Art. 18 Imitation Pearls a) Imitation pearls defined as such under B.2.3 must be so designated. The word 'imitation' must form an integral part of the designation; b) outside the designation or description of imitation pearls, it is forbidden to use the term 'cultured pearl' or any other adjuctions of that kind; c) it is inadmissible to use the word 'pearl' followed by an asterisk leading to a note at the bottom of the page which specifies whether it is a cultured pearl or imitation pearl. All imitations must be clearly and precisely designated (e.g. Majorcan imitation pearl, thus leaving no doubt that the object in question is an imitation pearl from Majorca).

Art. 19 Prohibiton of the term 'reproduction'. It is forbidden to call 'reproduction' or 'synthetic' or others, pearls which are cultured or imitation.

PART FOUR
PEARL WORKING AND SELLING

CHAPTER 13
Pearl Identification

In order to give a more precise definition of the origin and nature of pearls, man has long searched for more and more scientific methods to provide this precision.

In a report in 1921, Louis Boutan published the results of his experiments based on the hardness of the material. For this he placed a type of cardboard gutter on a table, which guided the falling pearls on to a glass tile placed on the ground 70 cm (27.6 in) below.

These were his conclusions:

False pearls rebound on average to a height of 50 cm (19.7 in)
Japanese cultured pearls 40 cm (15.8 in)
Natural pearls from Australia and Venezuela 40 cm (15.8 in)
Freshwater pearls 37 cm (14.6 in)
Eastern pearls (Persian Gulf, Ceylon) 35 cm (13.8 in)

I would discourage readers from attempting this sort of experiment because the fall can jar the pearl and cause internal cracks.

The Lucidoscope

In 1927, Dr. B. Szilard created the lucidoscope, a machine to differentiate between natural pearls and cultured pearls by the transparence of the material under a strong light and through various filters. With it, one can see the central core, successive layers, colours, patterns and characteristics.

Pearls with a foreign core (i.e. cultured pearls) can be distinguished by the mother-of-pearl in their centre, surrounded by fairly thick pearl layers. These cores are generally made from good-quality mother-of-pearl, cut into perfect balls, with the surface polished and rounded to an accuracy of about .001mm (0.0004 in).

The first observations that can be made with the naked eye are that the balls are made up from parallel mother-of-pearl layers. This parallelism is even more visible when the layers, even thin ones, have different opacities and colours. Cultured pearl cores are therefore striped.

If a natural oriental pearl is sliced one can see a structure of concentric rings around the same centre which is dense and so deeply coloured that the yellow shines out towards the outside. If one cuts a pearl right down to the centre, it can

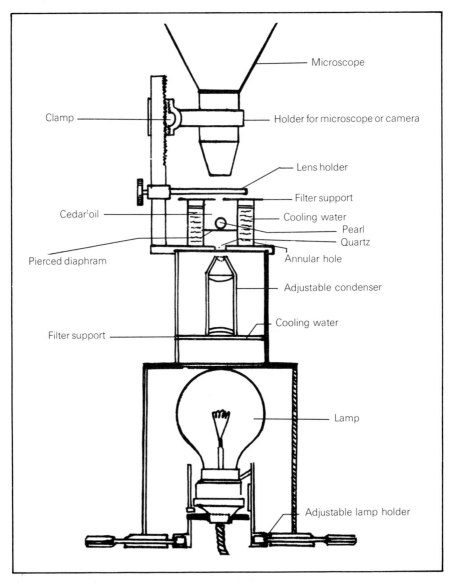

The lucidoscope, an early instrument to test pearls to see if they were cultivated.

also be seen that the transparency does not vary when turned in different directions.

The lucidoscope depends on these differences in the optical properties of mother-of-pearl and pearl. The pearl is placed in a dish attached to the machine, which is then filled with cedar-oil. Through various filters one can see that natural pearls have a relatively small core in relation to the size of the pearls; the colour of this core always appears to be orange, pink or reddish. The core itself is not very clearly defined and often melts towards the edges. In many cases a final layer, which is often thin and transparent, finishes off the pearl to form its outer skin.

When one turns the pearl, the colour and shape of the core do not change in appearance or transparency, as long as the pearl is not baroque.

By increasing intensity of the beam of light, the core seems to disappear. By looking at the pearl through a filter, the core appears to melt almost totally into the layers. Nothing is seen other than an almost uniform disc.

In the case of a cultured pearl, the core is normally immediately apparent as dense, geometric, round and perfectly defined. Around this core, small swellings can sometimes be seen which are embedded in the surrounding layer. This single layer, totally homogenous and uniform, a glassy and structureless mass, has absolutely no variation of density or colour.

By turning the pearl, one can see that most of the core is striped - the stripy characteristic of mother-of-pearl. But it would be imprudent to view the absence of any stripes as the indication that the pearl is natural.

Furthermore, by examining such a pearl through a special screen the core becomes accentuated and precisely defined, in contrast to the core's disappearance in natural pearls.

By changing the intensity of the lamp, the core does not change its dimensions as in the case of natural oriental pearls. This is a further indication of the presence of a mother-of-pearl core.

The Endoscope

The endoscope, invented in 1926 by C. Chilowsky and A. Perrin, and modified a year later by R. and S. Bloch, is intended to separate cultured pearls from natural pearls. It works only with drilled pearls.

The structure of a natural pearl is rather like that of an onion with spherical and concentric layers. The crystal structure of the aragonite of which layers are made refracts light round the layer and restricts it from passing from one layer to another. If a layer is lit at one point, it becomes totally illuminated, while neighbouring layers remain relatively dark. This is contrary to a cultured pearl, where light follows a flat layer of the core.

The endoscope looks like an old-fashioned magic lantern with a very bright arc light inside it, but instead of illuminating a slide, the light is directed through a hollow needle that projects horizontally towards the operator and is small enough for a drilled pearl to be pushed over it. The needle is not hollow all through. At the end is a short plug made of platinum with a mirror surface polished at 45 deg at each end of the plug. Above the mirror facing the light is a slot, rather like that in a penny whistle, facing upwards.

A lever is used to slide the pearl backwards and forwards along the needle and the end of the needle, is observed through a low-powered microscope which is part of the instrument.

When the pearl being tested is real, the light along the tube is reflected upwards by the first mirror and is refracted round a spherical layer of the asagonite structure. When the mirrors are in the centre of the pearl, the second mirror picks up the light and directs it out of the end of the pearl hole facing the operator. This appears as a flash of light as the pearl is moved along the needle.

If the pearl has a core, i.e. it is cultured, no flash occurs because the mother-of-pearl bead does not have a spherical structure. Instead, it illuminates slightly

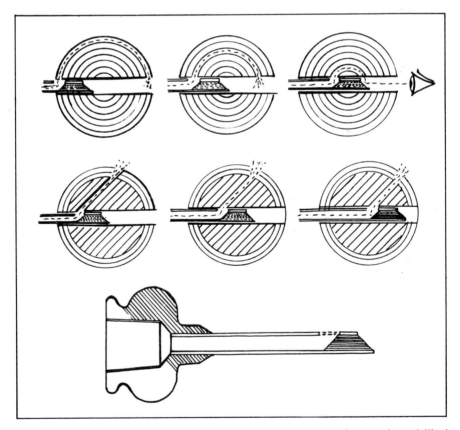

The endoscope was the most successful instrument for testing drilled cultured pearls when they first flooded the market. This shows the principle of its operation. Top natural pearl. Centre cultured pearl.

part of the outside of the pearl on which stripes can be seen because of the laminated structure of the bead.

In brief, the results are: in the case of a natural pearl, a maximum luminosity near the centre from an axial plane of observation and the absence of any stripes from any outside observation; in the case of a cultured pearl, there is no maximum luminosity from axial observation and the presence of clear stripes is seen from outside observation.

This process gives two criteria, one positive and one negative, for cultured pearls as well as natural pearls. Methods for telling them apart are totally safe.

Skilled operators can check pearls at the rate of about 150 an hour on the endoscope, the only inconveniences of which are that it can be used only for pierced pearls. They cannot be strung as they have to be checked one at a time.

In September 1925, the newspaper 'The Pearl' published an interesting report on the way to separate cultured pearls from natural pearls by their density.

To make this study, three lots of pearls were used: one comprised virgin natural pearls from Venezuela , the second natural pearls from Venezuela which had been worn, and the third, cultured pearls.

These were the figures obtained:

The densities of the 135 virgin natural pearls ranged from 2.73 to 2.506

The densities of the 101 natural pearls (worn) ranged from 2.35 to 2.73

The densities of the 30 cultured pearls ranged from 2.726 to 2.79

In the lot of 30 cultured pearls, only three had densities of 2.726, thus risking confusion with natural pearls.

There would seem to be little risk of error if this method were used to determine which pearls should undergo further examination, whether by x-rays, or by lucidoscope. It is important, however, not to use organic heavy liquids.

Radiography

Radiography of pearls is the most modern and the surest method of separating natural from cultured pearls (as well as in the identification of certain gems). The simplest method is the shadowgraph or skiagram, also known as the direct method. Its advantage is in speed of testing, as whole necklaces can be examined with one radiogram. Hard x-rays are used and the technique depends on the differences in transparency to x-rays of conchiolin and aragonite. Interpretation of the shadowgraphs is not easy, however. A natural pearl can look solid or as having a bead on the x-ray picture, but experienced radiographers can distinguish them as well as nucleated (cultured) and non-nucleated (Biwa) pearls.

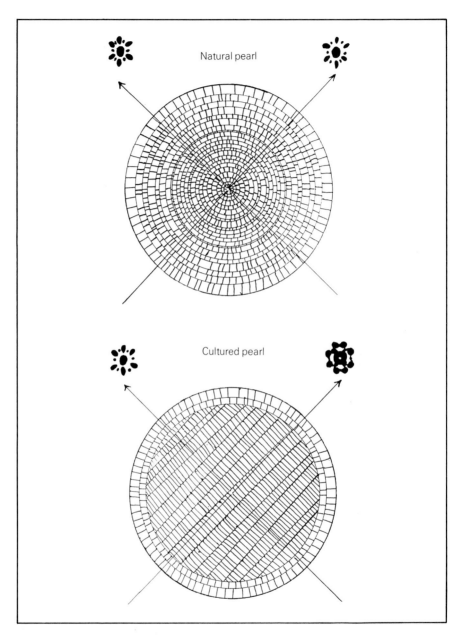

The lauegram, produced by x-raying, is a positive method of separating natural from cultured pearls. X-rayed from two directions, a natural pearl (top) will show similar hexagonal patterns, but a cultured pearl (below) will show a square pattern in one direction because of the approximately parallel layers of the bead.

Making up a necklace in a modern pearl business. Nearly all the necklaces today are uniform in size and colour. Matching is very important. Graduated necklaces are not as fashionable as they were.

Basic grading for colour is carried out rapidly by skilled sorters. The main colour range is from silver shades through cream to gold. Also often seen are blue-grey and grey (see Appendix).

Pearls are graded to millimetre sizes with sieves in the same way as diamonds. Uniform necklets have two sizes only, being referred to as e.g. 8-7½ or 7½-7. Graduated ones have about half as many sizes as there are beads, and obviously cost more to grade.

A range of colours in well-formed cultured pearls from Mikimoto fisheries in Japan. Colour – pink being considered the best – is one of the six important elements of grading (see Appendix).

Lauegrams

The most conclusive test for pearls is the x-ray lauegram, named after the German physicist Max von Laue (1879-1960). The method was applied to pearls by a Frenchman, Danvillier in 1924, later in collaboration with Shaxby. The lauegram shows a pattern of dots on film that are determined by the crystal structure of the material being x-rayed.

A natural pearl will produce a hexagonal pattern of dots no matter what direction of the narrow band of x-rays passing through it. On the other hand, in some directions, a cultured pearl will produce a pattern like a Maltese cross.

The method is, however, slow because of the several exposures often needed and the long exposure times.

Visual Methods of Identifying Natural and Cultured Pearls

When cultured pearls are very good quality, it is quite difficult to identify them as such with any certainty. The comparisons which follow are valid for only 80 per cent of cases. But they can help us to distinguish natural pearls from cultured pearls.

Look at a pearl under a lamp and rotate it; only a cultured pearl will reflect the light at each half-turn, thus revealing the presence of a core if the pearl is thinly covered by nacre.

For natural pearls, the diameter of the holes is rarely larger than .04 mm (0.016 in); for cultured pearls this is .06 mm (0.024 in) or more.

If when looking into the hole of the pearl through a lens, the pearl layer can easily be seen over a homogenous mass of white (the core), the pearl is cultured. Sometimes the layer between these is grey, a residue of the conchioline secreted at the first stage of the formation of the pearl-bag, before the pearl secretions are properly organised.

In natural pearls, this mass becomes darker, the deeper that one looks. A black mass at the centre of the pearl is a very good indication. This is generally a large residue of the organic matter typical of the natural pearls called 'blue pearls'.

Cultured pearls often have slight swellings beneath the surface, which are guessed at rather than seen, and look rather like veins. Natural pearls have no such features.

Cultured pearls often have points on them with a faint trail like the tail of a comet; natural pearls rarely have these.

The skin of cultured pearls is often very glossy and occasionally hammered. This hammering is a sign of very dense layers, more usual in natural pearls than cultured ones. Circles and growths which have been removed are frequent on cultured pearls, but are rare on natural pearls.

The colours of natural pearls are more regular than those of cultured pearls;

this can been seen by slowly twisting the pearls between one's fingers or on a wire.

Baroque pearls are not necessarily natural pearls, as many people seem to think.

If after all these observations, one is still unsure of oneself, the necklace or pearl should be sent to the British Gemmological Laboratory, 27 Greville Street, London EC1N 8SQ, or in France, to the Laboratory, 2 Place de la Bourse, Paris. In the U.S.A. contact the Gemological Institute of America, 1660 Stewart Road, Santa Monica, CA 90404.

CHAPTER 14
The Transformation

Pearl working or skinning is done by a pearl lapidary. His emotions and joy are like those felt by an adventurer searching for a treasure who, when he finds it, gives new life to something which has lain forgotten, lost and unknown for many years.

Since a pearl is made up of superimposed layers with different thicknesses, colours and qualities, it is very tempting to scratch away a fault, to remove one layer, then another in order to discover and reveal the most beautiful pearl.

In order to have any success in this venture, one must be familiar with the pearl's structure, which is very different in pearls from different places such as the Persian Gulf, or Burma, or Australia, or Panama, or Tahiti, or elsewhere.

A knowledge of the markets is also indispensable. In fact it is preferable to have a slightly dull white pearl than a bright yellow pearl. Flaws, depending on their shape and importance, will disappear or remain, but one may conceal another. It is possible to perfect the shape of a pearl. A pear-shaped pearl can be lengthened, but this work must be invisible because the slightest trace of interference will devalue the pearl by about 30 per cent.

Before undertaking the job, a lapidary must weigh up all his observations and remember what experiments he has done on similar pearls; must guess what is hidden at the heart of that small flawed ball which watches him like an eye and challenges him. The decision to take on work can take several weeks of thought.

Working with pearls is a constant struggle between weight and price. For example, let us take a pearl whose value is equal to the weight squared. A pearl of 30 grains is therefore worth 900 francs.

With a loss of 10 grains after work on the pearl, the remaining 20 grains would be worth 400 francs. If after the work the pearl is not worth more than its initial value when multiplied by 2.25, the lapidary has wasted his time.

Pearl of 20 grains (sq) = 400 x 2.25 = 900 francs. The work has therefore not been wasted in this example.

Contrary to what most people think, it is often possible to improve cultured pearls, but the permitted margin of error is often a lot narrower than in the previous case. For a natural pearl it is always possible to halt the work when one wishes and to accept the loss of weight, time and some money. For cultured pearls one realises one's mistake only at the appearance of the core, when everything is lost.

There, as well as in the previous case, the lapidary must struggle with weights and prices, by taking as his base not the grains or the weight squared but the price in momes or carats.

The Lengthening and Enlargement of Necklaces

Lengthening and enlargement are post-sale services which need a great deal of attention. Indeed the composition of a string of pearls demands a skill and technique for which several years of apprenticeship are needed. In order to avoid the risk of spoiling a necklace by the addition of three or four pearls, the work must be carried out by a professional using a large stock of pearls. This stock is comparable to the richly-coloured palette of a painter, from which he alone knows when to take a touch of grey, or green or blue to complete his work. Would anyone ever consider having a masterpiece restored by inexperienced hands?

Enlarging and lengthening a necklace is like restoring a painting. Several hours of research are needed to discover the desired pearls. For all these reasons, one cannot take as a base the average price of a choker's pearls; instead one must refer back to the price of individual pearls and add about 20 per cent.

Lengthening chokers poses no real problem because the pearls are of the same size. But for graded necklaces there are rules to be respected. Lengthening the ends must follow the decrease in size of the necklace. So the desired length is gained by adding pearls which have differences of several millimetres in their diameters.

An enlargement of the centre almost always requires at least four pearls: one like the present centre of the necklace, a larger one (the future centre) and two to bolster up the old centre.

The ideal enlargement consists of six pearls. An enlargement of six pearls, however, often gives the necklace an excessive length. So the pearl dealer or jeweller should suggest that his client has the excess pearls removed from the ends and have them mounted on a small gold or silver bracelet.

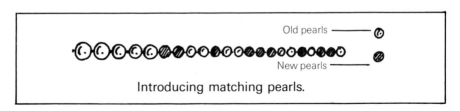

Old pearls

New pearls

Introducing matching pearls.

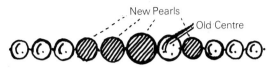

A necklace can be enlarged by adding four pearls at the centre, but they do not graduate properly.

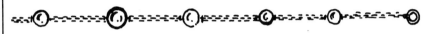

Six suitable chosen pearls provide the correct graduation.

If pearls are to be removed, suggest to the customer that they are made into a pearl chain.

Threading and Weaving Pearl Necklaces

A jeweller should know how to thread pearl necklaces, even if he is used to having them threaded elsewhere. It is unthinkable that he should not know how to attach a fastener, or tie a few knots. Such a gap in knowledge could lose quick sales or an urgent delivery. Necklaces are normally sold on nylon, but this is only a temporary support. Indeed nylon stretches rapidly and after a month the necklace has no tension.

Silk thread is by far the best material. There are various sizes from No. 0 to No. 24.

Natural pearl necklaces need threads from No. 8 to No. 12

Cultured pearl necklaces, threads from No. 16 to No. 22

Here is a list of the material needed:

A needle with a small eye

A small pin vice or handle with a large darning needle No. 1

Small thread No. 0 to No. 4, and a finishing thread

A wooden board covered in felt or chamois leather

It is worth washing one's hands carefully with lemon juice , so that the knots are white and to repeat this operation whenever the knots become dirty.

It is important to be very patient and not to count on succeeding at the first attempt. This is the order of operations to be carried out when re- threading a necklace.

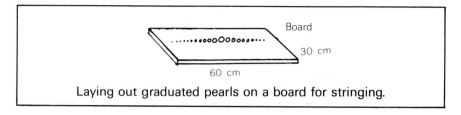

Laying out graduated pearls on a board for stringing.

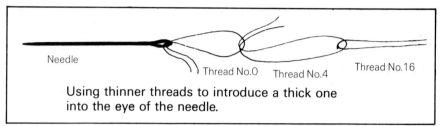

Using thinner threads to introduce a thick one
into the eye of the needle.

Place the necklace, laid out straight, on the wood.

Prepare the needle and threads as shown in the diagram.

Cut one of the end knots of the necklace.

Pass a few pearls along the needle and slide them up to the thread. (Never pull the needle, but slide the pearls along it.)

Pass the buckle into the fastening ring and close the fastener.

Make a simple thumb knot and guide it against the fastener using the broach. Hold one pearl against the knot with your index finger and remove the broach. Then make another knot and repeat the operation with the next pearl.

For the final tying up, pass the threads into the fastening ring twice, then make a figure-of-eight knot or pass the thread through the last pearl and make a knot.

Clasp

A snap end fastened to a double thread by passing
a loop over it. To use a gimp, see Appendix.

When the client buys a new graduated (chute) necklace, she often does not know what to do with the old one, unless she gives it to a daughter or niece. One solution often adopted is to transform it into a three-row bracelet.

If the necklace measures about 40 cm (16 in) with knots, for a normal bracelet, about 17 cm (6.5 in) of pearls are needed, plus the fastener. By supplying the client with an extra 11 cm (4.5 in) of pearls you can make her an original new piece of jewellery.

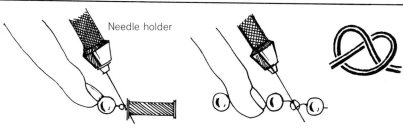

A darning needle in a pin holder is used to draw knots tight to the pearls. A simple thumb knot is used.

Pass the thread twice through the end fastener and finish with a figure-of-eight knot (left). Alternatively, pass the threaded needle back through the last three or four pearls using a thumb knot after each. To avoid abrasion, a gimp is usually threaded through the fastener. See Appendix.

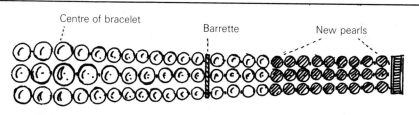

Old collars can be converted into bracelets.

Pearl weaving goes back to most ancient times. Numerous examples have been discovered in various tombs dating back before the Egyptians.

In the Middle Ages, when navigators such as Marco Polo, Christopher Columbus, Jacques Cartier, Cortez and many others departed for the New World, they always took on board a large quantity of glassware, including beads, to gain the friendship of the natives whom they would meet, and with whom they could deal. Natives everywhere were fascinated by multi-coloured glass pearls whose manufacture was the closely guarded secret of Venice.

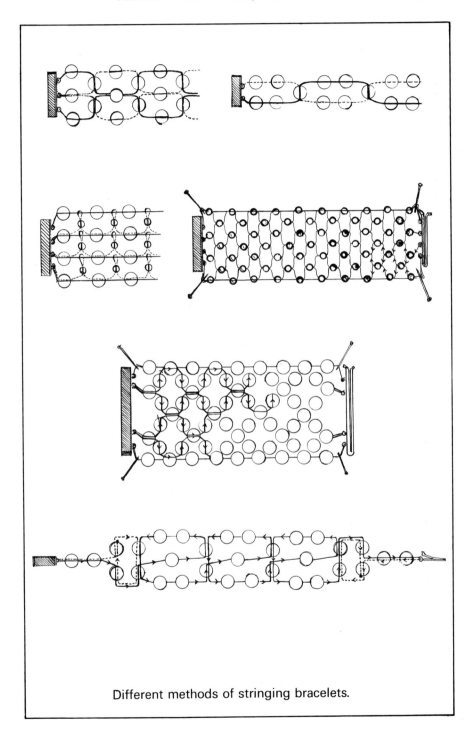

Different methods of stringing bracelets.

Almost everywhere, the natives had made beads of coloured clay to decorate their clothes and various objects, and also to count, pass messages by and pray with. Do not many religions have their rosary beads? But none of the beads manufactured by the natives or real pearls in some areas had the transparency of those from Venice, and business deals were soon struck. Indeed, natives bartered natural pearls, statuettes and golden necklaces for a few handfuls of beads.

The North American Indians used the pearls found in mussels and oysters as decoration and certain tribes, notably the Wampoun, offered moccasins, knife sheaths and game bags embroidered with pearls in order to obtain the friendship of neighbouring clans. Later on, the same objects were decorated with brightly-coloured glass pearls.

Some African tribes used pearls to adorn full dress clothing, more normal objects, and of course jewels. It is said that in the 17th century, the coastal peoples dealing in the slave trade often bartered four pounds of pearls with the negroes for one slave.

In Europe, weaving and embroidering with pearls have often been carried out by craftsmen to decorate ruffs, coats-of-arms, bracelets and necklaces.

The few sketches shown in this section will allow the reader to create different motifs for bracelets or necklaces. Once the basic rudiments have been learned, fertile imaginations are free to invent others.

Piercing Pearls

Piercing is one of the most delicate operations. As a general rule, if a pearl has not been pierced at its dead centre, it will turn awkwardly and its value will be much diminished. Sometimes it is necessary to take decisions contrary to this rule when one pierces a pearl at a pitted point in order to remove the flaw, regardless of the fact that the pearl will not rotate perfectly. Another important factor is colour. Practically no pearl has the same colour over all its surface. One must pierce the pearl at the centre of the darkest or lightest area while trying to maintain the curvature of the pearl after the operation.

A virgin pearl destined to become the centre of a necklace or pendant must be pierced according to the colour of the necklace, even if the piercing does not show the individual pearl in its best light. This is because once it forms a part of the necklace its value will appreciate.

Baroque pearls of a pear or button shape are normally pierced longways.

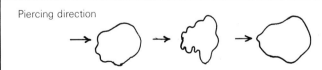

Piercing direction

The correct directions in which to pierce baroque pearls.

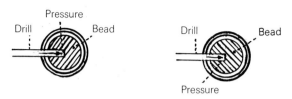

The angle of the laminations in beads of cultured pearls can deflect a drill.

Piercing a pearl always entails a certain risk. Once the drill enters the pearl, it must always be pushed perpendicularly from top to bottom or from right to left. For natural pearls, this is due to the asymmetry of the angle of the drill's entry, which, let us not forget, is powered manually. In the case of cultured pearls, this phenomenon is accentuated by the core because the incline of the mother-of-pearl layers deflects the drill.

Piercing a pearl has to be carried out in two stages. Firstly three-quarters of the pearl is pierced, then it is turned over and a new hole is made which meets the first one.

A serious accident can occur at the meeting point of the two holes if the force exerted by the drill is too strong. The drill may even break off in the pearl. The only way to avoid such accidents is to lessen the pressure on the drill at the moment when the holes are about to meet.

When pearls were pierced manually, the centre was found in the following way. The pearl was held in a wooden vice. With the aid of a horizontal drill bow, the piercer made a preliminary hole. Then he placed the pearl, still held by the drill, on an oiled stone; the mark left by the oil showed him the position of the second hole. The colour of the oil was black.

Nowadays, machines invented by the Japanese are used, which, as a general rule, find the pearl's centre extremely well.

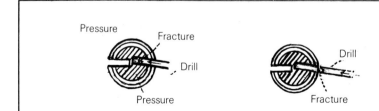

A pearl should be drilled from both directions, but beware of fractures that can occur because of the bead laminations.

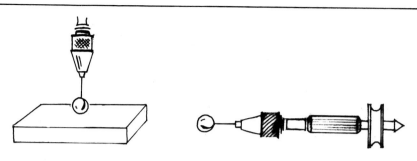

When piercing a pearl manually, centre the opposing holes by first drilling a hole in it, preferably by using a bow. Then place a flat honing stone with a smear of oil on it squarely against the opposite end of the pearl. It will make a mark where the opposing hole should be started.

The Chinese pierce pearls laterally through the base.

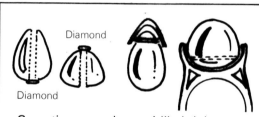

Diamond

Diamond

Sometimes pearls are drilled right through and the end capped by a small diamond. On the right are two methods of mounting with lateral holes.

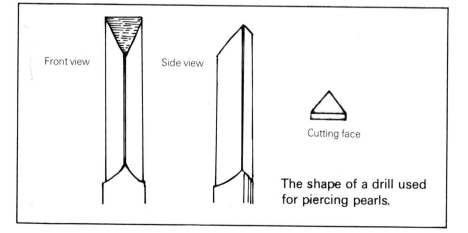

Front view   Side view

Cutting face

The shape of a drill used for piercing pearls.

Piercing has not always been carried out in the same way because of local customs and techniques. For example, pearls were pierced near the side by the Chinese. They were sewn on to mandarins' clothes and used as decoration or buttons.

In Europe, before the use of glue was widespread, pear and button-shaped pearls were pierced right through to be mounted. If the position of one hole could not be hidden when the pearl was mounted, it would be concealed by a small golden ball, or a brilliant or rose cut diamond.

Good results from piercing depend on the material being pierced and the shape of the drill. The Japanese have made extensive research in this area and this is their conclusion: The drill must be of hardened steel, carefully guided, and the shape must allow the powdered pearl to be ejected so that overheating is avoided.

Mounting Pearls by Glueing

Glueing is a very simple operation, which nevertheless needs some care for it to be effective.

A glued pearl will not come unstuck if this method is used:

1 First, it is necessary to half-drill the pearl, i.e. drill it to about the centre
2 Insert and glue a silver sleeve in the hole
3 Cut a thread in the sleeve
4 Screw the pearl on to the pin on the piece of jewellery, first covering this pin with glue.

A simpler method is to thread the hole in the pearl, then screw the pearl itself on to the stem, covered in glue.

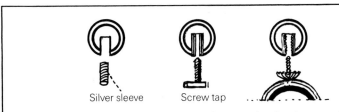

Silver sleeve   Screw tap

Peg setting for rings using a tube in the pearl.

Simple peg settings without tubes.

Simple glueing consists of enlarging the hole, then glueing it on to the stem. If the stem is too smooth, several grooves can be made with a file, to key the glue.

For all these operations, the choice of glue is fairly unimportant, so long as one possesses an appropriate solvent to detach the pearls if necessary.

Upkeep of Pearls

Both natural and cultured pearls require a certain amount of care if they are to last a long time.

Firstly they must be kept apart from other jewels, because they become scratched when touched by gold, diamond, sapphire and other hard materials.

When kept in an environment which is too dry, there is a risk of dehydration and they may change colour, or cracks may appear. Let us not forget that they contain 2.23 per cent of water. It is worth rehydrating them regularly by dipping them into salted water.

The acidity of a wrapping paper or case may tarnish the pearls, so it is worth wiping them with a chamois leather before putting them away in a jewellery case. Pearls should not be worn by someone who is ill or feverish, for a similar reason.

A good pearl necklace should be restrung about once a year to avoid running the risk of losing some pearls. This is also a chance for the jeweller to ascertain the state of the necklace and accordingly to congratulate or warn his client. If the necklace is slightly damaged, it is often possible to re-polish it.

Very old pearl necklaces are often so worn out that the pearls become barrel-shaped. This can be rectified if the pearls are large enough to justify the cost of a long and delicate piece of work. The same is true of old pearls mounted on rings or ear-rings.

When it is worn frequently the pearl is kept hydrated by its constant contact with the skin, which gives it an incomparable gleam, brilliance and orient.

CHAPTER 15
Commercial Considerations

Calculating the Value of Natural Pearls

In Europe traders have always reckoned the value of natural pearls by taking as a base the weight in grains squared, and multiplied by a co-efficient. A grain is a quarter of a carat (0.05 gramme) and the co-efficient depends upon the quality of the pearl.

For example, a pearl of 40 grains may be worth 4,800 francs or 800 francs, depending on the co-efficient which one uses for its weight squared (40 x 40), = 1600, with a co-efficient of 3 or 0.5. In pounds sterling, US dollars and other currencies, the co-efficient would be different. For example, a pearl of 40 grains could be worth £400, in which case the co-efficient would be 400 divided by (40 x 40) = 0.25. If the co-efficient were 0.05, the price would be £80.

The co-efficient is determined by a combination of the following criteria: shape, quality, colour, sheen, orient. The country of destination is always a factor which cannot be ignored. White, dull pearls which cannot be sold in France, for example, are very popular in Nordic countries.

Exceptions to this rule are natural pearls coloured grey, black and brown, which come mainly from Mexico, Panama and Tahiti. These are valued by grains, i.e. by weight alone.

For example, a pearl of 10.30 carats, 41.20 grains, might be valued at 3,296 francs, with a price of 80 francs a grain.

Without claiming it to be a golden rule, it is thought that nowadays, for the same quality of pearl, a natural pearl is worth 4 to 10 times more than a cultured pearl.

In order to limit any risk of error, one cannot include baroque pearls, large and small, or the small necklaces, which in Catholic countries are often grandmothers' presents at a girl's first communion. These goods are still traded, but their value is much closer to that of cultured pearls.

Arabs and Hindus value pearls by taking the 'shaw' as their base. This gives them a different base than multiplying the weight, because the method of calculation is different, but they use it in the same way.

Here is how to calculate it: the weight in carats squared must be taken; this is multiplied by 88, then divided by 135, then re-divided by the number of pearls. Thus the shaw is obtained, which is then multiplied by a number of rupees or riads, according to the nationality of the buyer or seller.

As an example let us take a lot of 82 pearls at 138 carats.

138 x 138 = 19,044 x 88 = 1,675,872 divided by 135 = 12,413
12,413 divided by 82 = 151 shaw
151 shaw x 40 rupees = 6,040 rupees

Valuing Pearl Necklaces

Valuing necklaces or lots of pearls demands a certain amount of complicated calculations, but nowadays, with a modern pocket calculator, this is child's play. But let us remember for the record that during the great era of the natural pearl markets in Paris and London, in every firm of great or moderate importance, some of the personnel were employed purely and simply to perform these calculations.

Let us take the example of a lot of 255 pearls which are divided as indicated in the diagram.

Pearls	Grains	1 x weight*	Estimation (Valuing)	Francs
3	24.36	197.80	20 ×	3 956
6	43.24	311.61	16 ×	4 985
12	74.88	467.25	12 ×	5 607
24	127.68	679.25	12 ×	8 151
24	97.92	399.51	14 ×	5 593
30	93.60	292.03	20 ×	5 840
156	333.20	711.68	30 ×	21 350
255	794.88	3.059.13		55 482

* 1 x the weight = square of the weight divided by the number of pearls

The total offer for the lot is 18 times its weight. If the lot is perfectly homogenous, by dividing it into three, one can see that it is possible to make up three necklaces. The bid will therefore be very high. If, on the contrary, the lot is very broken up as regards colour, the valuation will be made according to the number of sets that can be made from them.

COMMERCIAL CONSIDERATIONS

Example 1

1 Pearl	8.12 grains	1 ×	65.93
2 Pearls	14.08 7.04	1 ×	99.12
4 Pearls	24.96 6.24	1 ×	155.75
8 Pearls	42.56 5.32	1 ×	226.41
8 Pearls	32.64 4.08	1 ×	133.17
10 Pearls	31.20 3.12	1 ×	97.34
52 Pearls	114.40 2.20	1 ×	251.68
85 Pearls	267.96	1 × 1 029.40	

Example 2

1 Pearl	8.04 grains	1 ×	64.64
2 Pearls	12.60 6.30	1 ×	79.38
2 Pearls	9.44 4.72	1 ×	44.55
2 Pearls	7.28 3.64	1 ×	26.49
6 Pearls	15.40 2.56	1 ×	39.52
12 Pearls	23.20 1.93	1 ×	44.85
16 Pearls	26.32 1.64	1 ×	43.29
20 Pearls	26.30 1.31	1 ×	34.58
26 Pearls	23.60 0.90	1 ×	21.42
44 Pearls	25.28 0.57	1 ×	14.52
131 Pearls	177.46	1 × 413.24	

Example 3

1 Pearl	11.68 grains	1 × 136.42
2 Pearls	15.80 7.90	1 × 124.82
4 Pearls	25.32 6.33	1 × 160.27
8 Pearls	37.20 4.65	1 × 172.98
6 Pearls	19.20 4.65	1 × 61.44
10 Pearls	24.40 2.44	1 × 59.53
12 Pearls	23.80 1.94	1 × 47.20
24 Pearls	34.68 1.44	1 × 50.11
24 Pearls	25.08 1.04	1 × 26.20
24 Pearls	14.48 0.60	1 × 8.73
115 Pearls	231.64	1 × 847.70

If, instead of having three pearls of 8.12 grains, there are only two and the lot is homogenous, the valuations will be made on two necklaces and a number of possible sets. Finally, if the buyer possesses the missing pearl, his valuation will be entirely different. As one can see, the value of a particular lot is subject to many different factors.

The proportion of the graduation in a necklace is also an important factor. It is easy to calculate, but usually the calculations only confirm what the eye has seen.

The calculations that follow refer to three examples of necklaces as shown in the tables.

Take the necklace of 131 pearls totalling 177.46 grains in weight and in 10 sizes at 1 x 413.24. Now calculate the number of times weight in one size:
177.36 x 177.46 divided by 131 = 240.12

Let us calculate the difference between these two numbers:
413.24 - 240.12 = 173.12

Finally a third calculation must be made, by multiplying the number obtained by 100 and dividing it by the number of times weight in one size: 173.12 x 100 divided by 240.12 = 71.09 per cent

Example necklace No. 1:   string of 85 pearls 267.96 in 7 sizes 1 x 1,029.40
1 string of 85 pearls 267.96 in 1 size 1 x 844.74 = 184.66
    184.66 x 100 divided by 844.74 = 21.86 per cent
Example necklace No. 3: 1 string of 115 pearls 231.64 grains in 10 sizes 1 x
847.70 - 1 string of 115 pearls 231.64 in 1 size 1 x 466.58 = 381.12
    381.12 x 100 divided by 466.58 = 81.68 per cent

Valuing Cultured Pearls

In Japan, the basic valuing unit is the mome (also spelled momme), which can vary in weight between 3.75 g (18.75 carats) and 3.78 g (18.90 carats).

Chute necklaces, which are also called graduated necklaces, are identified by their total weight which corresponds to well-defined scales for a length of 43 cm (17 in).

Here are the four most important ones:
    3.5 momes centre of 7.5 ends of 3.5 mm
    5 momes centre of 8.2 ends of 4 mm
    6 momes centre of 8.5 ends of 5 mm
    7 momes centre of 8.7 ends of 5.5 mm

Small variations can exist in diameters as well as weight, but the bases given are valid, when one remembers that a cultured pearl is not a manufactured product.

Example: Purchase a mass of x rows of 5 momes at y yen a row. Chokers are sold at two different lengths of 35 or 45 cm (14 or 18 in). They are composed of pearls whose largest and smallest diameters vary by only half a millimetre.

Example: Chokers of 2 mm to 2.5 mm, 2.5 mm to 3 mm, 3 mm to 3.5 mm, and so on up to 10 mm pearls.

Purchases are not made by weight but by diameter and length.

Example: A bunch of x strings of pearls at 35 to 45 cm (14 to 18 in) and 6 to 6.5 mm for y yen a string.

Single pearls are sold in lots whose diameters vary by only 1 millimetre. Example: With a lot of 3 to 4 mm or 4 to 5 mm, the price is calculated by weight.

Example: A lot of 6 to 7 mm at 175 momes for y yen a mome. Above 10 mm, the pearls are sold singly or by carats, depending on the buyer.

In Europe, chute necklaces are generally sold according to differences in sizes.

Example: A necklace going from 7.5 to 3 mm is sold for a total sum.

Chokers are sold in the same way as in Japan by the millimetre for a given length and for a total sum.

Single pearls are sold by carat or by diameter.

The ideal method so that one does not become lost in these three categories is to separate them distinctly and to establish a scale of decreasing and increasing prices according to sizes and qualities, taking as a base the average price of current goods.

In order to avoid any risk of error, about four or five specimen pearls of about 6 mm should be kept and grids of comparison for quality, colour and price should be made.

As soon as five figures have been carefully written in this grid, one can determine the price of merchandise with a certain degree of assurance.

Men have often been drawn more to the brilliance of the diamond and the hues of coloured stones than to the gentleness of the pearl. If you are amongst them, do not refuse to sell pearls. Discover, somewhere in your organisation, a woman who loves pearls, and give her responsibility for this department. Both she and your supplier will do good business, even if the final decision always comes back to the boss. This system is used in many firms in France.

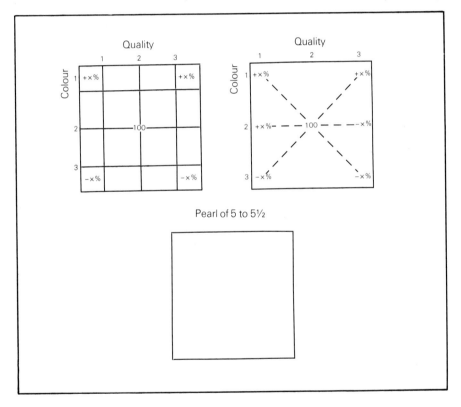

Pearl of 5 to 5½

Building up a Stock

Depending on the size of one's business, the evaluating factor of the stock to be built up can vary from to one to 20. The information which is summarised below is a personal preference. The owner alone will probably know the correct distribution of the stock as regards quantity, quality and price. Here again, for a pearl or a necklace of the same size, the price can vary from one to 20 times.

COMMERCIAL CONSIDERATIONS

As for necklaces (chute), the four most commercial sizes are those with the following characteristics:

Necklaces of 65 ct   7.5 mm at the centre 3.5 mm at the ends
Necklaces of 94 ct   8.2 mm at the centre 4 mm at the ends
Necklaces of 112 ct 8.5 mm at the centre 5 mm at the ends
Necklaces of 131 ct 8.7 mm at the centre 5.5 mm at the ends

Of course, there are variations of several millimetres.

Chokers are sold at very different lengths, generally between 35 and 45 cm (14 and 18 in). There is a small difference of half a millimetre between the largest and smallest diameters, so that it is necessary to specify two dimensions, 4.5 to 5 mm, or 5 to 5.5 mm, but never a choker of 5 mm.

Approximate weight of chokers 35 cm length		Approximate weight of pearls 1 hole for the fine pearls x4 = grains				
2 · 2 1/2 mm	15.00 cts	2 · 2 1/2 mm	0.08.5 cts	×4	0.34	grain
2 1/2 · 3 mm	18.75 cts	2 1/2 · 3 mm	0.16.3 cts	×4	0.65	grain
3 · 3 1/2 mm	28.12 cts	3 · 3 1/2 mm	0.25 cts	×4	1.	grain
3 1/2 · 4 mm	37.50 cts	3 1/2 · 4 mm	0.37 cts	×4	1.48	grains
4 · 4 1/2 mm	46.87 cts	4 · 4 1/2 mm	0.58 cts	×4	2.32	grains
4 1/2 · 5 mm	56.25 cts	4 1/2 · 5 mm	0.81 cts	×4	3.24	grains
5 · 5 1/2 mm	70.54 cts	5 · 5 1/2 mm	1.17 cts	×4	4.68	grains
5 1/2 · 6 mm	90.23 cts	5 1/2 · 6 mm	1.44 cts	×4	5.76	grains
6 · 6 1/2 mm	100.07 cts	6 · 6 1/2 mm	1.87 cts	×4	7.48	grains
6 1/2 · 7 mm	116.48 cts	6 1/2 · 7 mm	2.34 cts	×4	9.36	grains
7 · 7 1/2 mm	131.25 cts	7 · 7 1/2 mm	2.67 cts	×4	10.68	grains
7 1/2 · 8 mm	149.29 cts	7 1/2 · 8 mm	3.40 cts	×4	13.60	grains
8 · 8 1/2 mm	172.26 cts	8 · 8 1/2 mm	4.16 cts	×4	16.64	grains
8 1/2 · 9 mm	190.31 cts	8 1/2 · 9 mm	4.68 cts	×4	18.72	grains
9 · 9 1/2 mm	231.28 cts	9 · 9 1/2 mm	5.35 cts	×4	21.40	

PEARLS: THEIR ORIGIN, TREATMENT & IDENTIFICATION

The ideal is to stock three or four chokers in every pearl size from 2-2.5 mm to 10-10.5 mm, but since this is rarely possible one has to improvise. The most usual sizes are 5-5.5 mm to 8-8.5 mm.

Bracelets are made with chokers. By allowing 17 cm (6.7 in) for a wrist, it is easy to calculate the number of rows required, and the quantity of chokers to form them.

Pearls with a diameter of 6-10 mm and holes of 2 to 10 mm are very often used for rings: The very smallest diameters are very useful either for the manufacture of small cheap jewels or to repair old pieces of jewellery. Their low price means that there is no risk in stocking them. These small pearls are always useful.

Pieces of jewellery with pearls of 2 to 10 mm in diameter are very fashionable. But only mount a few, so that if the fashion changes you are still able to use the remaining pearls for rings, pendants and so on.

As for the large pearls of Burma, Australia and Tahiti, a jeweller ought to possess at least one of each, even if he does not like them very much. One must act on the principle that one only sells what one has on show.

Presentation in a Window

Too often pearls are not shown to their best effect in a window. Necklaces and chokers are wound around one another, giving the unfortunate impression of a caterpillar; that is, when they are not spilling out of a bowl in total disorder. Pearls certainly deserve more consideration. To enhance their brilliance, use busts covered in chamois leather, or round trays, or pearl shells and shellfish. Isolate expensive necklaces, and group together less expensive ones, by carefully avoiding any profusion which makes the client think, 'Which necklace should I choose? They all look the same'.

An outside window should always have its double in some inner display. Pulling out a shelf from a chest before a client always has a good effect.

By watching the windows of the great jewellers, I have always noticed the small number of objects shown, but also the great elegance of their display. There is a reason for this: so that we are sure that their chests are well stocked.

Do not imagine for a moment that such elegance is only worthwhile in areas which have a socially privileged clientèle. Do not forget that you are selling a dream, and that dream must be beautiful.

The Art of Wearing Pearls

Even though it has neither the sparkling brilliance of the diamond, nor the sheen of coloured gems, the pearl remains the most marvellous of all jewels. A pearl is full of discretion, and it is precisely this reserve, modesty and grace which seem to predestine it, as if through some mysterious affinity, to become the jewellery of femininity. When well matched, the woman and pearl appear as one.

If a woman declares that she does not like pearls, this is either because she has never worn them, or because she has been badly advised.

Nowadays, pearls are worn in various ways: a chute necklace of a length of 40 to 45 cm (16 to 18 in), a choker tight on the neck whose pearls only have half-a-millimetre's difference between them, a neck chain of 30 to 35 cm (12 to 14 in) or even longer at 50 to 80 cm (20 to 32 in), which is the same design as the choker, a ring mounted on a circlet of gold, or pearl-mounted ear-rings.

When worn on the ears, pearls will tone down anything excessive or unsightly in someone's features, such as a long nose, prominent cheekbones, or a bulging forehead. Imperceptibly, by their mere presence, pearls will re-establish the harmony and regularity of a face.

A double or triple row of pearls will conceal the wrinkles of old age. A chute necklace will lengthen a face or thin down a neck, whereas it will raise a neckline. A choker will underline the perfection of the shoulders and the purity of the bust.

A humble developmemt to feminine grace, the pearl, when it is well matched to the flesh tints of the woman wearing it, and whether it heightens or lessens features, illuminates her face and makes it radiant.

Here are some suggestions of what shades of pearl colours would suit various skin and hair colours:

Dark skin - golden tints of pearl

Pinkish skin - rosy cream colours of pearl

Pale skin - pinkish, rosy white, and rosy cream colours of pearl

Brunette hair - rosy cream pearls

Reddish hair - rosy cream pearls again

Blonde hair - rose colours of pearl

The suggestions should not be taken as absolute rules, because there are also green, black, blue-grey and other shades, even lavender. Another general guide is that chokers are best on long necks and graduated pearls on short and broader ones.

All women have within their reach the secret of developing and maintaining their beauty. A jeweller who helps them to discover it will earn their eternal gratitude.

Selling and the Education of Dealers

The cultured pearl would never have been sold if it had not been recognised as the rare and precious object which it deservedly is. I hope that the chapter devoted to the cultured pearl industry shows this.

A good dealer must have a sound knowledge of the article with which he is dealing, so that he can answer questions with precision and without using an excess of technicalities. But selling pearls is also an art, which consists of knowing how to play one's role in real life, just like a moment of happiness or dreaming. The value of a gift, whether given or received, always surpasses its mere market value. It is priceless, just as the love or friendship to which it bears witness. A good dealer must be able to help the client with his judicious advice and show that he is taking part in the celebration which makes up the purchase of a gift.

A lot of men do not suspect the place that jewellery has in the life of their companions. Women are scrupulous in loving their jewels out of fear of cornering for themselves an important part of the community's goods. Even a fair number of jewellers, whose vocation is to sell and make-up sets of jewellery, share this point of view to a certain extent. They also tend to put forward the notion of disposing and investing money before that of an objet d'art.

To this, one could object that any investment incorporates, by its very nature, an element of risk. Even investments which are gilt-edged are not safe. Placing an investment always represents a chancy operation. Moreover, as only perfect pearls and stones of impeccable quality offer the guarantee of a safe investment, then recommending to clients that they make an investment can bring discredit on most of our goods, which are imperfect.

Indeed, it is impossible to sell pearls without situating the requirements of the pearl and of the investment in their respective places. The first quality of a brilliant cut diamond is its sparkle, not its purity. Let us reflect on what happens in the skill of making stained glass. If the windows of Chartres cathedral occasionally transport us to a fantasy world, it is because the malformations and faults in the glass, owing to the crudeness of its manufacture, make the light undergo a mysterious process of diffusion and iridescence. In the same way, if one sets aside aesthetic considerations, the perfection of a pearl or a gem is only of subordinate value. The most beautiful gem is the one which gives the rays of light the mysterious effects of diffusion and iridescence, which are helped by its minor malformations and impurities.

As for pearls, none of them has a perfect shape, and none of their skins have geometrical regularity. Each one has its own peculiarities, characteristics and, one might say, its own personality. A small hole is only a defect if the pearl's iridescence is appreciably affected when seen from a normal distance. It is essential that a dealer knows how to put a value on the attraction and charm of a woman. But surely the first thing that a woman requires from the jewels she wears is that they exalt her beauty.

The sale of rings does not pose any particular difficulty. But that of necklaces, chokers, bracelets, long chains and ear-rings is much more delicate and demands a sense of the aesthetic. Indeed one has to take into account the shape of the face, the size of the neck, the beauty of the bust without forgetting the most important thing of all: the flesh-tint of the skin.

If a jeweller is not in the direct presence of the person for whom the pearls are destined, he or she should talk to the intermediary to gain the best possible image of this person. If by chance a sales assistant is free, do not hesitate to use her as a model.

Having discovered the tastes and budget of the client, select the articles which appear to be best suited and place them on a tray covered in chamois leather. At the same time, have a second selection ready, which may prove useful if the client's wishes have been wrongly interpreted, or if she suddenly changes her mind.

To sell pearls, even more than to sell gems, the layman's education must not be begun by placing the pearl in one hand and a magnifying glass in the other; that is only for the training school. Firstly, let us try to evoke some desire in the purchaser for the talisman which is being offered.

Between client and dealer, the mirror is the most eloquent intermediary. Show the first tray, try to ensure that she does not pick up the necklaces and note any small imperfections that may exist, because she would never pardon them. One by one, place the necklaces around her neck and watch her face well. Suddenly her face will light up and become happy and young. A settlement has just been reached between the woman and the pearls; she has just discovered the necklace for her. If she hesitates between two or three necklaces, one should proceed by a process of elimination.

At last the necklace has been chosen. Let her take it in her hand, stroke it, admire it. She is fascinated, she already loves it. It is *her* necklace. She has picked it from all the others and will now pardon any of the flaws and imperfections it contains.

If you are not persuaded that such an act works, try it on one of your saleswomen and judge for yourself. I assure you it is worth a try!

The sale of a necklace represents a precious advantage for a firm, since without any publicity it ties a client for some time to that firm. The client should return every year to have the necklace restrung, which will be an opportunity for the jeweller to show other jewels, to speak of one thing and another, and to keep in contact with his clients.

Things a Dealer Should Know

With every sale there is a necessity to give quick replies so that the clients know they are dealing with a specialist in which they have every confidence. These are the kind of questions which can suddenly confront the salesman.

How is a cultured pearl formed?

Man starts off the natural process by inserting a bead or core and a graft into the oyster's gonad. The graft is the secretor of pearl material, which will form the pearl bag enclosing the core and then form natural pearl material over it.

How is a natural pearl formed?

An irritant of some kind such as a grain of sand enters the oyster's flesh. On its

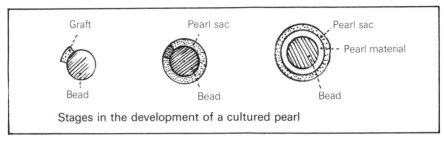

Stages in the development of a cultured pearl

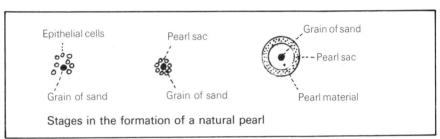

Stages in the formation of a natural pearl

way it is surrounded by epithelial cells, which form a pearl bag. The cells build up pearl material around the grain of sand.

What is the difference between the two types of pearl?
Cultured pearl has a core of several millimetres in diameter, and is the result of man's intervention. The natural pearl has no core and is the product of good fortune.

What is the core made of?
It is made of a ball of extremely pure mother-of-pearl.

Could cultured pearls be made with the oysters one eats?
Yes, but they would be chalky-white and thus lacking in any commercial value.

Do pearls (both natural and cultured) deteriorate?
No, but they may become tarnished if they are not kept properly. A gentle polish will often restore them adequately.

When should a pearl necklace be restrung?
Once a year, as a safety measure.

What are the criteria for making valuations?
Shape, size, colour, purity, rarity, orient.

Why do pearls have flaws?
Whether natural or cultured, pearls are fruits of Nature. Even a manufactured article such as a ball of steel, glass or plastic is rarely flawless.

Is a pearl a good investment?

No, not really, although its price may follow the evolution of the cost of living. Exceptions are large pearls and necklaces of more than 8 mm which can be resold.

If these questions are not entirely familiar to you, there is nothing simpler: question one of your associates, make up a list, give the answers yourself, then place them at the disposal of the salespeople in the business. It is like a game, but business can only benefit from it.

A Different View of the Pearl

Here we are in the presence of the pearl. Above all do not regard it with the austere look that stops at its outline. Try to view it with a wish to go beyond a superficial acquaintance. Let us try to find out why the ancients called pearls 'angel's tears', 'haiad's tears' or 'drops of rain fallen from heaven'. Nowadays the word 'pearl' signifies perfection, something ultimate and insurpassable, an impeccable accomplishment.

Wonder at pearls is a common reaction of every period. The great men of the world have always had a passion for pearls. The jewellery of the Roman patricians was adorned with them. Men of power, whether mandarins, maharajahs, sheiks, kings and emperors, queens and empresses considered them as the symbol of their majesty, opulence and power.

The fascination that a pearl evokes has never been unmerited. And yet its orient is fairly modest, when compared with the glowing brilliance of a diamond or the sumptuous richness of some coloured gems. But match a woman with the right sort of necklace and you will become aware of an imperceptible and subtle change. She will radiate with new charm. One has the impression that every pearl was waiting for the touch of her skin to justify its existence. It becomes like a drop of light that is delicately iridescent.

Light is a source of beauty and we have never tired of its varied and infinite tricks. Some can transform whole surfaces into magical enchantment to our eyes and minds, like the paintings of the Impressionists. Other phenomena play with light by transparency and iridescence; the sea, the sky, the rainbow, and mother-of-pearl, which interests us most especially, because the same is true of the pearl.

Iridescence of light is caused by a multiplicity of fine layers which the rays of light have to cross. A fine, partially transparent skin is sufficient to decompose light, as can be seen by a patch of oil on water. But when the layers build up, the iridescence grows deeper; as is the case with mother-of-pearl and pearls and human skin.

A pearl is formed by thin pearl parallel layers positioned concentrically. The epidermis has similar structure. Both cause a play of light which is appealing to the eye. So, are pearls and skin linked in some way? Everything happens between a pearl and a woman as if some mysterious natural affinity had caused a perfect harmony to be achieved.

From this comes a feeling of miraculous harmony when one sees a necklace on a woman's neckline. A precious substance, patiently formed in the ocean-depths inside the flesh of a shellfish, one day to be brought to the surface, the pearl seems to have no other raison d'être than to light the Venus-like skin on which it forms a halo with its discreet brilliance.

Without doubt, all jewels and gems communicate something of their brilliance to the hand, arm or bust, where they shine. But their inanimate mineral beauty remains foreign to one's skin, even though they lend it their magnificence. The pearl necklace uses the most refined resources to exercise its charm: it casts off its light so discreetly in order to beautify its mistress that it almost seems to fade away. And the man looking at his companion attributes her increased charm to her alone.

But let us allow a poet, Paul Claudel, to evoke the mysterious life of the pearl:

'The pearl, fruit of the sea, has no value other than its beauty and intrinsic perfection, which result from its simplicity, its beauty and its brilliance, and the desire which it inspires. It does not shine, it does not burn, it touches; a cool and refreshing caress for one's eye, one's skin and one's soul. We are in contact with it.

'And now I am holding it in the palm of my hand, that angelic virginity, that pearly curio, that petal, that pure hailstone that only the gods could have sent down, but from which, as from the flesh of a child, a sort of pink warmth emanates. It is something likeable, suave, unctuous, affectionate: I was going to say human. The humble mollusc is dead, but what it has unknowingly created, this extraordinary being which it has produced, will continue to live.'

The Future of the Pearl

Arriving at the end of the work, the reader might be driven to the hasty conclusion that the chapters devoted to the natural pearl deal only with the completed past, and those which concern cultured pearls, even when describing the present situation, only describe a technique which has halted because of its success and is destined to make no further progress.

For my own part, I am persuaded that the contrary is true. Let us imagine for a moment the routes that pearl production may take in the future and the consequences that these developments have on our profession, without forgetting that it takes only a few years for fiction to become reality.

Ever since the decline of the pearl fisheries because of the 1929 crisis, when pearl exploitation was restrained and even halted, a large number of oyster-beds which were abandoned to their own ends have been able to rebuild themselves and spread. This leads me to believe that there are vast reserves of molluscs lying on the sea-beds. Exceptions are the regions where the cultured pearl industry uses oyster-beds to maintain its own supplies.

If one objects to this by saying that the pollution of the seas and coasts has increased because of industrial development and thus hinders the growth of marine fauna, I would put forward the example of Japan, a country where the industrial concentration produces an alarming amount of pollution, but which remains the most important pearl-producing country in the world.

It seems to be worthwhile formulating a systematic prospecting plan for several sites, so that oyster-beds could be exploited again.

Searching for and locating them does not appear to present insuperable problems, despite the immense size of the oceans. With the assistance of a geographical institute, surely the sites of beds which were known in the past could quickly be rediscovered. In many countries where illiteracy does not allow for written documents, the oral tradition is still intact. By questioning the coastal population, as shown by Alex Haley in his work, *Roots*, it is possible to identify old locations exactly.

Finally, the immense progress which has been made in the last few years in the electronics field has produced on the open market a large range of viable and sophisticated equipment which can be bought for reasonable prices and will facilitate marine exploration. Sonars and acoustic depth-finders are capable of detecting the slightest distortions of the sea-bed, and infra-red rays can reveal animals hidden away in rock-faults. There is no doubt that these different instruments would save a great deal of time in explorations.

This being so, what is to stop us equipping a small team with such high-precision materials and prospecting areas which were previously restricted for one reason or another?

Sceptics will say that such an undertaking would be lengthy and expensive, and in any case news of the discovery of one or two beds would spread very quickly, and this would encourage a large number of fishermen to exploit these new sites. With modern industrial methods, they will claim, the beds would be totally pillaged and destroyed in record time for the profit of a few ambitious adventurers, but with little overall benefit for anyone else.

This would probably occur if research were not controlled and even subsidised by interested governments, or by an international organisation like the FAO. But if this were the case, the future of pearls appears very promising. Indeed, with modern knowledge, experience and methods it would be easy to determine scientifically the number, age and size of oysters likely to contain a pearl and thus be fished, without threatening the survival of the species; quite the contrary. Because, on one hand an excessive concentration of individuals from the same species in the same place causes a degeneration of that race and thus threatens its future in the long term. On the other hand, the rational exploitation of livestock stimulates the reproductive organs, so that a natural balance is kept by constant regeneration of the species.

Incomplete and by now old studies which have been made about the productivity of pearls in oysters have shown that in the best cases, 3 to 4 per cent of oysters produce a pearl and only two or three in a thousand a pearl of value. I have no valid means of confirming or denying these figures. They do not seem to err on the side of caution, when one considers the enormous number of natural pearls that arrived on the market between the wars. They seem to represent hearsay rather than realistic statistics. Let us not forget that the whole profession had an interest in minimising the figures in order to justify the high prices of certain goods. Whatever the truth, one must try to improve these proportions if one wants to exploit the natural beds successfully.

Since most pearls originate from larvae of gestods or other small animals, would it not be more utopian to grow the various parasites of pearl oysters (in the laboratory) and to contaminate a section of the registered beds, under strict control? The risks which could arise out of such experiments do not seem prejudicial to the survival of the species, because the oyster adapts very well to the presence of one or several pearls in its body and manages to expel them when they have reached a certain size. All that remains would be to try and foresee the exact moment when this phenomenon occurs, and to anticipate it so that the pearls are not lost at the bottom of the ocean.

Another method is probably well worth experimenting with. A lot simpler than the first, it consists probably of observing the phenomena which appears in the oyster's gonad when it has been grafted in order to produce a cultured pearl. When the pearl is harvested, several other small pearls are frequently found secreted by epithelial cells detached from the graft when it was inserted into the gonad. It is impossible to distinguish these pearls from classical natural pearls, whose structure and appearance they imitate, as they result from the same process.

Why not draw the obvious conclusions on the strength of these observations? For example, why not remove epithelial cells from one oyster and use a syringe to inject them into the gonads of other oysters, which could then be kept in the same way as those containing cultured pearls, e.g. in baskets suspended on ropes or tripod meshes?

The economic advantage of this process is certain, if one takes the time factor into consideration. Oysters live about 10 to 15 years. For present cultured pearl techniques, one has to wait for the oyster to reach four years of age, so that it is capable of withstanding the operative shock of having a graft taken. From this time onwards, it is watched for from two to three years, and for a further two years if too large a graft has been inserted. A harvest can only be expected from oysters aged about six to seven, then eight to nine years. And they have a mortality rate of 50 per cent because of the operation.

If the hypothesis of injecting cells were correct, and injections would work in the second years, harvests would follow every six to eight years. The mortality rate of the oysters would not exceed 20 to 25 per cent, since the intervention involves no operative shock.

The feasibility of such an experiment remains to be seen. But if one remembers that the price of a natural pearl is ten times that of a cultured pearl of the same quality and size; and if the pearls obtained had an average weight of 20 grains, then the operation has every chance of proving feasible.

The discovery and application of such techniques would certainly risk lowering the price paid for natural pearls, but it would have the advantage of launching on to the market a product that could not be found elsewhere other than at controlled sales. The beauty of natural pearls is incomparable and it is time to take some action to ensure their production, before we run the risk in a few decades of seeing them only behind the cold windows of museums, instead of being worn by the people.

On another point, the cultured pearl industry still has not exhausted its full potential. There too much work remains to be done. If one consults a map to locate countries where the cultured pearl industry exists, the small number of producing countries and areas will come as a surprise. The Persian Gulf, Ceylon, the Red Sea, Europe and America, at one time large producers, now seem to be unaware of the wealth on their coasts, lakes and rivers.

In none of these regions, where fishing was once so intensive that pearl fauna were in the process of becoming extinct, does the cultured pearl industry exist. It is unlikely that there are no species of *Malegrines* or *Anodontes* which man could revive and, with care, turn into a prosperous venture.

Pearl-growing techniques are now safe enough for an entrepreneur to search for suitable sites for farms, estimate the optimum percentages of shell concentration and finally calculate the feasibility of setting up such an operation.

The development of the cultured pearl industry offers a country numerous advantages. A cultured pearl business employs skilled and unskilled labour, for farm work as well as for laboratory jobs and office work when the pearls are sold. So it creates employment, a factor which is very important nowadays. It also brings into a country foreign currency and reduces imports, because throughout the world women never stop wearing pearls.

Sceptics do not cease objecting to high production because extra pearls put on the world market would risk forcing down prices. One can only agree with them. But one must not forget that Mikimoto's dream was that every woman should own a pearl necklace, and this is far from being realised.

Besides, even if cultured pearls achieved the enormous increase which I have portrayed, the most beautiful pearls would be just as rare. Nature guards its right in every enterprise, especially in the farming field, of which cultured pearl growing is a part.

Finally, a profusion of goods on a market does not necessarily result in a uniform lowering of prices for that particular commodity. Quality remains an essential factor in every sector, be it food, furniture, clothing, and especially in such a narrow field bound by aesthetic values as jewellery. Quantity, whose pursuit supposes open competition directed towards improving quality and constant promotion of products, arouses desire and longing, which in their turn create demand.

Jewellers, whose role it is to create necklaces and pieces of jewellery, would become even more selective in their purchases. Furthermore, they could make up collections whose price range would be far more extensive than it is at present. There is no doubt that the public would be the eventual winner.

Lastly, let us risk a final speculation on a totally different subject. The reader may have been struck by the persistence with which medical properties have been attributed to pearls. It is strange that ancient peoples of completely different races and customs and separated by thousands of miles, simultaneously became interested in the curative virtues with which pearls are endowed. It is no less strange that in most cases their observations check with each other. Pearls, reduced to powder or ashes or dissolved in various acids, stimulate or heal a good number of our organs and bodily functions. They are especially recommended for the treatment of eye, stomach and blood infections.

It is not foolhardy to suppose that the unanimity of their beliefs may be based on some truth. Consequently, may one suggest that it is up to chemistry and modern medicine to analyse the composition of pearls and to evaluate their effects on the human organism. Laboratory work might confirm a good number of the curative properties which ancient civilisations intuitively attributed to pearls, and may even discover new benefits.

It is the pharmacists' job to test the value of this hypothesis. It is clear that a positive answer would revolutionise all views on pearl production and pearl dealing thoughout the world.

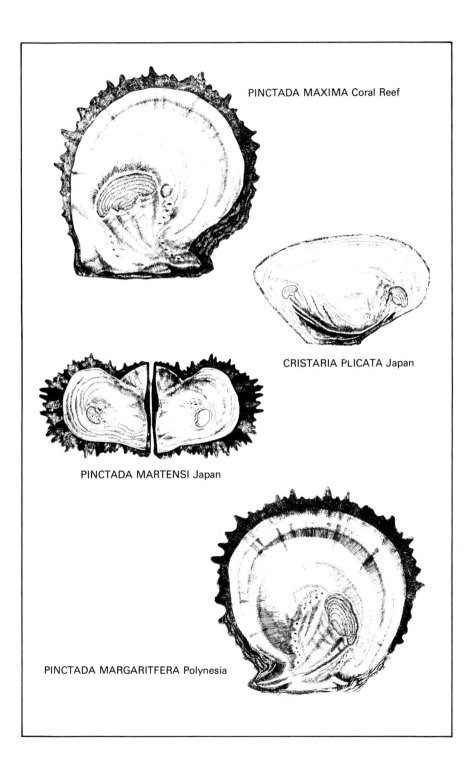

PINCTADA MAXIMA Coral Reef

CRISTARIA PLICATA Japan

PINCTADA MARTENSI Japan

PINCTADA MARGARITFERA Polynesia

Appendix

Evaluating Cultured Pearls

Like gemstones, each pearl is different and as individual as a fingerprint. Again like other gems, pearls are first sorted according to whether they can be used for the cultured pearl industry or not. The latter are used as a cosmetic or medicine base. The gem group is then further categorised into three sections: 'unmarked' pearls, pearls with one major blemish, and pearls with more than one major blemish. The first section is undrilled pearls, the second for half-drilled pearls and the third for necklets. Each section is then further sorted from the highest quality and price to the lowest commercial quality and price.

Of every hundred pearls harvested it is reckoned that only three reach the standards required by the top pearling companies.

The main grading considerations are:
1. Thickness of the nacre
2. Lustre
3. Colour
4. Shape
5. Surface perfection
6. Size

1. Nacre thickness is largely determined by the length of time the bead is in the oyster. The thicker the nacre, the higher the value, because of the longer life, usually better lustre, and the cost of the longer time of cultivation.

2. Lustre is the effect of reflection and refraction from inner layers of the skin as well as the surface. It cannot be measured quantitively, although most people can tell a good lustre from a poorer one if the pearl is examined against an opaque surface, such as white paper or plain cloth, and not on glass or a reflecting surface. To judge grades of lustre needs the skilled eye of a pearl grader. Nacre thickness and lustre are regarded as among the most important factors in grading.

3. Colour varies much more than is generally imagined. There are many shades

of cream, grey, green, blue and pink. Most popular are white and pink rose because they flatter a wide range of skin tones. However, choice of colour is a matter of taste in the end. The grader looks for richness of a colour and its evenness over the pearl. Most important, of course, is the sorting and matching of colours for particular necklaces. Mikimoto grades are as follows:

Flower pink

Silver pink rainbow.

(These two are normally only seen in Japan where the appreciation of pearls is greater than anywhere else. In the last two years limited stocks have been available in the United States and the United Kingdom.)

Silver light cream

Silver dark cream

Cream (this has a light golden appearance)

Dark Cream

Gold

Green (rare)

Blue, blue grey, black.

Normally, the price scales down with the grade, but higher factors other than colour do sometimes strongly upgrade the price. For example, a cream necklace with excellent lustre and almost perfect form would cost more than a silver light cream one that was less perfect. Even in colour there can be upgrading of price.

It should be noted that the length of a necklace also makes a difference in choosing the colour because, if most of the necklace is to be displayed against a coloured material instead of the skin, the colour of the pearl should not be too weak. For example a golden colour is fine on beige, plum and various other coloured materials.

4. The best shape is obviously spherical and generally speaking the rounder the pearl, the more desirable. Other shapes such as pear or teardrop, oval, button, and baroque are worth less, other things being equal. However, they are popular when a different style or fashion is needed. A large non-spherical pearl of excellent quality may make a particularly fine pendant and would therefore be priced accordingly. A quick way of checking the regularity of string pearls, used by dealers, is to lay the string on a desk top, hold one end down with one hand and move the other end of the string stretched in a semi-circle with the other hand so that the pearls rotate on their string. Any that roll unevenly or wobble are easily identified.

5. The more serious surface imperfections can also be seen while rolling pearls as explained above. A closer examination of individual pearls is obviously needed to find smaller imperfections. A broad classification of surface marks is as follows:

Clean; Small Spots; Spotted; Very Spotted.

It must not be forgotten that pearls are not manufactured and the word 'imperfection' does not denigrate a work of Nature; in fact, its presence, like that of an inclusion in a gemstone, is a 'hallmark' of Nature proving its genuineness. Therefore tiny marks on pearls can be considered as their natural texture, like the texture of raw silk, and do not detract from their value, or beauty for that matter.

6. The Japanese pearl industry has always quoted the price of loose pearls and necklaces by weight, using the momme (2.75 grammes) as the measure. The size, however, is always the diameter measured in millimetres. To add to the mélangé of measures, the length of a necklace for the U.S. and U.K. markets is quoted in inches. Therefore a retailer would order, for example, a 6 mm 15 in choker. Most pearl necklaces today are regular, i.e. not graduated. A good quality regular necklace, however, grades a half a millimetre, so that pearls of all sizes can be used. Such necklaces are recorded as 6½-6 mm, 7- 6½ mm, 7½-7 mm, and so on. Graduated necklaces are recorded to show the largest size in the middle to the smallest at the ends, e.g. 6x3 mm, 7x3½ mm and 8x4 mm. The end pearls are generally about half the size of the central one, but not always. Necklace lengths are grouped and named by Mikimoto as indicated in the diagram and figures below:

UNIFORMED NECKLACES

1. Choker	15 inches approx.
2. Standard	18 inches approx.
3. Matinee	22 inches approx.
4. Opera	30 inches approx.
5. Rope	40 inches or longer.

These names describe a 'look' so should only be used in conjunction with the exact length because of different body sizes.

GRADUATED NECKLACES

6x3 mm	16 inches approx.
7x3½ mm	17 inches approx.
8x4 mm	17 inches approx.
9x6 mm	18 inches approx.
10x7 mm	19 inches approx.

There are various other combinations. depending on availability of sizes.

EARRINGS

Pearls for earrings generally range in size from 4 mm to 9 mm.

Care of Pearls

Pearls are softer than almost all gemstones; only opal is really comparable in hardness. Consequently they can be scratched and otherwise damaged if they are jumbled with other jewellery in a jewel box. They are best kept separate in a soft cloth bag or case. After wear, they should be wiped with a soft cloth which should be slightly damp, but not wet. The object is to remove any perspiration, body acids, make-up, perfume, or hair spray which contain substances such as alcohol and acids harmful to the pearl. If the surface is attacked, the lustre is dulled. The string at the back of the neck is in constant contact with the neck and it is especially important to clean this part of the necklace as it can otherwise become severely damaged by chemical attack and through wear in course of time. Although some sources advise soaking pearls in warm water containing a little mild detergent or soap once in a while, it is probably best to avoid doing so because it can weaken the thread. It is better to wipe them with a cloth just moistened with mild soapy water.

Good quality pearls should be restrung once a year if worn regularly. They are strung on silk thread which is knotted between pearls to keep them from rubbing each other and also to avoid loss should the thread break. However, graduated and small size uniforms are often strung without knots because the overall look is better. Re-threading should always be done when there is any sign of fraying, stretching, bad soiling of the thread, or when the gimp that attached the silk to the clasp becomes discoloured.

On the subject of knotting pearls, the author explains the professional method on page 197 of using a beading needle or similar pointer pushed into the board to pull the knot tightly to the pearl.

Pearl Threading

The silk thread of a pearl necklace, where it passes through the loop in a fastener, should be protected by a gimp. A gimp is a very fine and flexible closed coil of gold or silver wire through which the silk is threaded, so that the gimp takes any wear caused by the movement of the fastener. Gimp can be brought in lengths from jewellers' supply houses and is cut to short pieces of one centimetre or more to suit the type of fastener used with the pearl jewellery.

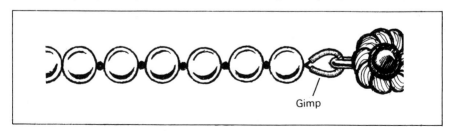

Gimp

Glossary of Important Technical Terms

ANODONTE
A variety of *Unionide*, with a brown smooth shell, capable of reaching about 15 cm (6 in) in length. Abundant in lakes and ponds.

AMAGE
Japanese name for the crude harvest of cultured pearls, when obtained by the farms, before they have undergone bleaching, piercing and stringing operations.

AMAH
Japanese name for female divers employed in preference to men for oyster fishing for the cultured pearl industry, as well as for edible oysters.

AQUA PERLATE
Medicinal potion with tonic virtues, used in the Middle Ages. It was prepared by dissolving pearls in an acidic substance (vinegar, lemon juice, vitriol or sulphur alcohol), to which various aromatic essences were added.

ARAGONITE
Calcium carbonate entering the chemical composition of the mother-of-pearl and the pearl material, under the form of microscopic crystals. The name comes from the province of Aragon in Spain, where a variety of analogous limestone is very widespread.

BAROQUE
Pearls of irregular shape due to Nature's caprices. Semi-baroques are baroque pearls which, despite their irregularities, are similar to round, pear and button-shaped pearls.

BIWA (PEARLS)
Biwa is the name of a Japanese lake. By extension, it designates all cultured freshwater pearls. The growing technique for these pearls is distinguished by the absence of a hard core, with only a graft from the mantle being inserted into the animal's gonad. They are also called non-nuncleated cultured pearls.

BLEACHING
Removal of an unaesthetic colour or stains from deposit of organic matter by immersion of pearls in a solution of oxygenated water and afterwards exposing them to light.

BLISTER
A more or less convex swelling on the surface of the internal wall of an oyster shell. These phenomena occur because of the introduction of animal or vegetable foreign bodies between the mantle of the oyster and the shell, and which became covered in mother-of-pearl cementing it to the shell. Sometimes a pearl expelled from the oyster's flesh, but having slid underneath the mantle, is the cause of the formation of a blister (blister pearl).

BLISTER, FINE
Pearl formation, which can attain a sizeable volume, caused by the decomposing gases of an animal or vegetable organism, introduced into the oyster's flesh and covered by pearl material. A fine blister looks like a large baroque pearl but has the characteristic of a hollow interior.

BLUE PEARL
Natural pearl which originates from secretions of corneous material (brownish), then covered in pearl material.

BUL-BUL
Description in colloquial Arabic of the variety of oysters collected from the Red Sea. Although their shells are fine, they are small and of little value, apart from the pearls they may contain.

BYSSUS
A fibrous substance secreted by the oyster's foot, which allows it to attach itself to some support.

CARAT
Unit of weight, correctly the metric carat, which is equal to a fifth of a gramme. It was first introduced in Paris in 1877 and over many years was adopted internationally. Previously, carats varied from country to country.

GLOSSARY OF IMPORTANT TECHNICAL TERMS

CARAT, ENGLISH
The old English carat was equivalent to 3.1683 grains. It was subdivided into fractions from ½ to 1/64. The metric carat became legal in the United Kingdom in 1914.

CARAT, FLORENTINE
Unit of weight used in the 17th century, which was equal to 3.04 grains troy.

CHOKER
String of pearls with a length of 30 to 35 cm (12 to 14 in). The pearls making it up are generally of equal number, and have a maximum difference of 0.5 mm (0.02 in) in their diameter.

CHUTE (GRADUATED NECKLACE)
Necklace composed of an unequal number of pearls. The central pearl has a diameter which is distinctly larger than the other pearls which diminish in size towards the ends.

CONCHIOLIN (pronounced 'konk-eye-ohlin')
From the Greek, konche - a shell. Substance of organic origin, arranged in a fine network, retaining the aragonite crystals which enter the composition of the pearls and the mother-of-pearl.

CONCRETIONS
Conglomeration of many small pearls initially formed near one another, which become fused together. The continued secretion of pearl material eventually covers them.

CORE
Ball of mother-of-pearl carefully polished, destined to be inserted with the graft into the oyster's gonad in order to cause a cultured pearl to be formed. Spherical cores are manufactured to obtain round pearls, and three-quarter spherical ones to grow blisters.

ENDOSCOPE
Instrument invented by Chilowsky and Perrin to set cultured pearls apart from natural pearls. Its principle consists of beaming a thin ray of light of great intensity into the pearl. It can be used only on drilled pearls.

EPITHELIAL CELLS
Cells constituting a tissue covering the oyster's mantle, which secrete the mother-of-pearl and pearl material.

GONAD
Sexual glands of the oyster. The most suited organ to receive the core and the graft in the production of a cultured pearl.

GRAIN
Unit of weight equal to a quarter of a carat.

GRAFT
Fragments removed from the epithelial membrane of the oyster and inserted with or without a core into the animal's gonad, to produce cultured pearls.

HALIOTIS
Shellfish of the gastropod family. Sought for its shell, its pearls and the edible flesh from its foot.

KAN
Japanese unit of weight, equal to 1000 momes.

KECHI
Pearls without a core, of small diameters, baroque shapes and obtained as a by-product of growing cultured pearls, when isolated epithelial cells from a pearl bag in the flesh of the oyster.

LAUEGRAM
Characteristic pattern of spots produced on photographic film by a narrow beam of x-rays passing through a single crystal. Used for positive identification of naturals and cultured pearls.

LIPS (SILVER, GOLD, BLACK)
Vivid description used for mother-of-pearl and pearl shellfish of Australia. The *Pinctada maxima* with perfectly white mother-of-pearl, the most beautiful in the world, is called silver-lip; certain species of the same variety, whose mother-of-pearl has golden reflections, are called gold-lips. Another variety of Pintadines, the *Pinctada margaritifera* whose shell has a black edge, has received the name of black-lip.

LOU-LOU
Generic name for the pearl in colloquial Arabic.

LUCIDOSCOPE
Instrument invented by Dr. Szilard to separate natural pearls from cultured pearls. His method was to expose the pearl to an intense light, which enabled the core to be seen through the layers of pearl matter which surrounded it.

GLOSSARY OF IMPORTANT TECHNICAL TERMS

LUSTRE
Property resulting from the reflection and refraction of light from a surface. Some of the light may just penetrate the surface before being returned to the eye. Pearly lustre is also known as 'orient'.

MABE
Cultured pearl obtained on the inside of the oyster's shell by attaching a semi-spherical core underneath the mantle, destined to be covered in pearl material. The extraction and finishing-work on the mabe once it is formed, involves very delicate work.

MANTLE
Part of the oyster's organism covering the internal organs and situated at the meeting point of the inner sides of the shell, whose mother-of-pearl it secretes.

MASSETTE
Small mass, composed of 6 to 10 rows of pearls (chutes and chokers).

MOME or MOMME
Japanese unit of weight used mainly for pearls which is equal to 18.75 carats. There are about 266 momes in a kilogram and 120 in a pound weight.

MUSSELS
Popular name for the shellfish specie Unionides.

NAISSAIN
Young oysters.

ORIENT
The lustre of the oriental pearls resulting from the distortion of light by aragonite crystals which gives them a special radiance and obliterates the contours. The finer the layers of pearl material, the better the pearls' orient.

ORIENT, ESSENCE OF
Invented in the 17th century by a Frenchman named Jacquin. Composed of fish-scales ground in water with added ammonia and dehydrated by adding alcohol. The product has a consistency of syrup and is used to coat glass or plastic balls in order to give them the appearance of pearls and become imitation pearls.

OSTREIDES
Family of molluscs comprising oysters, but not part of the Pintadines which produce most pearls.

PAIRING
A set of two pearls of the same diameter, colour and quality.

PEARL (NATURAL, CULTURED, IMITATION)
The word pearl without any qualifying adjective always designates, by convention, only natural pearls or fine pearls which are spontaneously formed in the organism of a pearl shellfish, without man's intervention. The cultured pearl, or pearl with a foreign core, results from man introducing an element (core plus graft) into the gonad of a shellfish, to encourage the oyster to cover the bead core with pearl nacre. The imitation pearl is manufactured from a glass or plastic ball, whose outside or inside is coated in a substance, essence of orient, producing the appearance, colour and effect of natural or cultured pearls.

PEARL CULTIVATION
The technique of growing pearls.

PINTADINES (PINCTADA)
Usual name for the Meleagrine or pearl 'oyster'. Type of mollusc, which produces most pearls and for its thin mother-of-pearl; *Fucata*, widespread on the coasts of China, Japan, Australia and New Guinea, and easily used for growing pearls; *Irradians*, plentiful on the Madagascan coasts; *Maculata*, widespread in the Red Sea, Polynesia and Australia, sought both for its pearls and its shell; this variety is also fished in Mexico and Venezuela; *Martensi*, plentiful in China and Japan; *Maxima*, widespread throughout the Pacific, Burma and Australia, renowned because certain specimens can weigh up to 3 kg (6.6 lb) and reputed for its pearls and mother-of-pearl; *Occa*, variety from Madagascar; *Radiata*, particularly plentiful in the Persian Gulf; *Vulgaris*, equally plentiful in the Persian Gulf, but also in Ceylon (Sri Lanka) and India.

PIG-TOE
A popular denomination of mussels living in the waterways of the USA from whose mother-of-pearl all the cultured pearl cores are manufactured.

PERIOSTRACUM
The outer crust of the shell, secreted by the outer edge of the mantle.

PINK PEARL
Pearl secreted by the *Strombus gigas*. The colours range from whitish-yellow to pale pink. The pink pearls can resemble balls of pink coral.

GLOSSARY OF IMPORTANT TECHNICAL TERMS

PINNA
Shellfish abundant in the Mediterranean, whose shell is long at its base. Sought for its flesh, it also produces pearls with a special structure constructed not of concentric deposits of layers of pearl material, but of a multitude of small prisms, arranged around the centre.

PLACUNA
Shellfish of the gastropod family, widespread in Asia, similar to a snail. Sought for its flesh, it occasionally produces unpopular pearls.

PTERIA PENQUIN
Type of bi-valve shellfish widespread throughout the Pacific used only to produce mabe pearls. Mabe is the Japanese name for this shellfish, which designates, by extension, all pearls obtained by this particular technique, even from other species of shellfish.

SADOF
Common designation in Arabic for the variety of shellfish, whose scientific name is *Margaritifera erythroensis*, particularly plentiful in the Persian Gulf and the Red Sea. These oysters are valuable both for the pearls that they contain and the mother-of-pearl.

SHAW
Reference base used by Arabs and Indians to value natural pearls. It differs according to the multiples of weight used in the East.

SOUTH SEAS
General description for all pearls produced by the large Pintadines (*Pinctada maxima*).

STROMBUS GIGAS
A widespread shellfish very common on the coasts of the Bahamas. Sought for its flesh, its bright pink shell and its pink concretions, called pink pearls.

TRIDACNA
Scientific name for the large shellfish commonly called 'stoop'. It produces pale pink pearls, analogous to pink pearls.

TRIPOD
Equipment used in the cultured pearl farms of Tahiti, consisting of a meshed trihedral frame resting on the sea-bed from whose sides the grafted oysters are hung.

TROY
The system of English weights once used for gems and precious metals, in which the pound is equal to 373.242 grammes.

UNIO
Variety of Unionide with a black irregular shell, capable of reaching 10 cm (nearly 4 in), plentiful in waterways and lakes. Extremely widespread throughout America, Europe and Asia, several sub-varieties can be distinguished: *Unio margaritifera*; *Sinuatus pictorum*; *Mongolicus*; *Dahuricus*; *Dipsas plicatus*.

UNIONIDES
Commonly called mussels. Family comprising almost all freshwater bi-valve shellfish, whose shell is dark brown on the outside, white and pearly on the inside. Most of the freshwater pearls come from Unionides.

WATER (OF MOTHER-OF-PEARL)
Property of mother-of-pearl to distort light on its passage through the aragonite crystals which form it. This phenomenon produces an iridescence. The finer the layers of mother-of-pearl, the more beautiful the water. Water is also used to describe the purity of other gems, particularly in early records.

Index

Numbers in italics refer to illustrations